Recent Advances
in the Reconstruction of
Common Slavic
(1971–1982)

by

Henrik Birnbaum and Peter T. Merrill

Slavica Publishers, Inc.

Slavica has published a wide variety of scholarly books and textbooks on the peoples, cultures, languages, literatures, history, folklore, etc. of Eastern Europe and the USSR, as well as on general and Indo-European linguistics. For a complete catalog with prices and ordering information, write to:

Slavica Publishers, Inc.
PO Box 14388
Columbus, Ohio 43214
USA

300615

ISBN: 0–89357–116–4.

This book was published in 1985.

Text set by University of Maryland Computer Science Center, Publications Office on a Mergenthaler Linotron 202.

Printed in the United States of America.

Recent Advances

in the Reconstruction of

Common Slavic

(1971–1982)

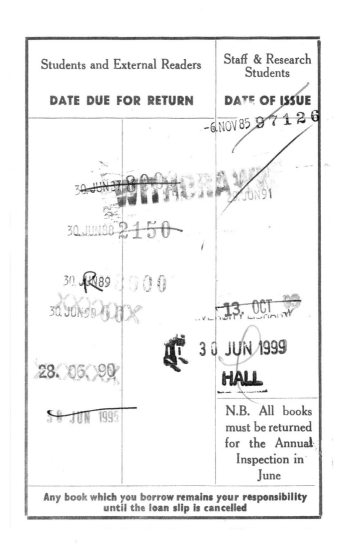

For Marianna and Susan,
with thanks for their patience.

Table of Contents

Prefatory Note

This bibliographic commentary is designed as a sequel to H. Birnbaum's *Common Slavic: Progress and Problems in Its Reconstruction*, Cambridge, Mass.: Slavica, 1975 (reprint, with corrections: Columbus, Ohio, 1979). While the general cutoff date for the previous survey was mid–1971, this follow-up covers the period of more than a decade through 1982, with the second half of 1982 reported on somewhat less systematically. Occasionally also a preliminary reference has been included to a work in the field not available at this writing, but about whose imminent publication the authors had advance knowledge.

The organization of the material surveyed in this overview generally follows that of the earlier volume so that the two can easily be used in conjunction with one another. It should be noted, however, that owing to the relative paucity of relevant publications the section on syntax has here not been divided into subsections as was the case in the earlier report. The key to the numerical symbols used for content identification in the Selective Bibliography of the previous work has, with some modification, been adopted here and corresponds to this report's Table of Contents.

As in the previous survey, no claims to exhaustiveness are made. The necessary selection was subject to limitations of space and access, as well as considerations of perceived significance.

Los Angeles and College Park, Md.
February 1983

H. B.
P. T. M.

Abbreviations

The following abbreviations are used throughout the text of this report (except in direct quotations and in headings and subheadings):

CS	= Common Slavic
OCS	= Old Church Slavic
(P)IE	= (Proto-)Indo-European
PS	= Proto-Slavic

In addition, the customary abbreviations for denoting languages are used to identify cited examples of relevant linguistic data or terminology; thus, e.g., **Bg** = Bulgarian, **Cz** = Czech, **F** = French, **Gk** = Greek, **Goth** = Gothic, **Hitt** = Hittite, **Lat** = Latin, **Lith** = Lithuanian, **OHG** = Old High German, **OPr** = Old Prussian, **OR** = Old Russian, **P** = Polish, **SC** = Serbo-Croatian, etc.

Abbreviations for series titles and journals used in the Selective Bibliography are spelled out in a note appearing there.

I. GENERAL TREATMENTS OF COMMON SLAVIC

(Including Common Slavic Viewed in a Broader Framework)

I.1. General Treatments of Common Slavic

In the decade that has elapsed since the previous report (Birnbaum 1979a) was prepared, work on reconstructing the CS protolanguage has continued vigorously. Thus, significant research has been published pertinent to the retrieving of the sound pattern, morphosyntactic structure, and etymologically elucidated lexicon of the ancestral language of all the Slavs. Moreover, important contributions have been made to our understanding of that language both in its broader Indo-European context and in its overall geographic setting as this pertains to contacts with other, non-related contiguous languages.

Of major general treatments of CS designed to be used as tools in more advanced academic instruction, mention should be made, in particular, of the second volume of P. Arumaa's *Urslavische Grammatik* analyzing consonantism (Arumaa 1976). Like its predecessor using essentially a modified neogrammarian approach, this is a thorough account of the consonant system of the Slavic protolanguage and its positionally conditioned modifications throughout prehistoric time. Though largely traditional in its underlying conception of linguistic diachrony, Arumaa's work considers recent findings and hypotheses concerning unresolved, controversial issues. Among such problematic topics is, for example, the author's assessment of the relevance of laryngeal theory for prehistoric Slavic (cf. 198–9). One of the virtues of this presentation is the integration of some of the author's own research in the field of onomastics and, specifically, the hydronymy of pertinent areas previously settled by Baltic tribes and, in part, Finnic ethnic groups. The author's thorough familiarity with, and masterful handling of, Baltic data shed new light on some of the intricate and difficult problems of the linguistic relationship between Baltic and Slavic. Given recent attempts to reorder the chronology of the Slavic velar palatalizations (cf. II.4., below), it should be noted that Arumaa adheres to the more traditional view concerning the chronology of these phenomena (cf. 27–42). For some assessments of this book, pointing out the merits of Arumaa's well-documented treatment but also voicing a few critical remarks, see, among others, Aitzetmüller 1977b, Micklesen 1977, Leeming 1980, and Birnbaum 1981d.

I.2. Comparative Slavic Linguistics

Of the current textbooks on comparative Slavic linguistics, the multi-volume works by Z. Stieber and A. Vaillant were completed during the period reported on here. Stieber's more concise and selective *Zarys gramatyki porównawczej języków słowiańskich,* part II, issue 2, treating verbal inflection, proceeds from the Late CS stage, thus presenting the author's view of that portion of the underlying system of Slavic morphology (Stieber 1973a). For pedagogical reasons Stieber reduces the number of remaining controversial points to the unavoidable minimum and, employing his usual terse style, presents a summation of the scholarly consensus regarding the data at hand. He thus refrains from exploring tentative hypotheses or offering controversial suggestions.

Vaillant's monumental *Grammaire comparée des langues slaves* was completed with the appearance of volume IV on nominal word-formation and volume V on syntax during the 1970s (Vaillant 1974, 1977). The first of these volumes contains a detailed discussion of Slavic nominal derivation using OCS data as its primary material. In addition, the French Slavist, as in previous parts of his work, adduces ample Baltic parallel evidence, thus adding an IE dimension to this reference work.

The fourth volume consists of three parts covering in forty-one chapters: I. "Flectional suffixes," II. "Productive suffixes," and III. "Other suffixes and composition" (i.e., compound formation). It should be noted that, given the largely prehistoric merger of *-o* stems and *-ŭ* stems, Vaillant does not treat the latter separately. Similarly, other "submerged" formational types are not singled out. Chapter 1 surveys the suffixes *-o-, *-ā-* and *-i-*. Chapters 2 through 18 subsequently examine deverbative nouns, subclassified according to their root vocalism. Chapters 16 and 17 discuss, in particular, disyllabic deverbatives, adjectives, and some aspects of deverbative nouns, while chapter 18 accounts for their accentuation. Part II subdivides the "productive suffixes" by gender: masculines in *-ьcь, -ъkъ, -nikъ, -teljь, -arjь,* etc.; feminines in *-ьca, -ica, -ъka, -ina, -ota, -ostь, -tva, -ynji,* neuters in *-ьce, -ъko, -ьje, -ьstvo,* etc. Adjectival suffixes are dealt with in chapters 25 and 26. Part III then discusses what the author has lumped together under "other suffixes", i.e., non-flectional and/or non-productive derivational morphemes. These are *-b-, -d-, -g-, -j-; -k-; -l-, -m-, -n-, -r-; -s-, -x-; -t-, -v-,* and, as a result of a secondary phonetic development, *-z-*. In chapter 37 the author investigates borrowed suffixes, primarily of an early date, while in chapter 38 he treats the auslaut of adverbs (from a historical perspective, justifiably subsumed under nominal derivation). The rubric of chapter 39 —"Verbal derivation"—is not entirely transparent since it deals with verbal prefixation ("preverbation") and deprefixation ("depreverbation") rather than with verbal derivation proper (suffixation, also infixation). Chapters 40 and 41, finally, sketch the principles of Early Slavic (and Baltic) compound formation.

Though there can be no doubt about the great value of this volume, if only for the wealth of the data presented and analyzed, problematic classification and subcategorization detract somewhat from its usefulness. Vaillant's organization of the material thus obscures the identification of broad chronological layers, namely, IE, Balto-Slavic, CS, attested Early Slavic borrowing and calques, more recent formations, outright neologisms, and so forth. Also the significant spatial divisions (general *vs.* regional *vs.* individual Slavic) and social dimensions (reflected in such oppositions as bookish Church Slavic, vernacular literary *vs.* vernacular colloquial, substandard, etc.) are not sufficiently defined. For a further discussion of the merits and short-comings of this part of the late French Slavist's impressive work, see, for example, Reinhart 1976 and Birnbaum 1981e.

Volume V of Vaillant's comparative Slavic grammar is, largely, an outline, where the emphasis on OCS data is clearly a restricting factor. The two parts of this volume treat first "the use of forms" and then "the phrase" (the latter, however, including also the full-fledged predicative syntagm, i.e., the clause and the sentence). Specifically, in part I are discussed the categories of gender and number, case, prepositions, and the use of verbal forms. Part II surveys various types of syntactic phrases, including sentences, followed by a detailed discussion of conjunctions and word order. Although the prominence of OCS syntactic data is somewhat dispro-protionate, Vaillant also provides exemplification from other Slavic languages, both early recorded and modern ones. This allows him to draw far-reaching conclusions regarding preliterate, in other words CS, grammatical functions and sentence structure. In his syntactic reconstructions, the author operates with hypothetical IE structures and frequently points to the attested parallel evidence of Baltic, which, here as elsewhere, is characterized by a high degree of archaism. In dealing with OCS functions and constructions much emphasis is placed on separating, wherever possible, genuine Slavic from borrowed Greek usage —an indispensable prerequisite for ascertaining the peculiarities of CS syntactic structure. Yet it must be said that, although in more than one respect insightful and important, this volume does not quite stand up to some of the previous ones, both as regards its theoretical foundations and the richness of data cited. For further evaluations of this volume of Vaillant's major work, see in particular Kortlandt 1978e, Gribble 1980, Pennington 1980, and Birnbaum 1983c.

While Vaillant saw the completion of his ambitious scholarly and, at the same time, pedagogical project, it is less likely that the Soviet Slavist S. B. Bernštejn will be able to bring his enterprise of equally far-reaching design to fruition. Yet a sequel to his 1961 *Očerk sravnitel'noj grammatiki slavjanskix jazykov* appeared in 1974, treating morphophonemic alternations and the formation of nominal stems. Although this volume, like its predecessor, has the format of an academic textbook, it also includes the results of its author's original research. Part one, on alternations, discusses specifically: phonetic changes and alternations, the formation and disintegration of morphophonemic alternations, the types and kinds of grammatical alternations, the kinds of morphophonemic alternations, the sets of morphophonemic alternations, and morphophonemic alternations of vocalic and consonantal variants. Separate sections treat: IE ablaut and its structure and development in the position before resonants; the modification of alternations after the monophthongization of diphthongs and restructuring of tautosyllabic groups; the grammatical functions of ablaut; and the utilization of ablaut in various CS dialects. A special section is devoted to the formation of consonantal alternations and another one to fleeting vowels. The remaining sections of this part survey the alternations of various stem classes: those in *-a*, masculine nouns ending in a hard consonant (old *-o* and *-ŭ* stems); diminutives in *-ъk*; possessive adjectives; adjectival formations in *-ъn*; nouns with the suffix *-ьnik-*; alternations in the infinitive, the present tense, and the aorist.

Part two of Bernštejn's work, on nominal stem formation, first discusses, among other things, the distribution of the various formational types of the noun in CS, the role of gender, shifting of individual stems from one class to another and, in addition, identifies traces of grammatical induction. Separate chapters subsequently examine the remnants of consonantal stems and *-s* formations; stems in *-n* (including those in *-men*); stems in *-ęt*; stems in *-r*, in *-ū* and *-ĭ*, as well as stems in *-ō/-jō* and in *-ā*. Though in no way a truly revolutionizing treatment, Bernštejn's work is a solid, well thought-out presentation testifying to its author's great erudition and ability not merely to summarize other researchers work, but to integrate his own observations and ideas as well. For a more detailed assessment of this volume, see Eckert 1975.

The CS evolution and pre-Slavic processes also take up a large part of the fairly traditional text by B. Gasparov and P. Sigalov, *Sravnitel'naja grammatika slavjanskix jazykov* (1974; for a review of volume one, see Kiparsky 1975b). Of the two volumes, the first one treats phonology while the second one covers morphology and its functioning. The first part of volume I discusses the relationship of the PIE sound pattern to its early CS (PS) counterpart. Not only is there a section dealing with the earliest retrievable stage of the PIE phonological system, but special sections discuss the loss of laryngeals and its consequences, the restructuring of the consonantal system and the earliest recoverable phase of PS phonology. The second part of volume I traces the phonological changes ascertainable in PS, but which belong in fact to the immediately preceding Balto-Slavic period. The authors thus survey the shift $s > x$, the loss of syllabic resonants and its consequences, Balto-Slavic prosodic changes, as well as some other, less significant phenomena of the Balto-Slavic period (assimilations of vowels: $e > o$ before $u̯$, $e > i$ before $i̯$; earliest vowel contraction of the type *ne-est-* > *nēst-*; loss of IE geminates; $ur > r$-, possibly paralleled by $u̯l- > l$; $sr > str$, $zr > zdr$). Subsequent parts discuss the history of the sound pattern of Early CS (PS) and elaborate on the major phonological modifications of the CS period. Here, in particular, the authors treat the first delabializations of vowels, the emergence of the tendency toward rising sonority, the subsequent evolution of that tendency at the close of the CS period, the evolution of the tendency toward syllabic synharmonism in CS, the restructuring of Late CS vocalism, and some of the main developments of CS phonology as they anticipate subsequent phonological modifications in the individual Slavic languages of the attested period. Volume II, after a brief discussion of the causes underlying morphological change, deals with the various word classes and their subcategories in traditional order, remarking on CS origins throughout the presentation.

I.3. Comparative Indo-European Linguistics

The Slavic, and specifically CS, component of IE has of course also been discussed, to various degrees, in recent general analyses of the IE language family. Thus, problems of prehistoric Slavic linguistics are considered in V. I. Georgiev's *Introduction to the History of the Indo-European Languages.* This is the English rendition of the Bulgarian scholar's revised and expanded text based on his notes for a lecture course given several years ago at Moscow University. Though focusing primarily on the fields of his special interest —Early Balkan, Greek, and Anatolian —Georgiev also treats such topics as "Balto-Slavic, Germanic, and Indo-Iranian" (chapter 8) and "Tocharian and Balto-Slavic" (chapter 9). In this context it should be noted that the Bulgarian Indo-Europeanist accepts the Balto-Slavic hypothesis in qualified terms, that is, recognizing the primacy of Baltic (especially archaic Lithuanian) over Slavic. Cf. the model conceived by V. V. Ivanov and V. N. Toporov; but see now also Trubačev 1982 discussed below (VI.4.). Operating, as usual, in a very wide-ranging framework, Georgiev repeats here his relevant views. Thus he posits the period of Balto-Slavic unity during the third millennium B.C.; a transitional period lasting from the late third through the early second millennium B.C.; the CS (or PS) period proper during the second and first millennia B.C.; a second transitional period at the beginning of the first millennium A.D.; and, finally, the crystallization of the major Slavic linguistic subbranches during the fourth through eighth centuries A.D. For this summation of Georgiev's views of preliterate IE, including Slavic, basically the same assessment holds true as for much of his previous work; the author displays a thorough control of the relevant data coupled with an imaginative, on occasion overly bold, interpretation of linguistic prehistory.

In a volume of studies tackling a number of still unresolved and controversial problems of IE linguistics, J. Kuryłowicz (1977) also discusses Slavic and especially CS linguistic data. Among issues addressed are both the form and function of certain morphological —in particular, verbal —categories and previously much debated prosodic phenomena. Thus, the Polish comparatist again considers the formation of the IE aorist and imperfect adducing Slavic along with other evidence (cf. 77 and 85–7); he further comments on the future tense and the subjunctive mood (cf., on the Slavic perfective present denoting the future, 95). Among problems of IE accentology Kuryłowicz devotes a whole chapter to Saussure's Law (157–63). It will be recalled that this law is considered by many scholars not to have operated in Slavic (but only in Baltic), and that the Polish linguist did not even consider Slavic prosody to be a direct reflection of PIE accentuation.

A general treatment of PIE syntax, and particularly word order, including relevant Slavic evidence can be found in Friedrich 1975 (for details, see below, IV.3. and IV.4.). For a discussion of some special problems of CS in its IE setting and the relationships of the Slavic protolanguage to its IE cognates, cf. also below, VI.1.

I.4. Common Slavic as Prehistory of Individual Slavic Languages (Diachrony of Individual Slavic Languages)

Of general treatments of the diachrony of individual Slavic languages which trace their origins to CS or even pre-Slavic phenomena and processes, the OCS grammar by R. Aitzetmüller (1978) deserves mention. Explicity designed as an introduction to comparative Slavic linguistics in its broader, IE context, this is essentially a historically oriented OCS grammar of the traditional, neogrammarian bent in which comparative evidence figures prominently. In the section on OCS phonology and its prehistory, the author recognizes a "law of open syllables," which he reformulates slightly, and a general trend toward palatalization (cf. the corresponding concepts defined by N. van Wijk and R. Nahtigal). He also assumes a special tendency said to have prevailed in CS by which earlier *a* would have been "renarrowed," however not to *ŏ*, but to *'a*. This latter view is, to be sure, highly problematic; cf. Birnbaum 1974, 146; 1979b, 202, 205–10. As regards CS and recorded Slavic accentuation, the author, in agreement with a majority of comparatists (but contrary to Kuryłowicz), considers it a direct continuation of the prosodic state of affairs prevailing in the IE protolanguage. In a similar vein he sees the origin of the formal designation of aspect in Slavic as residing in certain morphological categories characteristic of the PIE verb (cf. similar ideas previously expressed by C. G. Regnéll and N. van Wijk). For critical evaluations of Aitzetmüller's text, cf. Birnbaum 1978c and Jelitte 1980/81.

The comparative approach is also found in W. R. Schmalstieg's introduction to OCS (1976). Less immediately useful, perhaps, for classroom teaching concerned primarily with OCS itself, this is nonetheless a valuable tool for students interested in comparative IE linguistics and, particularly, in problems of Balto-Slavic. For some critical assessments, see Huntley 1976, Honowska 1976, and Dostál 1977, the last particularly pointing out the book's limited value for strictly philological work.

An OCS grammar of an entirely different kind is Lunt 1974, the sixth, thoroughly revised edition, which includes for the first time a lengthy epilogue, "Toward a Generative Phonology of Old Church Slavonic." This text, designed for use at American universities, is a strictly synchronic description of the earliest literary language of the Slavs, and as such it is a reliable reference work indeed. CS data appear here therefore only obliquely, as reflected in the attested OCS evidence. Moreover, in the added section on OCS phonology, now viewing it in generative terms, a great number of the underlying sounds and forms bear, naturally, a striking resemblance to those reconstructable for Late CS. Though the purely pedagogical value of this highly theoretical and technical treatment of OCS phonology, taking up almost half of the entire grammar, may be doubtful, it is, overall, more impressive than T. Lightner's early analysis of phonology and morphophonemics as they apply to the OCS verb. In general, Lunt's approach to generative phonology is fairly orthodox, reflecting the standard approach of the late 1960s. For some assessments of the new edition of Lunt's OCS grammar, see Huntley 1975 and Wukasch 1977.

Of historical treatments of Russian, A. Issatschenko's *Geschichte der russischen*

Sprache, the first volume of which appeared posthumously in 1980, deserves particular mention. The author combines an outline of the external (or cultural) history of the Russian literary language with a diachronic description of its structure and offers a number of refreshingly novel, if in part bold and controversial, interpretations. The volume also contains two chapters on "The Slavs and their language: From Common Slavic to Late Proto-Slavic" (13–23) and "The Eastern Slavs and Early East Slavic" (24–53). In accounting for the major sound changes usually attributed to CS and commenting on their partly controversial chronology, Issatschenko stresses, in particular, the peripheral nature of the Late CS dialect underlying Russian proper, particularly in relation to the prehistoric dialectal base of Ukrainian. In this respect the late Slavist echoes and amplifies on the relevant views of his teacher, N. S. Trubeckoj.

CS and occasionally even PIE provide the point of departure for two other recent texts treating contemporary standard Russian from a diachronic point of view. The first of these is R. Auty's sketch "The Russian Language," forming part of the second volume of the *Companion to Russian Studies*, which provides an introduction to Russian language and literature (Auty 1977). The other text is B. Panzer's *Der genetische Aufbau des Russischen* (Panzer 1978a). The former designed for British academic use, the latter for the same purpose in West Germany, both these textbooks are essentially traditional, offering only a few less common observations and explanations. Yet it should be pointed out that Panzer's book has a somewhat innovative format and presents abundant information also on the prehistory of Russian, including the evolution both from PIE to CS and from CS to Proto-Russian (Common East Slavic). For reviews of Panzer's introduction, see, e.g., Stolz 1980 and Leeming 1981b.

Volume three of V. Kiparsky's multi-volume Russian historical grammar, treating the evolution of the vocabulary, appeared in 1975 (Kiparsky 1975a). As is well known, historical lexicology has long been a particular forte of the renowned Finnish Slavist, and this volume is therefore of special interest also for the student of CS. In this volume the author treats at some length both the inherited lexical stock of contemporary standard Russian and its loanwords, including preliterate ones. Among the *Erbwörter*, the author distinguishes three chronological layers: Russian words of a) IE origin (for which an age of c. 3500 years is assumed); b) Balto-Slavic origin (at least 2500 years old); and c) strictly CS origin. Each of these layers is then subdivided according to semantic category (22–53). The particularly instructive section on Russian loanwords borrowed in pre-Petrinic times discusses CS loanwords from Germanic (54–59), Iranian (59–61), Turkic (here only the pre-Mongol loans are pertinent to our discussion, 61–4), Greek (76–84), Finno-Ugric (86–92), and Baltic (92–4). Of the CS loanwords from Germanic — a topic treated by the author already in his still not entirely outdated dissertation of 1934 — four groups are singled out. The first group consists of nine Proto-Germanic (pre-Gothic) loanwords: *glaz, duma, knjaz', skot, tyn, xižina, xlev, xolm*, and OR *šolomъ* Church Slavic *šlěmъ* (R *šlem*). With respect to *skot*, the author considers Germanic *-tt-* a reliable criterion indicative of borrowing from Germanic and not *vice versa* (cf. the contrary view propounded by R. Jakobson, E. Stankiewicz, V. V. Martynov, and others, with only minor differences; but, on the other hand, see Mańczak 1975, referred to below). The second group contains Gothic loanwords, totaling seventeen (including the name of the Danube: *Dunaj/Dunav*), while the third is made up of Balkan Germanic loanwords (among them *bukva*, *vinograd*, and *smokva*). Finally, in the fourth group are found West Germanic loanwords, that is, primarily German (mostly Old High German) borrowings. It should be noted that of the fifty-five Germanic loanwords assumed by the author to have entered CS, the vast majority are cultural terms, most of them nouns.

In discussing Iranian loanwords, Kiparsky takes note of O. N. Trubačev's revolutionizing view (expressed in a lengthy article published in *Ètimologija 1965*, published in 1967) according to which the Iranian loans found in East Slavic (Russian and Ukrainian) cannot be traced to the earliest phase of Slavic-Iranian relations. Instead, the Soviet etymologist considered twelve items found in West Slavic (primarily Polish and Czech) to be reflexes of "CS dialect words." Though not all of Trubačev's Iranian etymologies are fully convincing, Kiparsky acknowledges the significance of the Soviet linguist's findings, pointing to the difficulty of reconciling, in historical terms, the existence of Iranian loanwords (suggestive of early Slavic contacts) precisely in the Slavic West. After Trubačev's purging of Iranian loanwords in Russian, only the following items remain as reasonably certain: *bog, gunja, morda, sapog, topor,* and *štany.*

As for the Turkic loanwords in Russian dating back to preliterate times, only the name of the Avars, OR *Ob(ъ)re*, sg. *Ob(ъ)rinъ*, from which also the West Slavic designation of 'giant', P *olbrzym*, OP *obrzym*, Cz *obr*, Slk *obor*, is derived, must undoubtedly be considered of prehistoric origin (6th–8th cc.). In most other cases the exact date when a pre-Mongol Turkic word entered Old Russian, or preliterate East Slavic, is virtually impossible to ascertain.

Of the numerous Greek loanwords in Russian, the overwhelming majority entered Russian only in historical times (in the late 10th-early 11th cc., in connection with Russia's conversion to Christianity and its immediate aftermath; in the 14th–15th cc., during the so-called Second South Slavic Influence; and in the 17th c., as a result of Patriarch Nikon's reform and the subsequent church schism). Only *korabl'* seems to be a clearly prehistoric loan from Greek, while the "migratory word" *kad'* 'tub, barrel' is also possibly of preliterate date and borrowed from Greek.

As regards alleged borrowings from Finno-Ugric as early as the CS period, the notion of a Finno-Ugric substratum underlying all of CS can now be discarded. Only in a relatively small number of instances may some of the Finnic loanwords of Russian date back to a preliterate, dialectal CS (East Slavic) period and area.

Methodological difficulties are almost insurmountable in identifying possible Baltic lexical borrowings in prehistoric Slavic, given that Baltic attestation starts only several centuries after the beginning of Slavic literacy. In particular, it is extremely difficult to determine whether the correspondence of certain items of Slavic (especially of Russian, Belorussian, and Polish) with their exact counterparts in Baltic is due to borrowing from Baltic to Slavic or from Slavic to Baltic (the latter being the more frequent), or whether we are dealing here with parallel inheritance from PIE or one of its dialects.

Concerning the North Germanic (Scandinavian) loanwords in Russian (94–8), even the oldest ones (e.g., *varjag, vitjaz', grid', kolbjag, šelk, jabeda*, and a few others) mostly date from post-CS and partly early historical times. Only *vitjaz'* may actually be of CS origin (cf. also P *zwyciężyć* 'to win, conquer').

The preliterate evolution of the lexicon is further discussed by Kiparsky in a lengthy chapter on Russian suffix formation (181–305), as well as in a shorter treatment of prefix formation (306–43). Here the material is grouped by individual nominal suffixes and, with regard to the verb, according to the five present-stem (Leskien) classes; a further criterion for grouping the data is provided by individual prefixes. Some considerations concerning the prehistoric development are also included in a separate chapter on compounds (344–50). In particular, Kiparsky discusses here the archaic (IE) compositional types of copulative compounds (known as *dvandva*), determinative compounds (the two subtypes of which are sometimes referred to as *tatpuruša* and *karmadharaya*), and attributive compounds (*bahuvrīhi*). All these compound types are attested in Old Russian: e.g., *bratъsestra, malъžena; medvedь* (< *medъ-vědь* or *medъ-ědь*), *vojevoda, velьmoža, Vyšьgradъ, Novъgorodъ, Volčijxvost*. For a brief assessment of this volume of Kiparsky's impressive work, see Lunt 1976.

A survey of CS and a section on one of the dialects of Late CS are included in W. Kuraszkiewicz's historical grammar of Polish (cf. Kuraszkiewicz 1972, 13–20). Although reliable, as is most of the Polish scholar's work, this textbook does not contribute much new to our knowledge of CS (cf. for an assessment Cantarini 1973/74).

The fourth and fifth volumes of the monumental history of Slovak by J. Stanislav (1973) treat syntax. As in previous volumes of this work, CS data provide here the point of departure.

For some comments on recent general treatments of the historical phonology of individual Slavic languages (Russian, Ukrainian, Belorussian, Polish, and Slovak) by Kantor and Smith (1975), Kolesov (1980a), Shevelov (1979), Wexler (1977), Stieber (1973b) and Krajčovič (1975), see below, *sub* II.1.

II. PHONOLOGY

II.1. Monographic Treatments and General Problems of Common Slavic Phonology

Particularly deserving of mention among recent monographic treatments and discussions of more general problems pertaining to CS phonology is the study by V. N. Čekman, *Issledovanija po istoričeskoj fonetike praslavjanskogo jazyka*, subtitled *Tipologija i rekonotrukcija* (Čekman 1975). Čekman's approach to linguistic reconstruction is in part untraditional, relying as it does largely on a typological framework to retrieve the sound pattern of CS and to elucidate some of its modifications through time. The theoretical portion of the book discusses, specifically, the overall goals of comparative historical linguistics, commenting on the particular techniques used in reconstructing lost protolanguages. Typological irregularities, applicable to and informing the methodology of reconstruction, are emphasized and dynamic models of linguistic change are sketched. The author thus relates problems of change to language typology. Also treated are insights gained from areal linguistics and, in particular, the specific diffusion of linguistic phenomena in space. Of the various individual phonological phenomena and processes of CS, those discussed are palatalizations and jotations, including the controversial chronology of velar and other palatalizations, as well as the problem of the rise and ultimate disintegration of syllabemes, again, with unresolved issues of time sequence. Additionally, Čekman considers the general phenomenon of the tendency toward open-syllable structure and its implications for CS developments. Of particular problems in CS phonology, the fate of *ĭ* and *ŭ* (i.e., the prehistoric evolution and early attested phase of the history of the jers) is discussed.

In a review article by E. Stankiewicz (1973) on "The Historical Phonology of Common Slavic," the author discusses Z. Stieber's treatment of CS phonology as presented in his outline of comparative Slavic grammar. Though noting some shortcomings in the Polish linguist's textbook, Stankiewicz nonetheless considers it the most useful, informative, and manageable survey of CS phonology (the last qualification obviously aimed at G. Y. Shevelov's much more detailed and bulky treatment of the same field). Yet, the American Slavist calls for a "broader integration of historical and dialectological studies, a deeper approach to the reconstruction of prehistoric facts, and a stronger emphasis on general principles" (192).

In the volume honoring Roman Jakobson's contribution to linguistics and, indeed, scholarship at large, S. K. Šaumjan (1977) offers a highly positive reassessment of the great American linguist's contribution to the study of Slavic historical phonology. In particular, he emphasizes the then methodological novelty and the lasting impact of Jakobson's early classic, *Remarques*, including his pioneering treatment of preliterate, largely CS, phonological evolution.

W. R. Schmalstieg's "New Thoughts on Indo-European Phonology" advocates a "new view" of IE phonology, including also a number of facts and developments drawn from, or pertinent to, CS. In this context it may be mentioned, however, that even more far-reaching reassessments of PIE and comparative IE phonology have been proposed, and in part sketched, also by the Soviet linguists V. V. Ivanov and T. V. Gamkrelidze as well as by, in the West, O. Szemerényi, A. Bomhard, and others.

A more traditional overview of the phonological evolution from Late CS to Proto-OCS (Trubeckoj's *Urkirchenslavisch)* was offered by L. Moszyński (1978a). Using a structural framework adopted from the Prague School (and in more recent years applied successfully by Stieber to Slavic), Moszyński endeavors to suggest some broad systematizations of Slavic prehistoric sound evolution. Thus he points out that the vowel system remained fundamentally unchanged throughout the Late CS and Proto-OCS period. The consonant system, by contrast, was significantly restructured, rendering the softness opposition secondary or even redundant and showing first instances of dispalatalization, with the rise of a biphonemic value of palatalized labials as a result, and implementing a number of other related sound shifts: *$tj > t'$ $> št$, *$dj > d' > žd$; simplification of affricates $dž, dz' > ž, z' > z$. Further simplifications in the consonant system as well as other minor modifications are noted. Among the latter, the author comments, in particular, on the fact that Gk *ph* and *th* are not always rendered by *p* and *t*, but in addition yield the new phoneme *f*. Generally, it can be said therefore that while the OCS vowel system is markedly archaic, its consonant system is innovative as compared to that of CS.

W. Mańczak's treatment of Slavic historic phonology (1977a) views comparative historical phonology of Slavic, including its CS origin, almost exclusively in terms of the impact attributed by the author to word frequency as it affects phonetic change. Thus he examines the Slavic data according to word class and derivational as well as inflectional morphemes where these exhibit an irregular evolution. The Cracow linguist posits CS protoforms virtually throughout his discussion without, however, ever questioning their precise status and chronologically determined shape or origin. This, therefore, is yet another of his many contributions written in the spirit of Zipf's Law, emphasizing—indeed overemphasizing—purely statistical considerations.

Problems of CS and Early Slavic phonology are also addressed in S. Rospond's study (1975) on Slavic historical phonology in light of onomastics. Rospond demonstrates, once more, the value of toponymy and other geographic names in elucidating some insufficiently understood facets of prehistoric Slavic phonology.

Sections, of varying length and attention to detail, treating CS phonology are also included in a number of recent texts, or surveys, of the historical phonology of individual Slavic languages. This applies, for example, to V. V. Kolesov's introduction to the historical phonology of Russian (Kolesov 1980a). In chapters one and two are discussed "the earliest phonemic system of the East Slavic dialect as a constituent part of Common Slavic" (13–68) and "the completion of the dynamic tendencies of Common Slavic in Old Russian (mid–10th to end of 11th cc.)" (69–106). M. Kantor and R. N. Smith's "A Sketch of the Major Developments in Russian

Historical Phonology" is relevant to our discussion only insofar as it includes a set of generative phonological rules for converting PIE to contemporary standard Russian sounds and forms. The proposed rules thus parallel the pre-Slavic and CS, in addition to recorded, stages of development.

G. Y. Shevelov's monumental *A Historical Phonology of the Ukrainian Language* (Shevelov 1979), using the same approach, notational conventions, and format as his previous treatment of CS phonology, proceeds consistently from Late CS when viewing the subsequent, attested evolution of Proto- and Early Ukrainian. Thus, in particular, section two discusses "The Common Slavic Phonemic System Before the Beginning of the Formation of Ukrainian" (51–4), and section three dwells on "Peculiarities of the Proto-Ukrainian Dialects in the Common Slavic Palatalizational Processes" (55–77). For some reviews of Shevelov's recent work, see, e.g., Hüttl-Folter 1980 and Perfecky 1981 (leveling some harsh criticism particularly against the book's style).

Similarly, P. Wexler, in his matching treatment of Belorussian historical phonology (1977), takes CS as the point of departure when discussing subsequent Belorussian developments. Notably, this textbook contains a section on models of evolution and here traces the evolution from CS to Belorussian (52–64). For some assessments of this treatment, see Dingley 1979 and Naylor 1980.

Z. Stieber's *A Historical Phonology of the Polish Language* (Stieber 1973b) is a revised and expanded English rendition of his previous treatment of the prehistoric and historical phonological evolution of Polish, adapted to the format of the series of historical phonologies edited by Shevelov. Though adding little new to Stieber's previous findings, it should be noted that the book, in chapter one, contains a section on the preliterate period. Here the author discusses, among other things, "The Common Slavic Vowel System," "The Prosody of Common Slavic," and "The Common Slavic Consonantal System," as well as other prehistoric developments, partly of a CS dialectal nature. Stieber's work has been reviewed by, among others, Birnbaum (1981c).

R. Krajčovič's parallel treatment of Slovak historical phonology (Krajčovič 1975) also discusses in the introduction (23–41) such topics as the CS basis of Slovak, the relation of that basis to the CS macro-dialects, the CS basis of the western, eastern and central dialects of Slovak. In addition, a number of general conclusions are drawn from this discussion. For critical assessments of Krajčovič's work, see, e.g., Laskowski 1975 and Vavrus 1977.

II.2. Accentology

Considerable progress has been made over the last ten years or so in the field of Slavic accentology, particularly in the reconstruction of CS (and Balto-Slavic) prosodic structure. Here, the writings of two Soviet and two Western linguists are especially prominent. They are V. A. Dybo and V. V. Kolesov, and P. Garde and F. Kortlandt.

Two comprehensive essays by Dybo are particularly deserving of mention: "Baltoslavjanskaja akcentnaja sistema s tipologičeskoj točki zrenija i problema rekonstrukcii indoevropejskogo akcenta" (Dybo 1980 and 1979b) and "Rekonstrukcija sistemy akcentnyx paradigm v praslavjanskom (konspekt)" (1979a). The first of the two studies is a significant reinterpretation of Balto-Slavic prosody viewed both in typological terms and as it relates to the accentual facts of IE. Much of the author's previous work on CS accentology is summarized and integrated here, and Dybo also discusses the overall Balto-Slavic prosodic prototype as it underlies the Early CS (PS) accentual system. In the second part of the study, the Soviet linguist focuses specifically on the accentological status of oxytones found in what is usually termed "accent type c" (i.e., paradigmatically mobile stress) in CS. He proposes the reconstruction of the original "accentual curve" in this nominal paradigm, retaining Stang's view of the genetic identity of this paradigm and what is known as paradigm 3 in Lithuanian; yet Dybo modifies some of the details of Stang's conception. Thus, he takes into account, among other things, the reformulation by V. M. Illič-Svityč of Hirt's Law.

Dybo's second study presents a preview of his major work (Dybo 1981, discussed below). The analysis presented here makes novel use of data deriving from the accentual systems of Old Russian (or rather Russian Church Slavic from the 14th c.), of Middle Bulgarian (the evidence being also from the 14th c.), Old Serbian (with data from the beginning of the 15th c.), Croatian (with Kajkavian evidence stemming from the 16th c., Čakavian from the 17th c.); in addition, West Slavic data are reconsidered. As can be gathered even from these brief comments, Dybo resorts to the comparative method when attempting to reconstruct the Balto-Slavic state of affairs, or level of evolution, when the law of the development of syllabic accentuation (as formulated by Saussure and Bezzenberger) was operational. The present reconstruction is more complete than previous ones since it includes not only the system of accentual paradigms of the noun but also the accentual types of the pronoun, as well as a tentative systematization of the accentual types of derived nouns, with rules formulated for their generation. Moreover, this sketch presents a system of the accentual types also for the verb, commenting on the regularities of their distribution, as well as a separate system for generating the accentual types of deverbal nouns. Finally, the regularities occurring in the phrasal modifications of accentuation are briefly commented upon.

Dybo's *Slavjanskaja akcentologija. Opyt rekonstrukcii sistemy akcentnyx paradigm v praslavjanskom* (1981) is one of the two most important monographic treatments of CS accentology since C. S. Stang's *Slavonic Accentuation* (1957). It was Stang who correlated three distinctive tones (or pitches: acute, circumflex, neoacute) with three accentual paradigms, since then conventionally labeled a, b, and c. In paradigm a stress was fixed on an acute syllable. Paradigm b displayed neoacute tone in some forms, short accent on the immediately following syllable in others. (Since neoacute is due to stress retraction, paradigm b had fixed stress on a noninitial syllable at an earlier stage of CS or Balto-Slavic.) Paradigm c had circumflex tone on the initial syllable in some forms, final stress in others. Put differently, the paradigms can be described as having: fixed stress (*a*), partly shifted stress (*b*), and mobile stress (*c*). Complementing Stang's findings, Dybo (corroborated by Illič-Svityč) established a progressive accent shift which reduced paradigms *a* and *b* to a single earlier CS paradigm. Since type *a* had fixed stress on a non-final acute sylla-ble and acute vowels were shortened in CS, the accentual paradigms *a* and *b* were in complementary distribution. Thus, the rise of type *b* can be explained phonetically by assuming that a stressed vowel which was neither acute nor circumflex lost its stress to the following syllable in Slavic. The progressive accent shift (known as Dybo's Law) differs from Saussure's Law in that the shift is assumed to be independ-ent of the pitch (tone) of the syllable attracting the stress.

The new monograph by Dybo is, in fact, the first complete reconstruction of the CS accentual system ever undertaken in systematic fashion. As a result of a radical reevaluation and substantial reinterpretation of Slavic diachronic accentology (largely contained already in his previous pertinent writings), the author has been able to establish a uniform, general principle for setting up a coherent system of CS accentual paradigms. In addition to utilizing previously analyzed data, Dybo's stu-dy is based on evidence culled from early Slavic texts to which little attention has been paid in earlier accentological research.

Dybo's work contains, in addition to a general introduction (3–10), three major sections treating: (1) the accentual paradigms of the noun in Baltic and Slavic (11–54); (2) the accentual types of derivatives in CS and the rules for their generation (55–196); and (3) the accentuation of the CS verb and the fundamental principle of establishing the Balto-Slavic accent system (197–262). The author reassesses the validity of some previously formulated major "sound laws" pertinent to accentology—*viz.* Fortunatov's Law (i.e. Saussure's Law as applied to Slavic data, previously rejected by Stang), and Leskien's, Meillet's, Hirt's, and Illič-Svityč's Laws. He further comments on the prosodic correspondences between Slavic and Baltic (especially Lithuanian) and their relationship to the reconstructable accentual system of PIE (against Kuryłowicz's view of no direct link between PIE and Balto-Slavic accentuation). Operating with the three major types of accentual paradigms (*a*, *b*, *c*), Dybo arrives at the conclusion that all morphemes of CS can be assigned to one of two morphophonemic prosodic classes as regards their ictus (place of stress): I = the class of "recessive morphemes" (cf. the similar viewpoint presented in work by Garde, discussed below). To class I belong: (1) the roots of accent paradigm 1 (subsuming types *a* and *b*), (2) desinences receiving stress in accent paradigm 2 (corresponding to type *c*), and (3) the suffixes of words whose roots belong to class II. To class II belong: (1) the roots of accent paradigm 2, (2) thematic vowels, (3) the desinences of *enklinomena* (a designation of ancient Greek grammar, reintro-duced by R. Jakobson) of accent paradigm 2, and (4) the suffixes of words whose roots belong to class I. The prosodic characteristics of these two morpheme classes can be referred to as their accentual "valences"—with class I having higher, class II lower valence. A general law of the accentual "contour" of morpheme sequences in

Balto-Slavic may be formulated as follows: The ictus falls in the beginning of morpheme sequences (including one-morpheme sequences) of higher valence. The Balto-Slavic accentual system can be conceived of as a reflection of IE tonal relationships.

Finally, several more accentual contributions by Dybo should be noted. Dybo 1974 presents a study on Afghan accentuation and its significance for IE and Balto-Slavic accentology, while Dybo 1975 and 1977 concern reflexes of the Law of Vasil'ev-Dolobko (in Old Russian and Middle Bulgarian). Two studies treat the accentual types of the present tense of verbs: the first, of verbs with a reduced vowel in the root (Dybo 1972); the second, of verbs with roots ending in a non-sonorant (Dybo 1982). Stress patterns of derived adjectives are the topic of Dybo 1971.

Kolesov's accentological studies focus primarily on the evidence of Old Russian, commenting also on its unattested prehistory, however. His monograph *Istorija russkogo udarenija. Immennaja akcentuacija v drevnerusskom jazyke* (1972) thus treats the history of Russian nominal accentuation (feminine nouns, masculine and neuter nouns, short-form adjectives), including an analysis also of the Late CS beginnings of the evolution subsequently recorded in East Slavic. For an evaluation of this work, see, e.g., Kiparsky 1974. The other accentual study of similarly broad scope by Kolesov is his article on the relative chronology of prosodic changes in CS (Kolesov 1979a). Here he takes into account lasting and recent achievements in the field (referring to work by, among others, van Wijk, Stang, Jakobson, Kuryłowicz, Sadnik, Kortlandt, Illič-Svityč, and Dybo). The author concludes that in terms of prosodic restructuring, CS began with the rise of phonemic pitch at the word-form level. This led to the development of intonational word paradigms, and the emergence of the neo-acute. The culmination of this process was the redistribution of redundant prosodic features (of stress, according to the "principle of Križanić," studied by Dybo). Quantity arose on the basis of various rules for shortening positional length, subsumable under the Laws of Šaxmatov, Vondrák, and Trávníček. Only thereafter begins, in prosodic terms, the period of the independent evolution of the individual Slavic languages, each with its own characteristic accentual patterns and entities resulting from various modifications of neo-acute intonation.

Other pertinent studies by the same Soviet Slavist include articles on stress in prefixed nouns in Old Russian and CS, on stress in derived nouns with nonproductive suffixes in Slavic and, particularly, Old Russian, and on stress in derived nouns with the suffix *-išč-* in the history of Russian (Kolesov 1975, 1979b, 1980b). In the study on prefixed nouns the author, in surveying pertinent problems of accentuation in Old Russian and CS, arrives at a unified system as a result of various generalizations and levelings. He thus distinguishes among formations from: 1) an original mobile accent type; 2) a mobile accent type with jer prefix; and 3) an original oxytone type, namely, a) short roots, and b) roots with circumflex (falling) intonation.

Previous work by the two just mentioned Soviet scholars as well as some of their more recent writings were commented upon by, among others, R. Slonek and R. V. Bulatova. Slonek 1972 is concerned primarily with the reflexes of IE laryngeals in

Slavic, while Bulatova 1979 surveys the accomplishments of the preceding two dec-
ades, focusing especially on the contributions by Dybo and Kolesov.

Of P. Garde's accentual studies, it is above all his two-volume *Histoire de
l'accentuation slave* (Garde 1976a) that deserves our attention. Comparable in
overall scholarly significance only to C. S. Stang's and, now, V. A. Dybo's major
work on Slavic accentuation, Garde's contribution is superior to Stang's pioneering
monograph not only because of the former's more comprehensive character and integration of the most recent relevant findings but also in terms of its exemplary organization and presentation of the data. This is a highly original reinterpretation of the
evolution of Slavic prosody in its prehistoric as well as recorded phases. Part One
discusses systematically the Balto-Slavic origins and background. Chapter 1, on the
"Prosodic and Accentological Systems of Balto-Slavic," includes a discussion of the
Laws of Saussure and Illič-Svityč, among others. Chapter 2 treats "Accent in
Nominal Inflection," and chapter 3 concerns "Accent in Nominal Derivation."
Chapter 4 deals with "Accent in Nominal Compounds," and chapters 5, 6, and 7 cover "Accent in the Verb," both non-suffixed and suffixed and as it pertains to the verb
stem. Part Two, treating the evolution from Balto-Slavic to the modern period, first
discusses separately Baltic (chapter 3) and then CS (chapter 4). The remaining
chapters are devoted to the individual languages and language groups. Finally, Part
Three attempts to project backward from Balto-Slavic into IE. Thus, chapter 14
concerns the "Origin of Balto-Slavic Intonations," chapter 15 "The Accent System:
Generalities," and chapter 16 "Accent and Inflection." Chapter 17 deals with
"Accent in Nominal Compounds," chapter 18 with "Accent in Derivation," and
chapter 19 attempts to look "Towards the Origins of Free Stress in IE." Needless to
say, this significant contribution has already evoked a considerable scholarly debate,
mixing highly positive with a few critical notes. For reviews of Garde's work, see,
e.g., Kuryłowicz 1977, Cantarini 1977/79, Kiparsky 1977, Kortlandt 1978d,
Neweklowsky 1979, and Halle & Kiparsky 1981, the last going into particular detail
and gauging Garde's results against those obtainable by a different approach. All in
all, Garde's and Dybo's comprehensive monographs can be considered successful
summations of our present knowledge of Slavic accentology and its sources, with
proper attention paid to the intricate interplay between purely phonological
phenomena and morphological—inflectional as well as derivational—factors.

Some other accentological studies by the French Slavist may be considered largely
by-products of his major work, even though they too are of some significance as re-
ports on original findings and insightful conclusions. Thus, the paper discussing the
question of whether the oxytone stress pattern is of CS origin (Garde 1973) suggests
that the Balto-Slavic prosodic system (in Lithuanian modified only by Saussure's
Law) had but two chief paradigms: a barytone and a mobile one. A third paradigm
—the oxytone stress pattern —appeared only in East and South Slavic (according to
Illič-Svityč's Law) shifting stress from a non-acute (i.e. short or circumflex) syllable
to the following. This, however, cannot be considered a CS stress rule since it does
not operate in West Slavic, where the original place of ictus was at first preserved;

that is, the Balto-Slavic double paradigm prevailed here up to the period when stress was mechanically fixed (and up to the present in Kashubian). Thus, the counterparts of East and South Slavic oxytones at first (and in Kashubian until now) remained barytones in West Slavic. This new hypothesis, therefore, supplements that advanced by Illič-Svityč, who has shown that original barytones (posited for the distant past) survived in West Slavic. Consequently, Garde claims to have established a new phonological isogloss, separating West Slavic from the rest of the Slavic languages, thus explaining the place of stress in Kashubian as a genuine archaism. For a contrary view, see Kortlandt 1978d.

The other important paper by Garde (1976b) discusses "Neutralization of Tone in Common Slavic", focusing on such neutralization in monosyllabic stems, final syllables of bi- and multi-syllabic stems, long non-final syllables of non-monosyllabic stems, and long syllables in grammatical endings. The author concludes for CS that

the opposition acute *vs.* circumflex inherited from Balto-Slavic has been retained in Slavic only in the following positions: under stress, after stress. It has been neutralized in other positions ...: before stress; in unstressed forms. Thus Common Slavic had three types of long syllables: acute and circumflex, which occurred (in opposition with each other) outside the position of neutralization, and non-intonable length which occurred in that position (15).

Chronologically, pitch neutralization was the first strictly CS accentological innovation, i.e., the first development involving Slavic but not Baltic, and thus created a difference between the prosodic systems of Slavic and Lithuanian (as well as its sister languages).

Kortlandt's major contribution to Slavic accentology to date is his monograph *Slavic Accentuation: A Study in Relative Chronology*. The study reinterprets some, but not all, facets of prehistoric Slavic accentuation and is, as indicated by its subtitle, primarily concerned with the establishment of relative chronologies. It attempts to improve on the modern theory of Slavic accentology as it was ushered in by Stang's important work. Kortlandt subscribes to Illič-Svityč's rejection of Kuryłowicz's (but not Stang's) view that the pitch and ictus patterns of Balto-Slavic do not directly reflect a preceding, IE prosodic system. In particular, the Dutch comparatist discusses: 1) the origin and persistence of stress mobility in the -*l* participles; 2) the origins of differences in ictus, quantity, timbre, and intonation of various *o* sounds in diverse variants of Slovenian *konj*, with further implications for CS; 3) details of the presumed loss of IE laryngeals in Slavic, assuming for it a relatively late chronology (post-Balto-Slavic but pre-Late CS); 4) Dolobko's Law as it applies to the adjective (including the comparative); and 5) accent as it pertains to case endings, with special attention paid to the interaction of phonological and morphological factors. In appendices to his study, the author lists, among other things, Slavic lexical items with originally laryngealized vowels in the root and Slavic reflexes of instances of IE lengthened grade. It should also be mentioned that Kortlandt's study examines the detailed chronology of sound change in prehistoric and attested Slavic proposed by C. L. Ebeling in 1963 (and specifically for Slavic accentuation in 1967).

For assessments of Kortlandt's study, see, e.g., Comrie 1975b, Schelesniker 1975/77, Elson 1976, and Birnbaum 1983b.

Other recent accentological work by Kortlandt deals with the essentially post-CS neo-circumflex, attested in Slovenian and Kajkavian Croatian, for which he basically accepts Stang's view (1976), the overall state of the art (1978a), and problems of Slavic accentuation in deverbative nouns (1979b). As for the present state of the art, reflecting the twenty years of accomplishments since 1957 (including comments particularly on the findings of Dolobko, Dybo, Illič-Svityč, Ebeling, Winter, and himself), Kortlandt terms the progress spectacular. He is, however, critical of some more recent developments. As is usual in Kortlandt's work, there is much emphasis on detailed chronology. Regarding deverbative nouns, Kortlandt argues that the only subtype (for such nouns) where two different accentual pardigms can be reconstructed is that of prefixed masculines. The ascertainable semantic opposition seems to point to PIE. Feminine deverbatives, on the other hand, all had initial stress in Early CS (PS).

Of other recent research on Slavic and particularly CS accentology, mention should be made of M. Halle's "Remarks on Slavic Accentology" (1971). Here Halle applies a generative approach to some of the chief phenomena of contemporary Slavic accentuation, especially Russian, Serbo-Croatian (Štokavian, but also dialectal Slavonian and the Čakavian of Novi), as well as Slovenian. The author postulates throughout a set of synchronic generative rules operating on a uniform underlying accentual system, largely duplicating that assumed for CS. A similar approach is also employed by B. J. Darden when discussing "Rule Ordering in Baltic and Slavic Nominal Accentuation" (1972) where not only rule ordering but also an assumed change of status of the segments involved (phonetic *vs.* phonemic *vs.* morphophonemic) play a significant role. The notion of neutralization is crucial to the explanation proposed. Its diachronic significance lies partly in the fact that the author takes issue with, among others, Kuryłowicz and Illič-Svityč. He concludes that "both languages [i.e., Baltic and Slavic], taking different paths, developed in such a way as to eliminate the original ties between intonation and quantity." Darden 1979 contains some further criticism of Illič-Svityč's conception of Balto-Slavic nominal accentuation, as does Darden 1982 where account is, moreover, taken of the findings in Winter 1978 (see below, *sub* II.3.) and the author now in part sides with Kuryłowicz's view (as against Illič-Svityč).

P. Kiparsky's discussion of "The Inflectional Accent in Indo-European" (1973) includes a reinterpretation of phenomena pertinent also to Balto-Slavic. Thus, he reassesses the "correspondence" obtaining between the Lithuanian acute (i.e., falling) and the Slavic acute (i.e., rising) pitch in stem syllables with a contour reversal postulated for Lithuanian. Kiparsky further suggests that there in fact never existed "acute mobilia" distinct from "circumflex mobilia." The American linguist argues that "what is systematically different in Lithuanian, as opposed to the rest of Balto-Slavic, is only the falling character of the inherent accent on long stem syllables. Elsewhere it is rising and therefore distinct from the initial, falling movable accent"

(834). He thus rejects those theories which assume Balto-Slavic accentual mobility of -*o* and -*ā* stems.

Following Dybo, Nikolaev and Starostin (1982) are concerned with Slavic primarily to establish accentual types of the present and aorist stems. Where possible these stems are also correlated with their IE counterparts. The authors argue that the chief characteristic for Slavic of the two IE paradigmatic classes is their accentual distribution (class I = immobile, or fixed, stress; class II = mobile stress). Generally, the accentual paradigm can be correlated in Slavic with the formation of the aorist. Thus, a verb of class I forms a thematic, or "simple," aorist if the root ends in a consonant, a sigmatic-root aorist if the root ends in a sonorant. A verb of class II forms a sigmatic aorist if the root ends in a consonant, a sigmatic-dental aorist if the root ends in a sonorant. However, this system was modified slightly in CS as it applied to both accentual classes, and nonparadigmatic aorists of stems in -*a* spread widely by analogy.

Critical of Kuryłowicz's relevant views is Z. Junković in his contribution treating the problem of CS metatony and the complexities of intonation in the Slavic proto-language (Junković 1977). CS metatony, as observable in the present tense, and the application of Dybo's Law is further the topic of a recent paper by Johnson (1980), who suggests some major modifications in that law. Moreover, he doubts, in general, the validity of some of the recent findings in Slavic accentuation not only by Dybo but also by Ebeling and Kortlandt.

Here also some recent accentological contributions by R. F. Feldstein ought to be mentioned. Thus, in two papers he reexamines aspects of the neo-acute (Feldstein 1975 and 1978b), particularly in West Slavic, as compared to neo-acute, or rather its reflexes, in western South Slavic and in East Slavic. In particular he discusses the role of short high vowels (i.e., ь, ъ) in the rise of neo-acute intonation. Though only the prosodic feature of quantity can be found in West Slavic as a trace of former neo-acute pitch, two areas —Czech *vs.* Slovak and Polish—can be distinguished here and compared with the prosodic systems of Southwest and Northeast Slavic. This distinction is contingent upon whether it was tone or stress place that was crucial in preventing the merger of the reflexes of original acute and neo-acute intonation. In the second paper, on this and related subjects, Feldstein attempts to reconstruct the relative chronology of the loss of pitch opposition and neo-acute retraction of stress in Slavic nouns with short and long vowels. He suggests a causal connection between the merger of accentual paradigms with the chronology of neo-acute stress retraction (from word-final jers). He concludes that significant traces of pitch distinction can be identified despite the absence of precisely such distinctions in all of the West Slavic languages. In a third paper (Feldstein 1978a), the same linguist examines various aspects of the use of prosodic features in CS. Here he modifies the non-generative approach proposed by Jakobson (in his seminal contribution "Opyt fonologičeskogo podxoda k istoričeskim voprosam slavjanskoj akcentologii" of 1963) to fit a generative framework. In particular, he suggests a special diacritic feature in order to account for alternating (non-oxytonic) accentual paradigms while commenting on the pertinent work of, among others, Stang and Halle. An overall assessment of Jakobson's contribution to Slavic accentology, including its prehistoric phases, can be found in Birnbaum 1977b.

Some of the reflexes of the IE laryngeals as they appear in the prosodic patterning of Slavic paradigms were studied in a monograph by R. Slonek (1979). The dubious value of this work was justly pointed out by Shevelov (1980) in his review of it. For some additional work on the traces of lost IE laryngeals in Slavic, see below *sub* II.3.

Issues of Balto-Slavic prosody were further discussed by J. Prinz (1978) and V. Bubenik (1980). In an attempt at chronolgical systematization Prinz first discusses the "original intonational situation" followed by sections on "metatonies of the first type," "the oldest metatonies of the second type," and "the Late CS metatonies of the second type," assuming "a common Balto-Slavic heritage." Bubenik in his study first considers the account of Russian, Serbo-Croatian, and Lithuanian accentuation offered in recent years by M. Halle and M. J. Kenstowicz. He argues that the notions of specific levels ("autonomous phonology and lexology") are crucial to these accounts and claims further that the notions of "paradigmatic coherence" and analogy must be taken into consideration in order to avoid such complication as extrinsic rule ordering.

Old Russian accentological data are commented upon, and their relevance to the prehistoric evolution demonstrated, in studies by T. G. Xazagerov (1973) and A. A. Zaliznjak (1977). Xazagerov in his monograph on the development of accentual types in the system of the Russian declension, discusses in three early chapters (12–30) the prehistoric, primarily CS, evolution of the Russian accent system. In the more narrow study by Zaliznjak, an interpretation in terms of CS accentology is given for the distinction of two —open and closed —*o* phonemes in a 14th-century Russian Church Slavic text. In a recent paper, Micklesen (1982), though concerned primarily with stress patterns of a particular verb class in various modern Slavic languages (with mobile stress), reconstructs underlying forms largely coinciding with accentual patterns which can be posited for CS.

Problems of CS prosody take a prominent place, finally, in E. Stankiewicz's *Studies in Slavic Morphophonemics and Accentology* (1979), containing a number of mostly reprinted (but in part updated) studies by the American Slavist. Thus, some of the essays in this volume discuss "The Common Slavic Prosodic Pattern and Its Evolution in Slovenian" (32–41), "The Accent Patterns of the Slavic Verb" (72–87), and "The Slavic Vocative and Its Accentuation" (100–109), the last taking CS as its point of departure. Of particular interest is the partial reconstruction of the prosodic system of the Slavic verb offered in the second essay, where, on the basis of contemporary data, Stankiewicz suggests that "the phonologically and morphologically unmarked nominal and verbal forms of Common Slavic can ... be characterized as forms which carried *oppositional, marginal* accents and which were subject to *opposite, marginal* accentual alternations" (85). For a contribution to Slavic morphophonemics by the same scholar, including diachronic data reaching back to CS times, see below *sub* II.6. For some criticism of Stankiewicz's views as expresssed in this volume, see Becker 1981 and, particularly, Kortlandt 1980 (as well as the ensuing debate between the two linguists; cf. Stankiewicz 1982 and Kortlandt 1982b).

II.3. Vocalism (Including Ablaut and Modification of Diphthongs in Liquids and Nasals; Syllabic Liquids and Nasals)

Vocalic reflexes of Indo-European laryngeals, and in particular zero-grade laryngeals, were treated in a paper by M. Samilov (1975). The author points out that, in addition to the regular reflex *o* of a IE zero-grade laryngeal in Slavic, there are also two other developments of an IE laryngeal ascertainable in Slavic: IE **Hi* > CS *ě₂* and IE **Hu* > CS *u* under circumflex. Among the relevant lexical items with *o* discussed by Samilov are: *bo, ibo, nebonъ, ubo, bojati sę*, R *botat'*, *doiti*, R *drob'/droba, drobiti, droždiję, govorъ, grozdъ, koprъ, kovati, krojǫ, kromě* (and cognates), *krovъ, lopata*, Bg, SC *loš, lovъ, loxma, mokrъ, (sъ)motriti, neroditi*, R *ožina, ploskъ*, R *roču, snopъ, snobati, spodъ, sporъ, stojǫ*, P *stromy, toję* (gen. sg. f.), SC *tov, vъlovьnъ*, SC *zglobiti*. Reflexes of IE laryngeals were further discussed by H. D. Pohl (1974). In line with the standard view, Pohl assumes the erstwhile existence of three original laryngeals: *e*-coloring H_1, *a*-coloring H_2, and *o*-coloring H_3. In particular, he discusses the Slavic reflexes in terms of intonations, where acute points to an earlier laryngeal: the types EHR + C and ERH + C, in addition to original, inherited long vowels and long diphthongs marked by acute (cf. the relevant view of Stang). Pohl further surveys the presumed *o* reflexes of IE ə, and comments on such items as *damь* *<*dā-d-mi* < **deH₃-dH₃-mi*; *deždǫ* < **de-d-j-* **<de-dH₁-i-e/o-*, touching briefly also on reduplicated roots in Slavic. Other items commented upon, especially with reference to their ablaut are: *stojati* (: *stati*), *gorěti* (: *grěti*), *dojiti* and *pojiti* (: *piti*), further *dъšti* < **dhugh-H-ter*, **stryjь* < IE **pH-ter-(C)*, *spěti, spějǫ* < **speH₁-(C)*, *ženo* (voc. sg.) < **gʷenə*, as well as some others. In conclusion the Austrian linguist expresses the view that Slavic does not provide sufficient evidence to corroborate that IE ə here regularly yielded *o*.

The work *Studien zum slavischen und indoeuropäischen Langvokalismus* by T. Mathiassen, previewed in Birnbaum 1979a, appeared only in 1974. Here, the Norwegian comparatist investigates in some detail the IE lengthened vowel grade and its reflexes in Slavic and offers also a critical assessment primarily of Kuryłowicz's relevant views. In the first part of the book, he discusses length in the verb. Included here are subdivisions for the present and the past, the latter further subcategorized into sigmatic aorist and asigmatic formations. Also in the section on the past are excursuses on relevant data in Baltic, Germanic, Latin, Celtic, and Albanian, exhibiting long and/or lengthened vocalism in past-tense forms. Other instances of length in the verb include: long-vocalic nasal verbs, long-vocalic *-iti/ēti* verbs, long-vocalic iteratives and/or secondary imperfectives, verbs in *-ati/ěti*, long-vocalic causatives, factives, intensives, and iteratives in *-iti*. The second part of the book treats length in the noun, subdividing this category into long-vocalic nouns with and without verbal cognates, respectively, and commenting, specifically, on nominal *vṛddhi*. Mathiassen concludes that the IE languages discussed by him (especially Slavic, Baltic, and Germanic) reflect several layers of lengthening and that the PIE share of long-vocalic formations is considerable in all of them. For reviews of Mathiassen's work see, e.g., Erhart 1975 and Leeming 1976b.

Another important study providing new insights into the distribution of short and long vowels, particularly as they can be found in Baltic and Slavic, is the 1978 article by W. Winter. Its findings are of such significance that F. Kortlandt has even proposed to label them Winter's Law. In short, the paper in question discusses vowel lengthening and the rise of acute intonation in Baltic and Slavic. Winter notes that: 1) lengthening is not limited to verb stems; 2) lengthening in C_1VC_2-type roots depends on the nature of the consonant in the C_2 position; and 3) lengthening is also found in C_1VRC_2-type bases, again with C_2 as a conditioning factor. Specifically, Winter claims that "in [the] Baltic and Slavic languages, the Proto-Indo-European sequence of short vowel plus voiced stop was reflected by lengthened vowel plus voiced stop, while short vowel plus aspirate developed into short vowel plus voiced stop" (439). The German Indo-Europeanist concludes that the lengthening discussed is a genuinely Balto-Slavic phenomenon, while considering such lengthening in the position before PIE voiced stops an established fact. The author suggests that this particular development constitutes a strong argument in favor of postulating a separate stage of Balto-Slavic linguistic unity and speaking against an altogether separate development of pre- and Proto-Baltic and Slavic. The proposed reinterpretation can be integrated with the view on PIE voiced stops as having actually been glottalized, as expressed by T. V. Gamkrelidze and V. V. Ivanov (and, it should be added, in a somewhat different form also by P. J. Hopper). Winter's theory also jibes with Kortlandt's and others' conception of Balto-Slavic acute pitch as reflecting the loss of an earlier laryngeal; cf. also Kortlandt's comment to Winter's paper at the international conference on historical phonology at which it was first presented.

Problems concerning reflexes of IE ablaut as well as secondary Slavic ablaut were discussed also in contributions by Boryś (1981), Bezlaj (1971), Varbot (1981), and Hamp (1982).

Issues in part related to apophonic alternations but primarily concerned with the treatment of original diphthongs in CS were studied in a variety of papers. L. Moszyński proposes a thirteen-step chronology for such monophthongization; cf. Moszyński 1972c. E. Hamp (1976b) tackled the classic problem of the fate of *eu̯ in Slavic and proposed *ov* as its regular reflex, with a special explanation for the notable exception *devętь*, repeating an etymology proposed by him elsewhere.

Concerning the prehistory of nasal vowels, Kortlandt (1979c) applies his principle of relative chronology in order to enrich the diagnostic power of the comparative method. It should be noted that in his view a full-fledged system of nasal vowels never actually existed as a synchronic phonemic reality. This, he argues, is due to the loss of the unrounded back vowel (or rather functional diphthong) *yN* and the subsequent phonemicization of *ö* in the combination *öN*. Following his penchant for establishing detailed and refined chronologies, the Dutch linguist distinguishes ten evolutionary phases, spanning from PIE through disintegrating Slavic. For the evolution of nasal vowels, the author posits sixteen relevant phases: 1) raising of *ā, *ō before final resonants; 2) labializaiton of *ă and merger with *ŏ; 3) rise of the nasal vowels *iN, *eN, *oN, and *uN; 4) raising before final *-s; 5) delabialization of ŏ; 6) umlaut; 7) first palatalization; 8) monophthongization of diphthongs 9) second palatalization; 10) loss of *-s; 11) prothesis; 12) delabialization; 13) raising of *ā and *ō; 14) rise of new timbre distinctions; 15) loss of /j/; and 16) subsequent developments.

Though primarily concerned with presenting a general theory of diphthongization, Andersen 1972 makes use of CS data and developments. Thus, for example, the monophthongizations *ei, *ou > i, u are, according to him, analyzable by appeal to the acoustic parameter of diffuseness. Andersen argues that the diphthongs were reinterpreted as [-compact] monophthongs.

Both developments imply the existence of pronunciation rules — after the phonetic diphthongization or before the phonetic monophthongization ... which specify simple segments as unmarked with respect to compactness in their initial portion, but marked with respect to compactness in their latter portion (25).

The same process, operating in reverse fashion, accounts for the development *sr > str (e.g., OCS sestra, ostrovъ, similarly OCS izdrěsti). Here the shift is said to involve diphthongization of the sonorant (r) into tr: "in the phonemic diphthongization the initial, obstruent-like portion of the sonorant is interpreted as a stop whose specific resonance properties are determined by the preceding segment" (38).

Feldstein, in his study of Slavic diphthongs (cf. Feldstein 1976), attempts to simplify the analysis concerning the evolution of Slavic liquid groups (low -ǎr and high -ur). He posits two isoglosses specifying metathesis and loss of syllabicity in liquids. Further, he points out that the relative order in which the relevant shifts occurred varies from area to area in Slavic, and comments on those forms actually attested. Loss of syllabicity is viewed as contingent on the epenthetic mora caused by regressive compensation. Structurally, such epenthesis is linked with "leftward accent spread."

Marvan's 1973 paper on Russian and prehistoric Slavic contraction is merely a preview of his larger work of 1979, *Prehistoric Slavic Contraction*. The latter does significantly contribute to our understanding of this complex phenomenon of CS and disintegrating Early Slavic. In particular, the monograph outlines not only the origin and regional details of vowel contraction, but comments at great length also on the Late CS dialects underlying Czech, Slovak, Sorbian, Polish, Slovene, and Serbo-Croatian (9th–11th cc.) which exhibit, to varying degrees, this phenomenon. The author thus uses vowel contraction, which he views as a process consisting of several consecutive stages, in order to reconstruct areal, chronological, and structural strata of Late CS and Early Slavic. It should also be noted that he operates with a notion of surface- *vs.* deep-structural changes, sketching several of the repercussions of prehistoric Slavic contraction in the phonology and morphology of the attested languages. For some critical assessments of Marvan's book, see, among others, Leeming 1981a and Kortlandt 1982a.

Vowel contraction, including its preliterate facet, was also dealt with in F. Mareš's paper of 1971. Analyzing the phenomenon largely from a functional point of view, Mareš focused specifically on the Czech and only secondarily also on the Slovak evidence. Mareš further considered parallel, but not identical, phenomena in Polish and OCS, suggesting that vowel contraction outside the Czecho-Slovak and Polish area is mostly morphophonemically motivated.

Specific problems of CS vocalism were also discussed by a number of other scholars. J. I. Press (1977) reassessed the place of *y* in prehistoric and historically attested Slavic. J. Vuković (1975) contemplated the possibility of viewing *ě* and *y* as phonological diphthongs (given their morphological alternation). Z. Stieber (1976) supported the view that traditional CS *ŏ* was in fact a short *a* — and the sequence *CorC* thus *CărC* — but rejected the notion of East Slavic *akan'e* as an archaism reflecting a CS state of affairs (cf. below). L. Newman (1971) offered some original views on *-ě₃* in North Slavic, while M. Trummer (1978) reviewed the controversial correlation of *-y/-a vs. -ę/-ě*, and V. V. Kolesov (1973) attempted to identify certain trends in the post-CS treatment of CS *-ǫ < *-jăn(t)s*. B. Velčeva (1978) presented a generative phonological reinterpretation of the CS differentiation *ǫ : u*, including a survey of CS and pre-CS phonetic shifts analyzed in terms of distinctive features.

Of recent contributors discussing the origin of East Slavic *akan'e*, only V. K. Žuravlev (1974) continues to maintain that this phenomenon did in fact arise early, in preliterate times. Specifically, by resorting to the theory of neutralization (going back to Trubeckoj), Žuravlev claims that virtually all forms of attested unstressed vocalism as well as the very nature of vowel reduction in unstressed syllables can be thus explained. G. J. Stipa (1974), on the other hand, supports the substratum hypothesis, suggesting Mordvinian as the source and rejecting, therefore, V. Georgiev's and others' CS explanation. H. G. Lunt (1979/80), too, does not accept the "proto-*akan'e*" theory of A. Vaillant, G. Y. Shevelov, Georgiev, and F. P. Filin. In support of his view, Lunt refers to P. Ivić's and J. Riegler's compelling evidence adduced from South Slavic which refutes the CS nature of this East Slavic phenomenon. In this connection, however, he does not mention H. Birnbaum's similar stance (cf. Birnbaum 1979a, 133–4 and 152–4) and also fails to mention that Shevelov has since then "most emphatically" dissociated himself from Georgiev's extreme position (cf. Shevelov, *Teasers and Appeasers*, 1971, 303, esp. n. 4).

M. I. Lekomceva (1978 and 1980) considers the possibility of a Baltic (rather than Finno-Ugric) substratum effect triggering prehistoric and early historic *akan'e* (8th–12th cc.). Specifically, she corroborates Jakobson's early surmise about "three independent paths of evolution of *akan'e*" (cf. *Remarques*, 93). According to the Soviet linguist, *akan'e* emerged in the Sož-Desna basin in the 8th–9th centuries (a claim supported by archeological evidence), and reached its height of intensity in the 9th–12th centuries in the Upper Dnieper, Oka, and Volga regions, where Baltic presence is not attested since the 13th century but where the results of linguistic interference thus persist. A slightly different reinterpretation of the genesis of *akan'e* in East Slavic is provided by V. Čekman (1975), who suggests that *akan'e* appeared under conditions paralleling the Baltic tendency to differentiate the timbre of long *vs.* short non-high vowels. In East Slavic the same tendency is said to have been realized analogically in stressed *vs.* non-stressed position.

In a study on the reduced vowels in CS and Early Slavic, H. Kučera (1975) attempts to apply a generative approach to instances broadly falling under Havlík's Law. The proposed analysis relies on the existence of "iterative" (i.e., cyclical) rules in generative phonology to explain pertinent phenomena. Havlík's Law and other instances of jer fall are reeximaned by V. K. Žuravlev (1977) in terms of his "group-phonemic" concept. Thus he reinterprets the pertinent phenomena as explicable due to loss of syllabicity in vowels as a result of the transformation of two syllabemes into one syllable. This is considered yet another consequence of the disintegration of syllabemes in the Late CS period. In another paper, the same linguist (Žuravlev 1978) discusses the reflexes of reduced vowels in various Slavic languages. He takes the Late CS group-phonemes — in this instance *'(Cь) vs. (Cъ)*, that is, consonant plus jer viewed as a single entity — as his point of departure.

The problem of the distribution of reduced vowels in strong and weak position is the topic of a recent article by O. B. Malkova (1981). The author discusses, in particular, irregular reflexes of CS jers on the basis of Early Slavic, mostly Old Russian, evidence. A. Martinet in a typoligically oriented paper (1978) draws parallels between the CS jers and their subsequent fate and the treatment of the *svarabhakhti* vowels of Japanese (*i, u*). The same parallelism was previously observed by G. Y. Shevelov and J. Chew, Jr. in a paper contributed to the festschrift for the French linguist (1969; cf. Birnbaum 1979a, 268–9).

The CS reduced vowels are only part of the considerations in a paper by G. Y. Shevelov (1976) discussing the loss of jers in their relation to Early Slavic *y* and *i*. The American Slavist concludes his discussion by suggesting that: 1) *y* did not participate in the loss of the jers; 2) word-initial *i* (*ji*) did not participate in the loss of the jers; 3) word-medial and word-final *i* preceded by *j* was identified with and treated as *ь*, i.e., yielded *e* in strong position and zero (#) in weak position; and 4) *i* followed by *j* participated in the loss of the jers but was not identified with *ь* (in weak position it yielded zero, in strong its reflex was *i*, Ukr *y*).

A recent study by K. Polański (1982) explains the preservation and full vocalization of CS reduced vowels in word-initial position in Polabian (and its underlying CS dialect). Polański argues that the relevant factors are partly prosodic, partly morphological.

CS vocalism provides the chief data also in a somewhat eccentric paper by H. Schelesniker (1975) on the "Turan" influences on CS. Specifically, the Austrian Slavist discusses the impact of Early Turkic (i.e., "Turan") languages — notably, those of the Huns, the Avars, the Khazars, and the Bulgars — on prehistoric Slavic, emphasizing especially presumed Slavic-Avar linguistic contacts. He explains certain general tendencies of CS as a result of "Turan" interference, among them palatalization (making reference to Žuravlev's group-phonemic interpretation, or rather, a syllabemic view of synharmony). Thus he sees traces of Turkic vowel harmony in the Slavic syllable structure and in the effect that vowels had on each other across syllable boundaries. Schelesniker places these developments roughly in a period between the 6th and 9th centuries.

Various problems of CS vocalism, its prehistory and early attested reflections, are further discussed in a number of other studies reported on elsewhere in this account. These are: Kortlandt 1979a, Bernštejn 1974, Ivanov 1981b, Feinberg 1978, Birnbaum 1974 and 1979b, Aitzetmüller 1975 and 1979a, Slonek 1972 and 1979, Feldstein 1978b, Raecke 1979, Andersen 1977, Lamprecht 1973, Kočev 1978, Beleckij 1980, Kiparsky 1972, Hamp 1971, Georgiev 1974, Plevačová 1974, Mathiassen 1975, Mańczak 1977b, Trost 1978, Šaur 1978, and Wukasch 1974, 1976a, and 1976b.

II.4. Consonantism

Among studies dealing with the crystallization of CS, or rather of PS, from Late PIE (or an intermediary Balto-Slavic stage), and limited to the problems of consonantism, a paper by G. S. Klyčkov (1972) should be noted. Problems of PIE consononantism, including its reflexes in CS, were further discussed in a dissertation by L. Steensland (1973). The dissertation reexamines the controversial distribution of velars, including palatals and labiovelars, in the IE protolanguage. Assessing previous hypotheses propounded by various Indo-Europeanists, A. Meillet and J. Kuryłowicz among them, the Swedish linguist comes down on the side of those who assume two original series: velars and labiovelars. The palatal series is seen, therefore, as originally allophonic. For an assessment of this study, see Erhart 1974.

Related problems, and specifically the puzzling *centum* elements in Slavic, were discussed by Z. Gołąb (1969), who also provides a fairly complete list of the relevant items. His specific explanations rely heavily on considerations of chronology and prehistoric migratory movements rather than acceding to a more traditional interpretation in terms of "velar alternation" (*Gutturalwechsel*; cf. Meillet). A similar approach to the same problem was adopted by V. N. Čekman (1974a), who also discussed controversial *centum*-type reflexes of PIE $*k'$, $*g'$ in Balto-Slavic. The Soviet linguist attempts to explain such sporadic reflexes by assuming interdialectal interference or mixing, i.e., by making reference to hypothetical ethnogenetic processes. The somewhat questionable nature of such an explanation aside, it clearly presupposes the existence of a Balto-Slavic *centum* dialect given the absence of analogical reflexes in Indo-Iranian territory.

A related issue was further reexamined by F. Kortlandt (1978b), who focuses on the IE palatovelars in the position before resonants as reflected in Balto-Slavic. Taking into account, specifically, the controversial instances of *Gutturalwechsel*, the author arrives at partly new chronologies and a novel overall picture of the relationship between Balto-Slavic on the one hand and the rest of the IE languages on the other. The Dutch comparatist considers the possibility that the loss of palatality before *r was a common Indo-Baltic development, one not shared by Armenian. By the same token, Balto-Slavic and Albanian share the characteristic of depalatalization before other resonants, a development not attested in Indo-Iranian. The restoration of palatality in Indo-Iranian and Balto-Slavic is said to have occurred independently, in the latter branch of IE partly after the split into Baltic and Slavic. The loss of palatality is further believed to have preceded the rise of an epenthetic vowel before syllabic *r*, *l*, *n*, but not before syllabic *m*. The agreement with Albanian suggests to the author that this language originally formed a transitional dialect between Balto-Slavic and Armenian.

Inconsistencies in the implementation of the first palatalization of velars were discussed by N. I. Tolstoj (1978a), focusing on items derived from the roots *geg- and *gep-. H. Birnbaum (1978b), utilizing previous observations by Z. Gluskina (1966) and Z. Stieber (1968), discussed the only partial realization of the second (regressive) palatalization of velars on the northeastern periphery of the Slavic linguistic area. Data from North Russian dialects and some regional varieties of Russian in areas east of Moscow, suggest the incomplete implementation of this process usually considered CS. In addition, the isolated instances of the lack of the progressive palatalization in the etymon *vьx*- attested in Old Novgorodian texts were commented on in this paper; on this particular item, cf. also Savignac 1975. The CS and post-CS implications are considered both on the basis of contemporary dialectal data and Old Russian (Novgorod) evidence.

A. A. Zaliznjak (1982) is likewise concerned with data displaying the lack of the second and, partly, third palatalizations. His findings are based largely on evidence from the Novgorod birchbark letters; his conception of the Old Novgorod dialect is broad enough to include the Old Pskov dialect. The Soviet linguist generally confirms the data and hypothesis of Gluskina, which derived primarily from dialectal material and recorded evidence from the Old Novgorod chronicles and parchment (i.e., non-birchbark) *gramoty*. In a second, briefer section, Zaliznjak treats word-initial CS *tl (and partly *dl). As in word-medial position, *kl*/*gl* are the usual results. The author's general conclusion is that the Old Novgorod dialect, displaying a number of complex developments distinct from the rest of Common East Slavic (Old Russian), cannot merely be considered one of the Old Russian dialects. Rather, it must be directly related to a CS dialect (or even be considered one itself), thus reflecting disintegrating Late CS as a whole rather than merely Common East Slavic.

An argument for reversing the chronology of the first and second regressive palatalizations of velars was made by D. Cohen (1969). Cohen disputes the chronology of the prehistoric Slavic palatalizations proposed by Chomsky and Halle, and suggests a reordering of the relevant synchronic rules. Moszyński 1972b discusses only a specific problem relevant to the second regressive palatalization, focusing on the differentiated reflex of *sk* under the conditions of that palatalization.

The highly controversial traditional third, or progressive, palatalization of velars (also referred to as the Baudouin de Courtenay palatalization), and particularly its relative chronology, was the topic of a large-scale study by R. Channon (1972), *On the Progressive Palatalization of Velars in the Relative Chronology of Slavic*. Channon first describes the processes involved and summarizes previous views. He subsequently argues for the following relative chronology: 1) progressive palatalization: *k, g, x > k', g', x'*; 2) establishment of syllabic synharmony; 3) first regressive palatalization; 4) change of back vowel to front vowel after *j* or palatal consonant; 5) monophthongization of diphthongs; 6) second regressive palatalization; 7) shift of *k', g', x' > c', (d)z', s'/š'*; 8) change of *ě* to *a* after *j* and other palatals (as distinct from palatalized consonants). It should be noted that the essence, but not the elaboration, of this conception can be found already in M. Halle's treatment of this process in *The Sound Pattern of English* (1968). Appended to Channon's monograph is the relevant portion of Baudouin's first treatment of this phenomenon in *IF* 4 (1894). For assessments of Channon's work, see, in particular, Newman 1973, Steensland 1974/75, and Leili 1975. Of these reviews, Newman points out several novel considerations in Channon's treatment of relative chronology, while Steensland's evaluation is on the whole quite negative.

Early chronologies for the progressive palatalization are further assumed also by H. G. Lunt (1977a) and G. Jacobsson (1973, 1974, and 1977). Lunt considers the progressive palatalization "very early," prior not only to the first and second regressive palatalizations but also to the emergence of CS *x* and thus only affecting *k* and *g*. He conjectures, like Halle and Channon, that the process of palatalization actually occurred in two stages: first, the transition of the velars to palatovelars, and only considerably later a shift to affricates. Lunt further claims that an early chronology for the progressive palatalization renders possible reasonable explanations of certain irregularities in Slavic paradigms previously explained by analogy or as a result of other, interfering phonological evolutions. In this context it should be noted that prior to Halle, Channon, and Lunt, an early chronology of the progressive palatalization (though not preceding the first regressive palatalization) was assumed also by, among others, R. Ekblom, N. S. Trubeckoj, and F. V. Mareš. For some harsh criticism of Lunt's position, see Aitzetmüller 1979, expressing a preference for the traditional chronology.

G. Jacobsson's several contributions (1973, 1974, 1977) to the issue of the chronological order of the progressive palatalization are rather in line with some of the earlier work on this problem just mentioned. Thus, in addition to stating the precise conditions for this process, he merely claims that it occurred earlier than the second regressive palatalization. It should particularly be noted that in commenting on the phonetic conditions of the Baudouin palatalization, Jacobsson returns to the previously assumed shifts $* n̥ > ь$ and $*(C)un(C) > y$; he further assumes monophthongization of the sound sequence $*i/*u/*r/*l + n̥$.

The CS and Early Slavic palatalizations were, moreover, analyzed, using a generative approach, by D. Huntley (1978). He posits underlying forms to which synchronic rules are applied, these forms being largely identical with CS, and introduces a distinction between strong and weak generative models. The same phenomena were the topic of several papers using a similar approach by C. Wukasch (1974 and 1976a and b). In Wukasch 1974, the author suggests evidence that the first palatalizations of velars can, and in fact must, be interpreted by separate sets of synchronic rules. Wukasch also comments on the reordering of the vowel fronting rule and the rule yielding the results of the third palatalization, claiming that such reordering increases rule utilization, allomorphic regularity, and rule transparency. Essentially the same point is repeated in Wukasch 1976a, while in Wukasch 1976b the author again argues against rule collapsing as pertinent to the first and second velar palatalizations. It should be noted that although Wukasch in part supports the rule ordering solution proposed by Chomsky and Halle, he proposes to improve on it by offering an alternative analysis of -*i* ($\bar{i}_2$). He claims that the synchronic evidence for underlying diphthongal forms is weak and suggests instead a lexical marking of the morpheme -*i* (in the nom. pl. and the imperative) as an exception to the first palatalization.

General problems of the palatal correlation in CS, and particularly Late CS, consonantism were discussed by numerous authors. V. N. Čekman (1973) focused on the CS palatalizations of velars and the treatment of consonant plus *j*. Based on his group-phonemic approach, V. K. Žuravlev (1980) offered a new interpretation of the phonemic and phonetic status of consonants before front vowels, while H. Galton (1981) viewed the Slavic palatal correlation as an implementation of one of van Wijk's two main phonological tendencies of Late CS. A. G. Avksent'eva (1976) discussed the repercussions of the palatal correlation on the dialectal CS shift *tl, dl* > *kl, gl*. The correlation of hard *vs.* soft consonants is also at the center of the contribution by R. Krajčovič (1973), who claims that *fortis/lenis* (tense/lax) is distinctive for CS phonology rather than the traditional voicing opposition (cf. a similar theory elaborated by H. Andersen). The author claims that only where the *fortis/lenis* distinction was non-phonemic could the correlation of palatalization assume phonemic status: *l vs. l', r vs. r', n vs. n'*; in labials the *fortis/lenis* distinction is said to be partly absent (*m, v*).

Discussion of the *št/žd* reflex (< CS *tj, kt'/dj*) as a phenomenon of CS dialectology has been presented in recent years in Pianka 1974, Stieber 1974, Rospond 1977 (analyzing South Slavic onomastic evidence), Scatton 1978 (using a synchronic generative approach), and Timberlake 1981. B. Koneski (1981) suggests a seventh-century chronology for this shift in its core area, while the spreading of it to the Macedonian Slavs is said to have taken place only in the 9th–10th centuries. He considered the dialectal and standard Macedonian reflex *k', g'* to be of more recent date, attested since the 18th century.

Issues related to the modification of consonantal clusters were discussed by V. N. Čekman (1974b), B. Comrie (1975a), Z. Leszczyński (1977), H. D. Pohl (1980), and F. Kortlandt (1982c). Čekman suggests that the Early Slavic shift **gn (kn)* > **gn' (kn')* is a partly dialectal CS process. Comrie concludes that the regular CS reflex of the IE word for 'seventh' was **semъ*, whence the cardinal *semь* as attested in East Slavic. He thus claims that a form **sedmъ* cannot be posited for CS and that it supposedly arose by contamination of the inherited cardinal *set'* (or *sed'*) with the ordinal *semъ*. Comrie assumes that this form was possible in those CS dialects where the loss of weak jers prior to the loss of the form *set'* (*sed'*) led to the admissibility of the cluster *dm* (as in South and West Slavic). An examination and comparison of Slavic *sedmъ* and Gk *hébdomos* suggests a parallel and independent development of voicing in post-PIE times. Leszczyński comments on the duration and relative stability of the pre-Slavic and CS shift *sr, zr* > *str, zdr*, repeated in recorded Early Slavic. Kortlandt suggests that **p* was regularly lost before **t* in Slavic, never yielding *st* (as suggested by, e.g., Shevelov and, earlier, Vey). Kortlandt thus sharply attacks Pohl, who assumes *pt* > *st* "als Regelfall."

M. Karaś (1973) discusses the instance of prothetic, "mobile" *s*, largely of dialectal CS origin, considering both phonological and morphological factors for an explanation of this puzzling phenomenon. Some typical items are: P *skóra* : *kora, skra* (*iskra*) : *kra* (*ikra*), P *skrzydło* : SC *krilo*. Word-initial *x* in CS was the topic of a contribution by Z. Gołąb (1973). The author discusses the origin of this word-initial consonant, which regularly developed in CS only in the position *following* another segment (cf. the so-called *ruki* rule). Gołąb examines thirty-one pertinent lexemes where borrowing from Iranian may be assumed with a higher or lower degree of probability. For an opposing point of view, see Mańczak 1974/75, discussed below (cf. II.5.).

Problems of CS consonantism were further discussed in Andersen 1972 and 1977, Pohl 1974, Kortlandt 1979a, Gălăbov 1975, Lamprecht 1973, Kočev 1978, Browning 1982, and, at some length, Arumaa 1976, commented on elsewhere in this report (cf. I.1.).

II.5. Special Factors Conditioning Common Slavic Sound Change: Syllable Structure; Word-Final and Word-Initial Position; Frequency

The interrelation and mutual conditioning of phonological processes in the CS period was considered by S. B. Bernštejn (1977), who argues against the neogrammarian, atomistic view of linguistic phenomena. Among other things, Bernštejn points to the merits of the approach adopted by R. Nahtigal in determining the hierarchization of phonological processes and, in particular, his subordination of several relevant developments to the Law of Open Syllables (cf. also the relevant view of N. van Wijk). Syllable structure and, in particular, the tendency toward open syllables were also considered in a number of recent studies by H. Galton (1978, 1979, 1980a and 1980b). Thus Galton discusses certain aspects of the interdependence of the two main phonological trends of Late CS, first identified as such by van Wijk, i.e., open-syllable structure and palatalization. He further discusses the interrelation of syllable structure and intonation in CS from a general typological point of view. Here he makes use of other IE as well as Japanese data for comparison, and attributes to intonation a decisive role in the rise of CS open syllables.

J. Raecke (1979) attempts a comprehensive reinterpretation of CS monophthong-ization as conditioned by the Law of Open Syllables. In his discussion is included an assessment of previous pertinent explanations (esp. those of van Wijk and Nahtigal). The author arrives at a number of preliminary conclusions: 1) There was no single Law of Open Syllables operating. 2) The term "open syllable" is impre-cise and used with different meanings by different scholars. 3) The particular "law" (in any of its formulations) refers to the syllable auslaut, with monophthongization being one of the processes yielding open syllables; consonant syncope would thus not be subsumed here. 4) Van Wijk denied the existence of clearly defined syllable boundaries considered axiomatic for CS by Leskien. 5) Clarification is needed as to whether the rise of open syllables implies a shifting of syllable boundary or con-sonant syncope before or after monophthongization. Depending on the answer to this question, nasalization, liquid metathesis, and rise of syllabic liquids will or will not be included here. In addition, a clear motivation for the specific hierarchization and establishment of relative chronology for the individual developments is called for, and the nature of diphthongs as combinations of two vowels proper is discussed. 6) Whether "tendency" or "law," the subsuming of these interrelated processes amounts to an atomistic cataloging rather than a causal explanation. 7) Clearly, "tendency" and "law" cannot be equated since only the latter operates without excep-tion. Raecke submits that his observations and considerations are tentative and pri-marily aimed at pinpointing the difference between mere description and genuine ex-planation.

W. Gesemann (1975) seeks to define the function of j in CS phonology in light of synharmony and the specifics of syllable structure, applying a partly generative methodology. Further contributions already mentioned, concerned also with CS (and prc-CS) syllable structure, are Leszczyński 1977 and Kortlandt 1979c.

The reflexes of word-initial IE *u in Baltic and Slavic were discussed by F. Kortlandt (1977). He concludes that this vocalic anlaut yielded acute *vy*- under stress in CS while in pretonic position the result was *vъ*-; the equivalent reflexes in Baltic are *ŭ*- vs. *u*-. For stressed position, the Dutch comparatist assumes a prothetic laryngeal for the Balto-Slavic period. This hypothesis would therefore explain the attested distribution of Slavic *vy*- and *vъ*- forms.

As was mentioned above (II.4.), W. Mańczak (1974/5) has argued against Gołąb's thesis concerning the significance of the Iranian impact on Early Slavic, based on the origins of some items with initial *x*-. As usual, the Polish linguist here applies his statistical method and claims that only a minimal percentage (3%) of all loanwords consists of verbs and adjectives while of Gołąb's thirteen items in *x*- of alleged Iranian origin, as many as eight are verbs.

The new explanation by Polański (1982) of the treatment of reduced vowels in an-laut in the westernmost part of Slavic (and its underlying CS dialect base) was men-tioned above (*sub* II.3.).

Several studies of the last decade have again dealt with some aspect of CS auslaut. Thus J. B. Rudnyc'kyj (1971) elaborated on his earlier explanation of CS -ъ ($< *-os$)

as an analogical formation introduced from the old -*u* stems. In this connection he points also to some archaic, primarily onomastic data showing -*o* (*Samo*, 7th c.; Old Polish and Middle Ukrainian names attested from the 13th–17th cc.) as testimony of the claimed regular reflex of *-*os*. Basically in line with van Wijk's thinking, I. Gălăbov (1973) discusses a number of controversial auslaut developments of Slavic in terms of the CS tendency toward rising syllabic sonority, matching it with a trend to develop prothetic semivowels in vocalic anlaut position. Irregular developments are here considered strictly Slavic, not pre-Slavic or PIE, phenomena while only a secondary role is assigned to analogical (morphological) leveling (cf. V. Georgiev's different view).

A fairly detailed and sophisticated account of the evolution of the word-final position in CS prior to the operation of the Law of Open Syllables was given by J. Prinz (1977). Here a set of principles is formulated, grouped in five categories: a) general principles, b) special principles applicable to the position before undropped *s*, c) special principles applicable to other consonantal auslaut, d) special principles applicable to "weak" (i.e., never stressed) syllables, and e) special principles applicable to originally vocalic auslaut. The author formulates a set of intricate rules pertinent to each of these five categories. After discussion of these developments the German Slavist concludes that by the time word-final -*s* dropped, all major vowel modifications had been concluded. The apocope of -*s* is considered the last CS phase of the Law of Open Syllables while liquid metathesis is held to have been a post-CS phenomenon.

CS auslaut was also discussed by B. Velčeva (1980), who suggests a phonemic explanation to supplement some of Georgiev's morphological interpretations of controversial CS auslaut evolutions. The problem of the particular phonological evolution in word-final position was further considered primarily from theoretical and methodological premises by G. Holzer (1980). The author lists the reconstructed IE desinences subject to CS auslaut laws and attempts to explicate a maximum number of specific developments with a minimum number of separate rules of sound change. Troublesome irregularities in the development of CS auslaut, particularly the reflexes of *-*os* and *-*oN* were, moreover, examined by L. E. Feinberg (1978). Like Georgiev, Feinberg applies morphological explanations rather than a purely phonetic interpretation for the instances discussed.

Various aspects of CS auslaut were scrutinized in a number of studies concerned with specific grammatical forms. Thus H. Schelesniker (1976) reexamined the genitive doublets in -*y* and -*ę*. He suggests that the genitive singular desinence of the Slavic -*ā* stems can be identified with the nasalized locative ending of the Avestan -*ī* stems, while that of the Slavic -*i̯ā* stems is equated with the Indo-Iranian locative form of the -*ī* declension. The same set of grammatical endings was also reexamined by M. Trummer (1978). Concluding that the correlation -*y* (-*a*) : -*ę* (-*ě*) as well as -*ъ* (-*o*) : -*ь* (-*e*) and the desinence -*ǫ* all are phonologically contingent on a vowel system lacking rounding, Trummer traces them back to uniform endings *-*ān*/*-*ăns*, *-*ăn*, *-*i̯ăn*/*-*i̯ăns*, *-*i̯ă*. Mathiassen (1975) discusses the -*ь* ending in imperatives of the type OCS *daždь*, *viždь*. He suggests that imperatives, being interjectives, are subject to final syllable shortening or apocope.

Three interrelated studies dealing with auslaut by W. R. Schmalstieg (1971, 1972, 1974a) discuss the first person singular in Slavic, the development of the *-ā* declension, and some morphological implications of the IE shift $*-oN > *-\bar{o}$. In the first of these studies the author explains the thematic ending *-ǫ* as a reflex of $*-on$ (with $*-\ŭn$ as an alternate reflex). This originally occurred only before a following consonant but subsequently was generalized in the present tense, whereas the aorist generalized the other variant. In his discussion of the *-ā* declension, Schmalstieg attempts to provide an integrated explanation for its several controversial reflexes. Finally, in the third paper the American linguist concludes that the IE ending $*-oN$ originally denoted a non-singular form of the noun. This ending is also assumed for the verb where the original third person non-singular is said to have been in $*-oN$ as well (at least in the thematic verbs). He further proposes that the $*-o$ stem singular desinence $*-om$ had a sandhi variant in $*-\bar{o}$ attested also in a number of other IE languages. Also, Schmalstieg claims that the traditional Balto-Slavo-Germanic isogloss $*-m$ as a dative marker cannot be upheld as such. The ending $*-om$ (with its variant $*-\bar{o}$) is also found in Indo-Iranian, Italic, and Greek.

As was the case with W. Mańczak's treatment of Slavic historical phonology (1977a), his brief discussion of the evolution of the numeral *jedinъ* in Slavic is again primarily concerned with the effect that frequency is said to have had on such irregular developments (Mańczak 1977b). Affective phonological change, previously given much consideration by G. Y. Shevelov in his monumental text on CS phonology of 1964/65, is discussed in a paper by T. M. S. Priestly (1978). Thus the affective factor is considered in such changes as $k > x/š$, various palatalizations, nasalization, voicing, affrication, lengthening, and aspiration. The author is particularly interested in some of the theoretical implications of less regular sound changes of this kind, with attention paid to such aspects as peripheral *vs.* marginal phonological features and secondary articulation. Priestly offers synchronic (generative) and psychololinguistic comments and touches also on some of the specifics of poetic language.

II.6. Morphonology (Morphophonemics, Other Than Ablaut Alone)

Problems of Slavic morphophonemics, including its prehistoric facets, were reexamined by E. Stankiewicz in his 1979 volume on that topic and on Slavic accentology (cf. II.2., above). For the most part, morphophonemics is dealt with here in its interrelation with prosodic patterning. Thus, in the essay on "Slavic Morphophonemics, Its Typological and Diachronic Aspects" (42–71) the author points to, among other things, the unsophisticated nature of accentual morphophonemic studies on CS due to the lack of comprehensive approaches and integrated theories. Morphophonemic considerations play an important part also in his papers on "The Accent Pattern of the Slavic Verb" (72–87) and "The Slavic Vocative and Its

Accentuation" (100–109), both considering CS data.

V. V. Ivanov's study of the morphophonemic alternations in the IE verb (1981b) can be considered a by-product of his major work on the IE verb (Ivanov 1981a, crucial in particular also to prehistoric Slavic; see below *sub* III.5.). Ž. Ž. Varbot (1978) discussed morphonological aspects of compound nouns in relationship to their etymologies, citing a number of CS forms. Only in a qualified sense morphophonemic is the approach of J. Vuković (1975), who reviewed the status of CS *ě* and *y* as members of phonological oppositions. Given their morphological alternation, the author considers the possibility of regarding them as phonologically opposed diphthongs in the CS vowel system.

T. Browning (1982) offers some critical comments on previous treatments of the morphophonemic alternation *v~vl'* in CS and OCS, considering also the dual reflex of the sequence **owj* (> *uj* or *ovl'*). The author proposes that closer attention be paid to chronology and environmental conditioning for a better understanding of these seeming irregularities.

Morphophonemic considerations were further included in work by, among others, Čekman (1973), Kolesov (1975), Garde (1976a), Dybo (1979a and 1981), and Timberlake (1981), discussed elsewhere in this survey.

III. MORPHOLOGY

III.1. Monographic Treatments and General Problems of Common Slavic Morphology

While, to the best of our knowledge, no major monographic treatments of CS morphology (limited to that component of CS linguistic structure alone) have appeared in the decade reported on here, three articles addressing general problems of CS morphology deserve mention. V. K. Žuravlev's "Vvedenie v diaxroničeskuju morfologiju" (1976) is a general statement and commentary on the principles of diachronic research in morphology. The author utilizes, with some preference, Slavic prehistoric and historic data. Referring to work by V. Georgiev, R. Jakobson, W. Mańczak, and others, Žuravlev considers the close interrelations between phonological and morphological change. In another paper, authored jointly with V. P. Mažiulis (1978), a number of specific Slavic and Baltic morphological evolutions are discussed with a focus on the twin theories of phonological and morphological oppositions. Among phenomena discussed are: the loss of the dual; the strengthening of the genitive *vs.* locative, dative *vs.* instrumental, and nominative *vs.* accusative oppositions; instances of "weakened" paradigms; the strengthening of the accusative-genitive, dative-locative, and dative-genitive neutralizations; as well as the specific correlations occurring in the category of gender.

V. I. Georgiev in his "Principi na slavjanskata diaxronna morfolgija" (1978) states some general principles of Slavic diachronic morphology, and illustrates them with numerous examples partly from the CS and pre-CS periods. The Bulgarian comparatist is thus concerned both with the recorded evolution (usually commenting on changes occurring between OCS and modern Bulgarian or contemporary standard Russian) and with the prehistory of forms attested in OCS. Here he focuses, in particular, on the evolution of auslaut and grammatical endings from IE to CS times. Moreover, he discusses the relationship and relative weight of phonetic solutions as compared to explanations resorting to analogy as a factor in linguistic change.

III.2. Inflection

Recent studies in case theory which focus on or, at any rate, consider CS data, include the paper by B. Comrie (1978) on the "Morphological Classification of Cases in the Slavonic Languages." Comrie discusses Jakobson's structured approach to case, using Slavic diachronic, including CS, material. The author suggests that in CS (or even earlier) "there was a two-fold functional division of ... cases (excluding the vocative)": syntactic cases (nom., acc.) *vs.* semantic cases (gen., dat., instr., loc.). This was paralleled by a formal division whereby the nominative usually was identical with the accusative. Within the semantic cases, the closest formal relation obtained between the genitive and the locative.

A number of less general papers focus on only one or two cases. Thus, the nominitive singular masculine is discussed in Mathiassen 1978, while the genitive, particularly in its relation to the accusative, is reexamined by Georgiev 1973a. The latter operates with notions of "isomorphism" and "isosemanticism" against the IE background and cites, in particular, also Baltic data. Kortlandt 1978c comments on the genitive plural in Slavic and other IE languages, reconstructing the CS ending -ъ as going back to PIE *-om (not *-ōm), with a Balto-Slavic intermediate stage *-ŭN. Analyzing the chronology of relevant accentuation, the Dutch linguist assumes that IE *-om "developed from an uninflected predicative form in late I-E" (294). He points out how one incorrect assumption (in this instance, the positing of PIE *-ōm) led to a chain reaction of misinterpretations, and stresses the necessity of "detached analysis of the internal chronological evidence which the daughter languages supply" (296). The Slavic genitive-accusative was further discussed by V. Pisani (1974a) in a brief excursus (54–5).

The specific problem of the origin of the genitive singular of the -o stems in Baltic and Slavic was considered by K. H. Schmidt (1977). The German Indo-Europeanist, acknowledging that the regular Slavic form reflects an earlier ablative (< IE *-ōd), suggests that the archaic genitive type represented by OCS česo reflects the pronominal origin of the genitive. The Old Prussian development (loss of the ablative) is said to represent an early branching off within Baltic, with Slavic here following the East Baltic evolution. Yet, he claims, this particular agreement cannot be used as an argument for a presumed Balto-Slavic linguistic unity. Schmidt's article further comments on the special East Baltic evolution *-ōd/ōt > -ad/at. V. N. Toporov (1975a) reexamines the origin of the Slavic genitive and especially the controversial instances of -y < PIE *-ās (?), proposing a holistic, integrated view of the genitive and its syntactic prehistory. The genitive-accusative (as well as the origin of the Štokavian gen. pl.) is explained in terms of the archaic so-called divine *dvandva* in Early Slavic, and especially Old Russian, by K. Liukkonen (1973 and 1974). Subsequently this IE construction was extended also to certain saints of the Christian era (cf. Peter and Paul, Cosmas and Damian, Boris and Gleb).

The origin of the Balto-Slavic thematic instrumental plural was reconsidered by V. Mažiulis (1973). The author reconstructs two Balto-Slavic adverbial forms in *-ais and *-ōs and assumes an earlier non-differentiated function of the instrumental and locative. He further hypothesizes a subsequent identification of *-ais with the instrumental plural and *-ōs with the locative plural in Baltic while for Slavic he suggests that a reversed distribution occurred: *-ōs yielded -y in the instrumental while *-ais, patterned on the athematic model and restructured to *-aisu > -ěxъ, was used for the locative.

The evolution of the Slavic -ęt declension was recently discussed by Kragalott (1977), who however only briefly comments on the underlying CS evidence. K. E. Naylor (1972) attempts to find the causes for the residual evidence of the Slavic dual (attested in Slovenian and Sorbian) in some structural pecularities of this category in CS (and partly PIE). The CS athematic declension was again discussed by K.

Polański (1979), noting in particular the suffixation of old root nouns in CS *-y* (< PIE *-ū*) by means of a *-k* morpheme. V. K. Žuravlev (1977/78) discusses the dynamics of Balto-Slavic morphological oppositions, focusing primarily on modern synchronic data. He concludes that, as shown by the Balto-Slavic example, the weakening of one opposition (ultimately leading to neutralization; here, specifically, the case oppositions in the dual: nom.-acc., dat.-instr., gen.-loc.) usually entails a strengthening of other oppositions and vice versa. Moreover, he sees a parallelism obtaining between such mechanisms in morphology and phonology.

Problems of CS declension were further treated in R. Eckert's study of the IE heteroclitics in *-l/-m* in Slavic and Baltic to be discussed below (cf. Eckert 1979; III.3.). Certain aspects of CS declension were also touched upon in Schmalstieg 1972 and 1974a, Schelesniker 1976, Trummer 1978, and Feinberg 1978 referred to elsewhere.

The diverse endings of the first person plural in Slavic are the topic of a study by M. Enrietti (1977), who considers the etymologies and the phonological and morphological development underlying the desinences *-mъ, -mo, -me, -my*. The author contemplates the possibility that some endings, e.g. *-mo*, may have influenced adjacent languages inside the Slavic area (for example, Serbo-Croatian having an effect on Slovenian). In surveying the relevant question, he also points to the diversity manifest in this ending in other IE languages, e.g., Greek. F. V. Mareš, in a paper on the Slavic present tense system viewed diachronically (1978), is primarily concerned with the evolution from CS to present-day Slavic. He suggests, among other things, that syntactic agreement in CS is indicated formally in the third person (sg. and pl.: *-tь*, OCS *-tъ*). The plural is marked by means of a nasal infix and/or the particular grade of the thematic vowel: sg. *-e-, -i- vs.* pl. *-ǫ-, -ę-.*

The controversial formation of the Slavic imperfect was again treated by, among others, H. D. Pohl (1975a), V. Georgiev (1976), and J. Ferrell (1974/75). Of particular interest is Pohl's discussion, suggesting that: 1) the inherited imperfect fused in Slavic with the aorist, initially of primary verbs, forming a new Slavic "aorist;" 2) a new imperfect based on the past-tense morpheme of Balto-Slavic, *-ē-*, was formed; 3) the Slavic reflex *-ě-* was expanded by the formant *-x-*, attested from the earliest period, to achieve a viable paradigm; 4) since *-ě-* yielded *-a-* after palatals and *j*, two allomorphs came into existence: *-ěx-* and *-(j)ax-*; 5) since *-jax-* was prevalent, analogical formations appear; 6) at the beginning of the attested period *-ějax-* and *-ajax-* are contracted and the OCS morpheme *-(j)ax-*, serving as the point of departure for all further developments, arises. In a quite different vein, Georgiev proposes that the Slavic imperfect goes back to a syntagm consisting of a participle and the imperfect form of the verb *byti*. In the course of its morphologization, this new paradigm is said to have been partly adjusted to that of the aorist: CS *zavā + *jāsъ, *bijā + *jāsъ > zovaaxъ, bijaaxъ*; cf. also the OCS phrase *bě umiraję*. Ferrell postulates a Late CS imperfect formant *-ěiax-* (with *i* being a glide), and claims that there is no substantive evidence for assuming a Late CS formant *-ěax-*. The author further traces the subsequent modification of the imperfect in Early Slavic, especially OCS and Old Russian.

On the basis of the evidence from a single South Slavic language (Serbo-Croatian), O. N. Trubačev (1980a) posits the existence of a dialectal CS verb *něti, integrated into the paradigm of nesti, as an example of grammatical suppletivism. He identifies the reconstructed CS verb with cognate forms attested in Ancient IE (Skt náyati 'he leads,' Hett nāi-, ne 'to direct, lead,' etc.). Trubačev reconstructs an original IE root *nai- or *noi̯-, as opposed to *nei̯ə-/*nī-, assumed, for example, by J. Pokorny. The IE reconstructions of Trubačev would thus also fit the Slavic evidence.

As mentioned above (cf. II.5.), the athematic imperative of the type OCS daždь, viždь was discussed by T. Mathiassen (1975), who suggested a phonetic explanation for the unexpected -ь. The relationship of thematic and athematic verbs in Slavic (and Baltic) was reexamined also by D. F. Robinson (1977), focusing on some of the well-known specific problems: the spread of imperatives in *-jь to the thematic type; the intermediate position of iměti; and the origin of the desinence -ǫtъ. Only with some qualifications can Z. Stieber's note on the CS supine (1970/72) be considered to fall into the area of inflection. Pointing out that the ending of the supine in CS was *-tǔ, the Polish Slavist claims that for verbs such as *mokti, *pekti one should expect the supine forms *moktъ, *pektъ (> *motъ, *petъ). However, the OCS evidence shows only mostь, peštь. Equivalent reflexes, pointing to CS *kt' (rather than *kt) are also found in Old Czech, Slovene, and Lower Sorbian. It must therefore be assumed that the infinitive form here analogically modified the old supine already in CS.

Problems of prehistoric Slavic verb inflection were further discussed at some length also in Stieber 1973a, Ivanov 1972a and 1981a, Kuryłowicz 1970/72, Schmalstieg 1971, Stepanov 1978, Trubačev 1982, and Nikolaev and Starostin 1982, reported on below (cf. III.5.).

III.3. Derivation (Including Other Processes of Word Formation, Primarily Composition)

The two monographic treatments of Slavic derivation, particularly of nominal word formation, including its preliterate phase, by Bernštejn 1974 and Vaillant 1974 were accounted for in a previous section of this bibliographic commentary (cf. I.2.). An excellent outline of CS word formation was also provided by F. Sławski in the introductory part of the CS dictionary published under his general editorship (Sławski 1974-: 43–141). Here the derivational and compositional processes involved in the formation of the prehistoric Slavic substantives are treated in some detail (58–141).

Of studies treating nominal derivation, the paper by R. Eckert (1974) deserves particular attention. The East German Slavist and Baltologist discusses nominal formations based on the verbal root *ēd 'to eat,' tracing old -r, -ǔ, and -i stem derivations and examining also early formations in -sl and -sn, attested both in Baltic and Slavic. Moreover, he considers the possibility of traces of an old -n stem, also derived from *ēd. In two earlier studies, the same scholar discussed nominal stems in *-i* in Baltic and Slavic and, in particular, the extent to which they illustrate the separate development of the two linguistic branches (1972a, 1972b).

The *nomen agentis* in CS was treated in a monograph by M. Wojtyła-Świerzowska (1974a). The author surveys the relevant formations with the suffixes *-ъ*, *-'ь*, *-a*, *-'a*, *-ь*, *-ьji*; *-ějь*, *-tajь*, *-tel'ь*, and *-junъ*. She further investigates those suffixes containing *-k-*, *-l-*, *-x-*, *-n-*, and *-r-*, as well as suffixes in *-tь*, *-tvъ*, and *-ogъ*. Additionally, the author discusses further aspects of the rich formal system of suffixation found in this semantic group. Finally, she points to some major factors instrumental in the renewal and differentiation of that subsystem, namely, the addition of suffixal elements, either purely structural (formal) ones or more productive, functionally identical derivational morphemes. A by-product of this monograph is Wojtyła-Świerzowska 1974b, discussing Slavic *nomina agentis* in *-ь* < IE *-i-s*.

Individual Slavic suffixes, going back to CS and pre-Slavic — Balto-Slavic and PIE—times, were further discussed in a variety of articles. Thus Taszycki 1972 examines *-y* < *-ū*, while Sławski 1974 considers formations in *-d-*, together with their IE background. Sławski 1976, looking at CS *-tъ*, distinguishes various semantic subtypes: *nomina instrumenti*, *nomina acti* and *loci*, *nomina agentis*, all primarily from earlier *nomina actionis*. Sławski 1980 treats CS *-ęt* clarifying internal Slavic and broader IE relationships. Complex suffixes going back to CS and earlier periods were further examined in Kiparsky 1972 (*-ьsk* and *-ьstvo*), Jeżowa 1975 (*-ika*), and Grošelj 1972 (*-in*).

Individual nominal formations were also reexamined by Schuster-Šewc (1971a), who suggests suffix alternation with *-ika*/*-ica* in analyzing CS **kъniga*, while according to Otrębski (1972), Slavic *měsęcь* and Lithuanian *měnuo* both reflect a common Balto-Slavic word. Boryś 1976 examines three reconstructed items and their attested cognates, all presumably derived from a verb **sьkati*. Regarding Moszyński 1981, see below, V.3., for details.

The mechanics of gender-shifting derivation in the CS noun were discussed in a paper by R. Bošković (1976). The author holds that the CS gender-shifting derivations in *-iā* and *-iiā* are secondary but ultimately of identical origin. The first type is claimed to have originated with stems in *-ĭ* which have the reduced vowel grade of the stem suffix to which was added the IE gender-shifting element *-ā*; the second, with stems in *-ĭ* which had the full vowel grade of the stem suffix to which was added the same gender-shifting suffix (represented by CS **gospod'a vs. gostьja*).

Problems of nominal prefixation were discussed in a monograph by W. Boryś (1975), dwelling in particular on the prefixes *pa-*, *pra-*, *sǫ-* and its phonetic variant *sъ(n)-*, and *ǫ* and its phonetic variant *vъ(n)-*. In addition to certain phonological and purely morphological aspects of these prefixes, their productivity, function, and origin are discussed. A specific subtype of nominal prefixes containing an original velar, previously not necessarily identified in this function, was discussed in Moskov 1978 and 1980.

Adjectival derivation in Early Slavic — as well as prehistoric Slavic and pre-

Slavic — was examined from various points of view by V. Šaur (1981), tracing the deverbative origin of certain Slavic adjectives (CS *glupъ*, *gluxъ*, *slěpъ*, *prostъ*, *pustъ*, *prǫdъkъ et al.*). Adjectival derivation is also at the center of attention in the monograph by H. Keipert (1977) on the adjectives in *-telьnъ*. This work, however, moreover sheds light on the origin of CS *-telь* and its adjectival derivative, both largely emulating Greek and Latin models. Certain CS deverbative adjectives, all showing the ablaut alternation *o* : *ь*, were further discussed by W. Boryś (1981), (cf. above, II.3.). The relationship of CS *velijь* and *velikъ(ь)* and its reflex in OCS were discussed by A. Zaręba (1976) and F. V. Mareš (1980b). While Zaręba is primarily concerned with the present geographic distribution of the two forms (the *k*-less variant today being a dialectal and peripheral archaism), Mareš mainly treats the original functional difference of the two competing forms, one being definite the other indefinite. The original adjectives in *-l* were considered by J. Kuryłowicz (1970/72) in his discussion of the provenience of the Slavic perfect and its specific functional background. Adjectival derivation and inflection were treated by T. Mathiassen (1978), who assumes an original opposition of the long *vs.* short forms of the Slavic comparative/superlative degree in the nominative singular masculine. He suggests that the original heteroclitic of the comparative paradigm was subsequently lost and that, as a result, various paradigm levelings occurred in the individual Slavic languages. A paper by A. Zaręba (1978) maintains that the adverbial formations represented by Church Slavic *drugъda*, *drugъde* were probably restricted to a portion of the Early Slavic linguistic territory. Consequently, no reflexes of them can be ascertained in East Slavic and eastern South Slavic (Macedo-Bulgarian; OCS has only *drugoide*, *drugoici*). New light on the origin and semantics of CS *drugъ* (and cognates) is further shed in Sławski 1982. Marojević 1982 touches upon the fate and traces of a certain suptype of CS possessive-adjectival formations in recorded Slavic.

Problems of IE and, particularly, CS pre- and postpositions were discussed from a typological point of view by V. V. Ivanov (1973). He treats especially *nadъ-*, *podъ-*, *perdъ-*, *zadъ-*, and *pozdъ-*.

Issues of expressive derivation in the Slavic verb were broached by I. Němec (1979a). The author traces the prefix *la-* to an onomatopoetic morpheme *lŏ-* suggestive of intensive, excessive activity; cf. also *lopati*/*lapati* 'to devour,' *lobъzati* 'to kiss, flatter,' *labužiti* 'to consume excessively.' On other studies investigating various facets of verbal derivation, see below *sub* III.5.

Word formation by means of composition (i.e., formation of compounds) was treated, with particular attention paid to CS, by H. D. Pohl in his monograph *Die Nominalkomposition im Alt- und Gemeinslavischen* (1977). Here the author reexamines nominal compounds in Early Slavic (CS and OCS) viewed in their IE context. He attempts a redefinition of IE and Slavic nominal composition by proposing a principle of classification different from the traditional one (as practiced by Brugmann, Wackernagel, Schwyzer, and others). In his discussion is included an analysis of lexical calques, especially those which entered Slavic from Greek in the process of coining many new compounds. J. Kurz (1971) has examined a particular problem pertinent to CS and Early Slavic compounds: their reanalysis, or recomposition, considered both from a phonological-morphological and a semantic point of view.   K. Handke, in an article on CS models for West Slavic nominal compounds (1979), further elucidates this process.   Discussing anthroponymic compounds with a non-final verbal component expressing government in Slavic and IE in general, H. D. Pohl (1973) surveys the various subclasses of this formational type with original predicative function in the verbal element.   In particular, he distinguishes two (basically) nonproductive and one productive subcategory, represented as follows: 1) *Ča-slav*, root noun with the root *ča-* < **čě-* < IE **kʷē(i)-* 'to hope, expect;' 2) *Pri-by-slavъ*, *Ne-da-měrъ*, indeclinable root nouns with root *by-* < IE **bhū-* 'to be' and *da-* < IE **dō-* 'to give;' 3) *Ljubi/o-měrъ*, verbal stem, partly modified noun; cf. *ljubi-/ljubo* 'to love'/'dear' (on the last, see also Birnbaum 1978a).   Derivational considerations are also in the foreground of a toponymic paper by I. Lutterer (1971). Discussing the evolution of various formational types of Slavic geographic names, Lutterer in part traces them back to CS sources.   For further research in Slavic onomastics, largely analyzing prehistoric toponymy, hydronomy, and anthroponymy and mostly also including derivational considerations, see below, section VI.4. Particularly relevant are the studies by S. Rospond (1974/76), O.   Kronsteiner (1975), J. Udolph (1979a), and O. N. Trubačev (1982).

Problems of prehistoric Slavic derivation were further discussed, partly at great length in: Martynov 1973, Polański 1979, Tschiževskij 1977 (discussing various aspects of the CS and Balto-Slavic noun and its declension); Vaillant 1971 and 1975, Klepikova 1976, and Stieber 1980 (discussing individual items); Rospond 1978 (discussing the suffix *-ynja* in toponyms); Dybo 1971, Kortlandt 1977, Kolesov 1979b and 1980b (discussing various aspects of accentuation and partly also vocalism); Fisher 1977, Bezlaj 1977, and Förster 1979 (discussing CS and Early Slavic prefixes from various points of view); as well as Mathiassen 1973 and 1974, Jeffers 1975, Ferrell 1974/75, Georgiev 1976, Kuryłowicz 1973 and 1976/78, Koch 1976/78, Kølln 1977, Pohl 1975a, Stepanov 1978, Machek 1980, Nikolaev and Starostin 1982, and, in particular, Ivanov 1978a and 1981a (all concerned with one or another facet of the Slavic verb).

III.4. Morphology of the Noun (and Pronoun)

I. Duridanov (1973) differentiates among seven chronological layers of nouns in Balto-Slavic and, separately, Baltic and Slavic.   The first layer is said to include Common Balto-Slavic formations inherited from PIE which are found also in other IE languages.   The second layer contains nominal forms derived by means of suffixation found only in Balto-Slavic; hence the items of this layer are of particular significance in elucidating the intricate Balto-Slavic problem.   The third layer consists of residual Balto-Slavic isomorphemes attested only in a part of Slavic.   Layer number four consists of nouns found in either Baltic or Slavic, and with known equivalents in other IE languages, while the fifth stratum also exhibits items found in either Baltic or Slavic but without IE counterparts. The sixth stratum includes uniquely Slavic nominal formations (e.g. such characterized by a -*k* suffix: OCS *sladykъ*, cf. Lith *saldùs*). Finally, the most recent layer contains nominal derivations formed by a suffix which were borrowed by the Balts from the Slavs, or vice versa, only in historical times.

CS and Balto-Slavic nominal derivation by means of suffixation is also the topic of a paper by V. V. Martynov (1973). Here, methodological problems and difficulties in establishing a unified theory of nominal derivation for Balto-Slavic and CS are discussed. The author sketches the Balto-Slavic and CS derivational systems of the noun and points to an alleged "great shift" in the relevant evolution of word formation. This shift would imply that old singulatives were to a large extent replaced by diminutives, with the latter serving as a base for the formation of new singulatives marked by -*k* suffixation not found elsewhere in IE. Moreover, Martynov comments on Baltic and Slavic formations marked by the suffix -*j*.

A recent study by V. I. Degtjarev (1981) investigates the origin of nouns used exclusively as *pluralia tantum* in Slavic. Degtjarev suggests that the history of this nominal subclass in preliterate Slavic presupposes the existence of number as a universal grammatical category of inflection which allowed its utilization also as a derivational means in secondary nominalizations. J. Kurz (1973) discusses the problems of the very existence and meaning of the Slavic pronoun *jь, *ja, *je, and particularly the question of its original demonstrative function.

The prehistoric Slavic noun is viewed in an entirely different manner in a paper by W. S. Hamilton, Jr. (1974), who explicitly constructs "the deep structure of Common Slavic ... on a synchronic basis," i.e., as a point of departure for the attested Slavic evidence. He thus deliberately disregards all diachronic changes that occurred in the course of CS as well as comparative evidence from other IE languages. Instead, the author charts the assumed generation of CS nominal surface structures derived from their underlying deep structures, both in the singular and the plural, and subsequently develops a model for generating the modern Slavic surface structure forms from the deep structure of the noun in CS. Though strictly generative and synchronic in its approach, this paper nevertheless takes into account the passage of real time between the CS and the modern period of the Slavic languages.

The noun in CS and specific aspects of nominal (as well as pronominal) inflection and derivation were treated during the last decade also in a number of other reference works, monographs, and studies. These have been reported on elsewhere in this survey. Foremost among them is volume four of Vaillant's comparative Slavic grammar (1974). Other relevant studies treat accentuation (Dybo 1971, 1977, and 1981; Kolesov 1972, 1979b, and 1980b; Kortlandt 1979b), as well as vocalism and auslaut (Schelesniker 1976, Trummer 1978). Problems of the noun in CS and pre-Slavic were also discussed in work on declension (Schmalstieg 1972, Georgiev 1973a, Mažiulis 1973, Liukkonen 1973 and 1974, Toporov 1975a, Kragalott 1977, Schmidt 1977, Polański 1979) as well as on nominal derivation (Kuryłowicz 1970/72, Schuster-Šewc 1971a, Otrębski 1972, Taszycki 1972, Grošelj 1972, Eckert

1972a, 1972b, and 1974, Sławski 1974, 1976, and 1980, Wojtyła-Świerzowska 1974a and 1974b, Boryś 1975, 1976, and 1981, Zaręba 1976, Bošković 1976, Pohl 1977, Keipert 1977, Feinberg 1978, Mathiassen 1978, Moskov 1978 and 1980, Mareš 1980b, Marojević 1982). Some aspects of the CS noun were further discussed in a couple of papers whose focus was on syntax (Basaj 1971 and Dejanova 1977). The prehistoric forms of the Slavic noun are, of course, discussed in great detail in various Slavic etymological dictionaries (cf. V.1. below) as well as in a few special studies on Slavic lexicology (Hamp 1973 and 1975, Vaillant 1971, Tschiżewskij 1977) and in work on Slavic topo- and hydronymy (cf., e.g., Rospond 1978 and other studies reported on *sub* VI.4.).

III.5. Morphology of the Verb

The all-overshadowing work treating the prehistoric evolution of the verb in Slavic and some other IE languages is V. V. Ivanov's 1981 monograph *Slavjanskij, baltijskij i rannebalkanskij glagol. Indoevropejskie istoki* which in its importance only can be likened to C. S. Stang's 1942 classic on the Slavic and Baltic verb (partial and preliminary version: Ivanov 1978a). In this book, the Soviet comparatist further develops his theory of the reflection of the two series of verbal forms, represented by the Hittite -*mi* and -*ḫ* conjugations respectively. The Ancient (or archaic) IE comparative evidence considered by Ivanov includes, in particular, Slavic, Baltic, and Early Balkan IE, the latter represented by the Phrygian and Albanian verb systems. In addition, he adduces a considerable amount of Hittite data, using it as the most appropriate point of departure for reconstructing the PIE verb system (however, with due attention paid to the significant separate Anatolian development). The book further develops the author's idea of the formal identity of the medio-passive and the perfect, considering this latter tense form a secondary category. The author also explains the origin and function of various -*s* formations attested in the IE verb and reassesses the form and function of the specific category ususally referred to as the injunctive.

Specifically, Ivanov's monograph is organized in the following manner. Chapter 1 is devoted to IE prototypes of the Slavic, Baltic, and Early Balkan verbal desinence systems. In chapter 2 the author treats the athematic verb class and the reflection of the IE verb forms of the first series in Baltic and Slavic (discussing, among other things, the verb roots *s-, *ed-, *ei-). Chapter 3 covers the reflexes of the PIE verb forms of the second series in Baltic and Slavic (discussing, for example, the roots *doH- > *dō-, *dheH- > *dhe-; the derivations of the root *stoH-). Chapter 4 concerns Baltic, Slavic, and Albanian suppletive paradigms resulting from the unification of the two verbal series, while some archaic sigmatic forms and stems with the suffixes *-s- and *-sk'- in Baltic, Slavic, Phrygian, and Albanian are the topic of chapter 5. Finally, in chapter 6, Ivanov discusses archaic derivations with a nasal affix. The problem of the thematic *vs.* the athematic verb in Slavic and Baltic was recently also discussed in a brief note by D. F. Robinson (1977) as was mentioned above (cf. III.2.).

The reconstruction of the Balto-Slavic verb system was further the topic of an incisive article by F. Kortlandt (1979d), who views such reconstruction with an eye to what it can tell us about the PIE verbal system from which it developed. In particular, the Dutch linguist considered the following problems: 1) Slavic *idǫ* (as well as *jadǫ* and *bǫdǫ*) and the PIE imperative; 2) Slavic *xoštǫ* and the PIE optative; 3) Slavic *mogǫ* vs. *vědě* and the PIE perfect; 4–9) the personal endings of the Slavic (and Baltic) verb; and 10) a note on the PIE verbal system. In this last section the author posits seven "partly compatible sets of mutually exclusive suffixes."

A largely generative approach to the structure and development of the Slavic verb system was attempted by B. Panzer (1978b). The author combines the two historically based classifications of the Slavic verb, according to the present-tense stem (introduced by Leskien) and the aorist-infinitive stem (adopted by Diels). He thus formulates a set of rules which generate the actually attested forms, taking as his point of departure a set of theoretical constructs essentially identical to the forms reconstructed for CS. A similar approach was taken also by L. R. Micklesen (1973). This article attempts a reinterpretation of the CS verbal system in terms of synchronic morphemicization, achieved by the application of a formal set of ordered rules roughly of the generative type.

Problems of the prehistory in Slavic of aspect and related phenomena, viewed in their broader IE context, were discussed by M. L. Palmaitis (1981). In addition to Slavic and Baltic data, Palmaitis also cites Greek evidence in his discussion of the emergence of the aspect correlation, and applies a typological point of view. Similarly U. S. Stepanov (1978) analyzes the genesis of Slavic aspect as it relates to the category of voice in Baltic along lines previously followed by H. Kølln, among others. In particular, he reconstructs apophonic and non-apophonic classes of thematic verb stems, discusses the perfect in its relationship to the category of state, and considers stem formations in *-(a)e/o-* and in *-i-* (iteratives and causatives). Moreover, he draws some general conclusions pertinent to the semantic structure of the utterance in Baltic and Slavic.

A number of other articles dealing with various verbal suffixes and their functions as they can be reconstructed for CS (and Baltic or Balto-Slavic) have appeared. J. Kuryłowicz considered iteratives in *-eie/o* (1973), as well as *-nǫti/-ěti* verbs and their semantic hierarchization (1976/77). Kølln 1977 concerns infinitives in *-ěti* and present stems in *-e/o*, while Koch 1976/78 discusses a hypothetical present stem class in *-v*. Further, Mathiassen 1973 treats nasal suffixation in CS and pre-Slavic.

K. Trost (1978) reexamines the relationship of the Slavic forms *idetъ* : *šьdъ* : *xoditi*, adding some general comments on the subclass of verbs of motion. V. Machek (1980), continuing earlier work, comments in this posthumous publication on the parallelism between, on the one hand, the Slavic and Baltic verb systems and, on the other, that of Latin. Specifically, he compares the Slavic iteratives-intensives in *-ati*, *-tati*, *-sati*, and *-stati*, with the matching Latin intensive verbs in *-tāre* and *-sāre*.

In a brief clarifying article on the IE prefix *po- and its reflexes in Slavic and Iranian, R. L. Fisher (1977) points out that the reflex of this prefix in Iranian Ossetic (where it is used as a perfectivizer) must be considered a Russianism and not, as was previously thought, an early East Iranian-Slavic isogloss. In Slavic, he finds this prefix more strongly attested in Russian while in Baltic it only plays a peripheral role.

In a broadly ranging essay on the IE infinitive, R. J. Jeffers (1975) remarks that the agreement of the infinitive stem with the aorist stem in Balto-Slavic ought not to be interpreted as implying a tense/aspect role for the infinitive. In particular, he points to the fact that in such forms as OCS *vrěšti* and *iti* the infinitive stem is different not only from the present but also from the aorist formation.

The prehistory of the Slavic verb was further discussed, or at least mentioned, in a number of other publications. In particular, this applies, of course, to Stieber 1973a, but also, for example, to Kuryłowicz 1977a. Specific problems residing in the Slavic verb were further treated in: Dybo 1972 and 1982 and Johnson 1980 (accentuation in the present tense); Nikolaev and Starostin 1982 (accentual types of present and aorist stems); Schmalstieg 1971 (the phonology of the first person singular); Enrietti 1977 (on the first person plural); Mareš 1978 (the present tense); Ferrell 1974/75, Pohl 1975a, and Georgiev 1976 (on the imperfect); Kuryłowicz 1970/72 (the perfect); Mathiassen 1975 (on the athematic imperative); Stieber 1970/72 (on the supine); Trubačev 1980a (on verbal suppletivism); Pohl 1973 (verbal components in compounds); Němec 1979a and Kurz 1971 (discussing verbal derivation); and Huntley 1982 (on semantics). Problems of the prehistory of the Slavic verb were at least touched upon in Dejanova 1977 (on the emergence of the gerund) and Vaillant 1975 (on the etymology of an OCS verb). Finally, relevant Slavic evidence is cited in Karaliūnas 1972 (discussing cognates of CS *pasti*) and Ivanov and Toporov 1980 (assessing the overall contributions of Kuryłowicz and Stang).

IV. SYNTAX

Relatively little work devoted specifically to the reconstruction of CS syntactic structures has been done over the last ten years or so. Among contributions to this field can be mentioned an article by B. I. Skupskij (1978). He discusses problems inherent in the reconstruction of the syntax in the earliest, Cyrillo-Methodian texts of the OCS gospel. The author considers, among other things, the necessity of separating genuine Slavic, i.e., inherited, constructions from those that must be considered Greek loan syntax in Early Slavic (cf., however, previous more significant work in this area by J. Bauer, R. Růžička, J. Kurz, R. Večerka, and H. Birnbaum reported on in Birnbaum 1979a).

Another paper belonging in this section is Comrie 1978, discussing Jakobsonian, semantically based case classification. The analysis utilizes Slavic diachronic material, including reconstructed CS (for details, see above III.2.). Also primarily syntactic is the discussion in Press 1973 and Harvie 1978; both papers discuss the dative absolute construction of Slavic. Press suggests some reasons for the choice of the dative in Slavic and Baltic and attempts an explanation for the diversity of case forms in these absolute constructions in various IE languages. Drawing on typological comparisons with Finno-Ugric, the author proposes a number of factors relevant to the particular choice of case. Such factors are, supposedly, the noninsistence on identical subject; the pre-main-clause position; the antiquity of some of the forms involved; the variability of the semantic message inherent in different case forms; the close semantic ties between the genitive, dative, and locative; and the lack of number and gender in personal pronouns. Harvie, noting evidence of dative absolute constructions in Russian and suggesting structural parallels of this construction with other IE languages, thus sees a historical base also for the Slavic dative absolute. He does not, however, deny its strong reinforcement through Greek influence (on OCS and Russian Church Slavic).

A. Timberlake, in his 1974 dissertation on the nominative object in Slavic, Baltic and West Finnic, discusses the construction of the type R dial. *voda pit'*, *zemlja paxat'*. He rejects one of the more common traditional explanations elaborated on by, among others, V. Kiparsky, and claims instead that this construction goes back to CS and is ultimately of IE origin. The structural, system-inherent explanation which he offers is not applicable to prehistoric times, however. Syntactic tendencies in the evolution of Slavic numerals, partly reaching to CS times, were discussed by M. Basaj (1971), while CS underlying forms are used as the point of departure for the historical development of Slavic gerunds by M. Dejanova (1977).

C. Bartula, in a paper on CS elements in the complex sentence of OCS (1972), identifies some of these elements and calls for further comparisons with Old Czech, Old Polish and Old Russian for a more detailed and refined identification. I. Bujukliev (1977) briefly discusses the origin of the relative subordinate clause in Slavic in terms of its IE and CS background. Relative clauses are also the topic of an essay by Z. Gołąb (1972), discussing CS data and the evidence in North Slavic. Identifying areas for future in-depth research, the author points to the priority of relative pronouns over subordinating conjunctions and hypothesizes that in languages with relative pronouns "these are syntactically the most expansive morphemes." While reinterpreting and summarizing the known facts, this contribution does not add any new data.

V. V. Ivanov, in a broadly comparative paper (1978b), examines Slavic "enclitic complexes," consisting primarily of pronoun plus verb, in the context of related phenomena in other IE languages (among them, particularly, Hittite and Mycenean Greek). A theoretically founded attempt at reconstructing fragments of CS phraseology, or to be specific, idiomatic expressions, was made by N. I. Tolstoj (1973). This rather programmatic study takes into consideration both chronological and spatial factors, while operating with linguistic (including stylistic) as well as extralinguistic (cultural, especially mythological) parameters.

C. Vasil'ev (1973) discusses the question of whether the construction type *u menja est'* is Russian or CS. The author conjectures that it in fact goes back to CS times because traces of it can be found in OCS, Old Russian, Old Serbian, and Old Croatian (in addition to the more persuasive evidence of contemporary East Slavic and Serbo-Croatian). Thus he is able to undermine the thesis that this construction is due merely to Finno-Ugric substratum influence in Russian. However, he considers the possibility that the Finnic impact may have caused a functional realignment of this construction, shifting the meaning from local to partitive, and further to possessive. To be sure, this can be fully clarified only when it is established which languages east of the CS linguistic area actually were neighboring, and whether CS or part of it ever had a Finnic substratum. That these questions will some day be answered seems rather unlikely, however.

Finally, it should be mentioned that P. Friedrich's 1975 treatment of PIE syntax, or rather of word order, in the IE protolanguage also briefly discusses relevant reconstructions for CS. Friedrich suggests VSO and SOV as the main word-order types for CS on the basis of the attested surface syntactic evidence. In so doing, he refers to E. Berneker's pertinent study of 1900.

Prehistoric Slavic syntactic structures and patterns were, moreover, discussed at some length also in volume five, devoted to syntax, of A. Vaillant's monumental Slavic comparative grammar (Vaillant 1977); for details, see above *sub* I.2. Similarly, dialectal CS is the basis for the two volumes of J. Stanislav's history of Slovak, treating syntax (Stanislav 1973); cf. above, I.4.

Syntactic, or in part, rather, phraseological, problems and phenomena of CS also take up considerable space in work by V. V. Ivanov and V. N. Toporov (1973 and 1974; further discussed below *sub* V.3.) and by R. Eckert (1981, treated in the same section below). Finally, syntactic considerations enter marginally also into Hamp 1976a, Ivanov 1973, Bezlaj 1977, Degtjarev 1981, and Mareš 1980b, accounted for elsewhere in this volume.

V. LEXICOLOGY

(Including Etymology and Lexical Semantics)

V.1. General Problems of Common Slavic Lexicology

Of reference works treating general problems of CS lexicology, it is primarily the etymological and comparative dictionaries of Slavic which go beyond one single Slavic language that should be mentioned here. The *Słownik prasłowiański*, under the general editorship of F. Sławski, began to appear in 1974 and to date (1982) the first four volumes have been published. In volume one, the succint treatment of CS derivation and other word formation, particularly as it pertains to the noun, is worthy of note (cf. III.3. above). For some early reviews, cf. Aitzetmüller 1977a and Moszyński 1977b. Equally, if not more, important is the *Ètimologičeskij slovar' slavjanskix jazykov. Praslavjanskij leksičeskij fond*, under the editorship of O. N. Trubačev, which also began publication in 1974 and by 1981 had reached its eighth volume. For some assessments of the earlier issues, see Schuster-Šewc 1975a, Moszyński 1977b, and Ondruš 1977b; cf. further also Trubačev's own account (1979b), discussing the methodological and practical problems attendant upon the various stages in the preparation of this major etymological reference work. A somewhat less ambitious endeavor is the *Vergleichendes Wörterbuch der slavischen Sprachen*, authored by L. Sadnik and R. Aitzetmüller. The first volume (covering the letters A and B) was completed in 1975 (Sadnik & Atizetmüller 1975-). Here the reconstruction of the CS vocabulary is not quite as much in the foreground as in the etymological projects centered in Cracow and Moscow. The fourth comparable project, with its base in Brno, the *Etimologický slovník slovanských jazyků*, whose managing editor is F. Kopečný, is also somewhat different in overall design (Kopečný 1973-). The two parts of this work published to date (1973, 1980) cover only the synsemantic words and pronouns, or, specifically, prepositions (and prefixes), word-final (attached) particles; conjunctions, (free) particles, pronouns, and pronominal adverbs. Though limited so far to grammatical items, each entry lists the comparative evidence and discusses each etymology with much attention paid to CS. It goes without saying that the wealth of the etymological material contained in these large-scale collective enterprises cannot be evaluated properly in this report.

Similar considerations hold true for the serial publication *Ètimologija*, edited by O. N. Trubačev and containing a number of important studies, mostly by Soviet, but occasionally also by other scholars in the field. In the period covered here, eleven volumes (*Ètimologija 1970–1980*, published between 1972 and 1982) have appeared.

Of etymological dictionaries of individual Slavic languages, it should be noted that a new reference work of this kind has begun to appear for Bulgarian under the editorship of V. Georgiev (1971-). To date, two volumes (1971, 1979) have appeared; for a review, see Šaur 1980c. An etymological dictionary of Slovenian by F. Bezlaj (1976-), so far covering the letters A-J, has also appeared in the decade under review. Further, the etymological dictionary of Polabian, originally initiated by T. Lehr-Spławiński with the assistance of K. Polański (the first issue of which appeared in 1962), has continued, now with Polański as the sole author (cf. Polański 1971-). For an assessment, see Schuster-Šewc 1975b. Further, a historical etymological dictionary of Upper and Lower Sorbian, authored by H. Schuster-Šewc (1978-), has made its appearance and has already prompted some critical reactions (Ossadnik 1979, Stone 1980); cf. also the sample issue (Schuster-Šewc 1973a) and an early review (Reinhart 1974). The significance of the Sorbian lexicon for Slavic etymology, with implications also for CS and pre-Slavic, was, moreover, discussed by Schuster-Šewc in a theoretical article devoted to that subject (1979). Of ongoing publications in this category, F. Sławski's Polish etymological dictionary (1954-) continues and has occasioned responses by, among others, E. Hamp (1971a and 1977), discussing individual items.

CS and dialectal CS material in the vocabulary of OCS was recently analyzed by A. S. L'vov (1978), who attempted to separate such OCS lexemes of CS origin with the same derivation in all Slavic languages as opposed to those whose formation exhibits dialectal restrictions. The CS component of the Serbo-Croatian lexicon was reexamined by B. Pizłówna 1972, (following the model study of 1938 on the same subject by Lehr-Spławiński, as applied by him to Polish). Pizłówna touches, in particular, on the problem of the CS dialectal base of Serbo-Croatian. Possible lexical ties, or perhaps merely parallels, between South Slavic and Northwest Slavic (Kashubian), which conceivably point to a Late CS dialectal base, were examined by H. Popowska-Taborska (1975). She is skeptical, however, about any common origin of the items considered and prefers to see in them accidental analogies and/or archaisms characteristic of the peripheral zones of the Slavic linguistic territory. The Polish Slavist further discusses lexical loans and their semantic modification, especially in connection with transhumance (i.e., shepherd migrations to and from mountainous regions).

The major contribution to Russian historical lexicology and its chronologically complex prehistory made by V. Kiparsky in the third volume of his Russian historical grammar (1975a) has already been summarized above (cf. I.4.). Here, a more theoretical discussion of the same problem by Kiparsky (1971b) should be mentioned, however. In another theoretical paper (Kiparsky 1971a), the Finnish Slavist discussed some general principles of modern etymological research, especially J. Rudnyc'kyj's complex and highly abstract formula, making reference also to illustrative Slavic data.

Problems related to the chronological and geographic stratification of the CS vocabulary as they pertain to the ethnogenesis of the Slavs were discussed by Z. Gołąb (1977). The author views the lexicon of the earliest Slavs in its IE dialectal context, while taking into account findings by Lehr-Spławiński, K. Moszyński, Stang, Trubačev, and others. Gołąb thus attempts to establish six sets of relevant lexical layers: 1) a *centum* layer; 2) an eastern layer (reflected in Slavic-Indo-Iranian lexical correspondences); 3) a northwestern layer (showing links with Italic); 4) a northern layer (characterized by lexical ties with Germanic); 5) the Balto-Slavic layer; and 6) the purely Slavic layer. Statistical and semantic considerations lead Gołąb to reassess the gradual emergence of the Slavic ethnic group. He surmises that the ancestors of the Slavs and the Balts originally belonged to the eastern (or *satəm*) portion of IE, remaining in close contact with the forebears of the Indo-Iranian Aryans. According to this view, an early westward move (possibly about 2000 BC) brought the pre-Slavs into contact with speakers of *centum* dialects, especially the ancestors of Italic and Germanic tribes. This suggests that the forebears of the Slavs were only peripherally involved with the Proto-Balts, and, naturally, sheds some new light on the controversial problem of an alleged early Balto-Slavic unity.

Methodological issues of Slavic etymology were further considered in Trubačev 1973 and 1982, Němec 1979b, Kopečný 1979, and Polák 1980. Trubačev comments on, among other things, the origin of CS *s* < IE *k'* (cf. II.4. and VI.4.). Němec discusses various criteria (archaic idioms, stylistic features, etc.) and suggests techniques for identifying items of foreign, yet Slavic origin in individual Slavic languages, especially Czech. Kopečný offers a few methodological considerations relevant to etymological reconstruction using primarily Slavic, including CS and pre-Slavic data. Problems of methodology are also addressed by Polák on the basis of Slavic and, in particular, CS linguistic evidence.

The recent introduction to etymological studies by Erhart and Večerka (1981) addresses both the substance and methodology of relevant research and is designed for academic use. The rich "etymological index" at the end of the book (192–274) lists such reconstructed IE etyma which have survived into Slavic, citing both Slavic and other IE cognates. The text portion contains: an introduction which defines the field of etymology, illustrating it with Slavic, mostly Czech data (7–14); a bibliographic commentary on major etymological research beginning with antiquity and running through modern times (15–30); a discussion of linguistic evolution and the methods for reconstructing linguistic prehistory, focusing on CS and PIE phonology (31–70); a section on phonological change and its subtypes (71–80); a treatment of morphological entities and their modification, including ablaut (81–90); a chapter on word formation and its various techniques (91–113); a discussion of specific morphological changes caused by fusion, analogy, folk etymology, and contamination (114–26); a presentation of semantic change, including metaphorization, tabus, expressive meaning, etc. (127–44); a survey of the concrete devices available to establish the origin of words (145–69); and an account of the major etymological dictionaries available or in progress, commenting on the strategies applied in each. A selected, but representative, listing of secondary literature concludes this useful textbook.

Specific problems of Slavic etymology were further addressed in a volume of proceedings resulting from the 1972 Leipzig symposium on etymology and historical lexicology. Particularly deserving mention here are the contributions by Schuster-

Šewc, Trubačev, Němec, Müller, Martynov, Eichler, Jacobsson, Kisse, Ondruš, Kopečný, and Varbot (Schuster-Šewc 1975b). For a review, see Šaur 1977b.

Individual Slavic etymologies were, of course, discussed by a number of authors. Thus, J. Zaimov (1976b) and V. V. Martynov (1972) each considered a number of such items. H. Leeming (1971) suggested some non-IE influences, while H. Schuster-Šewc (1971b) focused primarily on West Slavic items. Boryś 1979 is concerned with the geographic distribution of some CS dialectal items and Boryś 1982 treats lexical archaisms of Kajkavian Croatian in part dating back to CS times. J. Udolph (1980) and J. Zaimov (1976a) discussed the significance of Slavic onomastics for etymology. Some new etymological explanations or suggestions were further offered in Trubačev 1982.

V.2. Common Slavic Vocabulary Inherited from (Proto-) Indo-European

A. Gluhak (1978) discusses the etymologically obscure *rešeto*, contemplating an IE-Uralic parallel as conceived in a wider, Nostratic framework. Given this likely parallelism, Gluhak considers the fact that the lexical item in question is found only in a limited number of East IE languages (Slavic, Baltic, and Indo-Iranian, but possibly also in Italic). An alternative possibility, namely that the word is a common innovation of Finnic (Permian), Ugric, and some IE languages, is also discussed.

Slavic, or rather Balto-Slavic, plays only a secondary role in the paper by A. J. van Windekens (1971). The author tries to show the "occidental" nature of the Tocharian vocabulary by comparing Toch A *talke*, B *telki* 'sacrifice' with Balto-Slavic *dhḷgh-* (R *dolg*, etc.) 'debt, obligation' (cf. also Goth *dulgs* 'id.'), and the similar Toch B *talkā-*, Slavic *tolka-* (P *tłoka* 'Sunday pleasure, communal labor without remuneration'). Both point to a common original meaning 'feast, festivity organized by labor community.'

Balto-Slavic lexical correspondences were again investigated in Eckert 1977, while Plevačová 1974 examined the Slavic root *ner-/nor-* (with further ablaut variants) 'to submerge,' commenting also on the contamination with the verb root in *nuriti* 'id.'. Leeming 1978 discussed the Slavic metal name *želězo* in its IE context and Fermeglia 1977 investigated a number of Slavic etymologies with controversial IE and partly non-IE (Turkish or Arabic) cognates.

Hamp 1971b offers some comments on the relationship of Russian and Slovenian *omela*, on the one hand, and OCS and SC *imela*, on the other, considering, in particular, other possibilities than the straight ablaut variation usually assumed for these items. The same linguist (1973a) makes some new observations germane to the second component in Slavic *jed-inъ, jed-ьna*, deriving the former from IE *einos*, the latter from *-inā̃*. Hamp 1975 further attempts a new interpretation of the controversial Russian form for '90', reconstructing *devjanosto* from *devьnó-sъto* < *Heneun̥-ó-*. For this etymology, he subsequently considered the possibility of bilingualism with a Turkic language as an influence (cf. also Hamp 1976b). A few new surmises regarding the etymology of the same numeral were also advanced in

Pisani 1974, who accepts the traditional explanation of *d-* as analogical with the anlaut in *desętь*.

An IE origin was assumed by A. S. Mel'ničuk (1978) for the CS verb *větiti* 'to speak, advise' and congnates, tracing it back to an IE root **voit-/věit-/vīt-* 'branch' and establishing connections both with Lat *invītāre* 'to invite' and CS *vitati 'to dwell.' Skeptical about too much emphasis on early Latin-Slavic lexical isoglosses, advocated by V. N. Toporov and others, K. Kostov (1980) criticizes, in particular, the assumption of a common root **rěg'-* as the source for a number of lexical items in Latin and Slavic.

For some other etymological studies dealing with the IE background of individual items, but with the emphasis primarily on semantics, see below, section V.3.

Problems of Slavic lexicology with implications for CS and a wider IE background were also considered in a paper by G. Nagy (1974). Nagy discusses the old issue of the relationship between the Baltic and Slavic designations for the god of thunder (*Perkúnas, Perunъ*), and comments specifically also on the possible rhyme-word relationship of these items with their closest counterparts in Greek and Hittite. An attempt at reetymologizing the puzzling discrepancy of OCS *rozga* and *razga* was made in Georgiev 1974. He posits an underlying form **(v)arzgá*, the double anlaut vocalism supposedly reflecting intonational differences.

Lexicological items attested in individual Slavic languages or reflected in German place names, having ramifications for CS were further studied by W. Boryś (1978), W. Budziszewska (1974), H. Schuster-Šewc (1976), and H. H. Bielfeldt (1970/72).

The South Slavic item *vatra* 'fire, etc.' Schuster-Šewc 1980 holds to be a CS lexical dialectism rather than a loan from Avestan, Albanian, or Daco-Moesian, as previously believed. The East German scholar believes that it is reflected also in OSln *jatra* 'morning' and that it has cognates in Lekhitic and Sorbian (partly with *-str-* rather than *-tr-*) as well. He explains the phonetic difficulties (*v-* : *j-*, *-str-* : *-tr-*) as due to CS phonological fluctuations and considers the attestation of the equivalent of the South Slavic word also in Albanian and Romanian explicable in terms of shepherd migrations ("transhumance"). Sławski 1982 sheds some new light on the origin and semantics of CS *drugъ* and its cognates, while Hamp 1982b discusses some color designations and related items (*siv-/sin-*, *sěd-/sěr-*, with the variant *šěd-/šěr-*, further *ra-n-*) against their Balto-Slavic and broader IE background.

Considerations of CS lexicology, focusing on various aspects of derivation, enter into work by R. Eckert (1972a, 1972b, 1974 and 1979) and by M. Moskov (1978 and 1980), referred to above (cf. III.3.). Finally, issues of the CS vocabulary were raised by I. Duridanov (1973, primarily concerned with the morphology of the noun), N. I. Tolstoj (1973, in an attempt to reconstruct CS phraseology), V. V. Martynov (1978, in a discussion of possible Balto-Slavic-Italic lexical isoglosses), E. Dickenmann (1980a, analyzing Early Slavic lexical relics as mirrored in toponymy and hydronymy), and J. Udolph (1981c, on North Slavic toponymy and hydronymy; 1982, on the Slavic designation for 'salmon') all reported on elsewhere in this bibliographic commentary.

V.3. Semantics (Specific Problems of Lexical Meaning)

Methodological problems of Slavic etymology with an emphasis on semantics and semantic change were discussed by A. de Vincenz (1975), who uses, in particular, the Slavic designations for 'frog' and 'child' as examples. General problems of semantics were also discussed in O. N. Trubačev 1980b, where his methodological considerations on reconstructing lexemes and their meanings are illustrated with Slavic data; on the utilization of semantic considerations, see now also Trubačev 1982.

Of specific semantic groups, lexemes with mythological content have continued to attract much attention. Among relevant studies we can mention an essay by V. N. Toporov (1975b), which discusses items with such meaning or at least association—R *ten'*, *telepat'(sja)*, *pčela*, *koza*, and others—suggesting possible linguistic links reaching beyond the Caucasus. Another paper in this vein is by A. V. Desnickaja (1978), who identifies some Southwest Balkan-East Slavic etymological and sematic isoglosses, partly of cultic-mythological origin. Methodologically innovative (not to say programmatic), the study by N. I. Tolstoj and S. M. Tolstaja (1978) discusses techniques for reconstructing Early Slavic spiritual culture. They emphasize, in particular, the relationship between popular and literary culture and comment on various types of sources, different kinds of ritual symbolism (illustrated with previously untapped material from the Poles'e region), as well as the "deep semantics" and some formal aspects of ritual habits and their reconstruction.

The bulk of the mythologically oriented papers, however, deals with the notion of 'god' and its various designations in Slavic. Thus, Georgiev (1972) discusses Slavic *divъ* and its cognates, as well as *bogъ*, considering the first item a direct inheritance from PIE *deiṷo-s*, the second a loan from Iranian (OPers *baga-*, etc.). For Slavic *gospodь*, the Bulgarian scholar assumes an underlying PIE form *ghosti-poti-s*, which however would have to have entered Slavic through Germanic mediation to account for its attested phonetic shape (rather than the expected *gostьpotь*). Georgiev further views the three terms discussed as representative of three phases of CS mythology.

Primarily concerned with semantic change, Rudnyc'kyj (1974) discusses the replacement of earlier Slavic *div-* by *bog-* after *divъ* had been degraded to mean 'evil spirit.' This semantic shift was paralleled in Iranian, whereas the reflex of *div-* in Baltic retained its original meaning 'god.' The same lexical items were further discussed in Gołąb 1975b, where *div-* was also compared with *dik-*, given the special use of the latter, along with *čist-*, in idioms of the type *dikol čisto pol'e*. In addition, other lexical items with connotations of primitive life were discussed. The lexemes *divъ*, *dikъ*, and *bogъ* are only among several items pertinent to Slavic demonology (cf. further *běsъ*, *čьrtъ*, *Velesъ*—in Old Czech also attested as a common noun—*vila*, *jęza/*jęga*, *diva*, and *děva*) commented upon in Polák 1977. Slavic *div-* (and its competitor *bog-*), with IE cognates, is also in the foreground in two papers by E.

Hamp (1974 and 1978).

The mythological name *Div*, attested only in the controversial Igor Tale and texts related to it, and the "eighth deity" of the reconstructed East Slavic pantheon *Simargl* (believed to reflect the divine bird *Simūrγ* of the Iranians) are discussed in Worth 1978. suggests a relationship between the two deities leading to the replacement of the latter by the former under pressure brought about by representatives of the then recently embraced Christian faith. The two chief Slavic designations for god were also examined in Sławski 1979, assuming *bogъ* to represent a specific Iranian-CS isogloss and positing a zero-grade variant for the PIE form underlying *divъ*.

The Slavic designations of pagan deities (among them *Perunъ* and *Velesъ/Volosъ*) were further discussed in a paper by V. V. Ivanov and V. N. Toporov (1973). They explored the reconstruction of CS texts on the basis of etymologizing a semantically restricted sphere of the lexicon, in this case a set of mythological names. M. Shapiro (1982b) propounds the interpretation of the mythological names *Volos* and *Veles* as "an instantiation of the IE divine twin myth." This conclusion is problematic, however, because of the phonetic closeness of the items. Various terms for wizard and witch, including some items on the periphery of mythological terminology, were further discussed in Slupski 1981, where the material is divided into lexemes with, as opposed to such without, indisputable cognates.

Contributions etymologizing early ethnonyms also deserve mention here. O. N. Trubačev (1974), considers a number of early Slavic ethnonyms in terms of the light they shed on the much debated issue of the Slavic protohome and the Slavs' assumed early crossing of the Carpathians. Moreover, he draws some interesting parallels between the early dispersal of the Slavs outside their original homeland and such a phenomenon as the Russian colonolization of Siberia. Trubačev also suggests a tentative identification of early West and East Slavic civilizations with certain archeologically defined prehistoric cultures datable to the period 3rd/2nd cc. BC to 2nd/3rd cc. AD. This paper has now been superseded by the more comprehensive and even more imaginitive study by the same scholar (Trubačev 1982; cf. VI.4., below). The name of the Slavs, *Slověne* (and derivatives), was reexamined in two studies by H. Schelesniker (1972) and J. P. Maher (1974). In their speculations, however, these authors do not go much beyond previous research even where earlier findings or surmises are being rejected. The etymology of the ethnonym *Veneti/Venedi* was, again, studied by Gołąb (1975a). He postulates a semantic shift: **Uenétes* 'ruling class of warriors' $>$ **Uenétes* 'Veneti,' as a designation of the prehistoric and early historical Slavs. To be sure, it is not certain that this new hypothesis is viable. Gołąb also discussed recently (1982), the semantic association between certain kinship terms and the two Slavic ethnonyms **Sъrbi* and *Slověne*. Here he sheds some additional light not only on this possible link but also on the controversial etymologies of the ethnic designations themselves.

Terms with some religious or ritual connotations referring to early, pagan burial practices were investigated in Maher 1973. Leeming 1973 offers some etymological considerations pertaining to words designating writing, with suggestions about early

Slavic-Iranian and Slavic-Germanic contacts, in addition to ties that Slavs may have had with an Asian, presumably Turkic, people in the Balkans or Pannonia. CS and Early Slavic legal terminology was surveyed in two articles. The first, by Toporov (1973), views CS *vьrvь and věno, věniti against their IE background. The second, by Ivanov and Toporov (1978), discusses archaic legal terms and constructions gleaned particularly from OR sources, along with some items of mythological-poetic and social origin in their relation to IE. In surveying various Slavic terms denoting 'love,' Birnbaum (1978a) commented, specifically, on the two CS roots ljub- (< PIE *leubh-) and mil- (< PIE *meil-/*mīl-). The concepts of gift, barter, and exchange, and the broader field into which they fall, were discussed on the basis of Slavic data, viewed in their IE context, in Ivanov 1975.

Names for metals were analyzed in Mareš 1977, who assumes the knowledge of the following seven metals among the Slavs while still in their assumed protohome: gold, silver, iron, bronze, lead, a tin-lead alloy, and mercury. By contrast, familiarity with steel and brass, introduced from the West, can be dated only to the sixth/seventh centuries AD. The etymology of the "migratory word" for silver in Slavic (with counterparts in Baltic and Germanic) was reconsidered in Trubačev 1978. The Soviet etymologist suggests that the Slavic form reflects an ancient practice of covering glass with a layer of silver on the facing side. For further thoughts on Slavic metal terms, see now also Trubačev 1982 (details below, VI.4.).

Konnova (1972) examined some lexical and semantic isoglosses pertaining to grain terminology as they are distributed in modern Slavic, allowing certain conclusions also for dialectal Late CS. A number of building terms, all going back to the CS period, were discussed in Lindert (1978). Pointing out that different ways, kinds, and forms of construction yielded a complex terminology, the author asserts that some of the pertinent terms, e.g. *kǫt-ja, *vez-ja, *by-dlo, go back to PIE, while others, e.g. *xyz-ja, *jata, *xata, are early loans. Some of these CS terms were dialectally limited; this applies, for example, to *bydlo, * obitělь. *termъ, *xata, *xalupa, the latter said to be a modification of *xalǫga. Moreover, as Lindert points out, a more differentiated—mostly already post-CS—reality gradually required also a new and correspondingly more differentiated terminology. Slavic tree designations were once more discussed by Tolstoj (1978b). In particular, Tolstoj comments on recent views by Bernštejn, Filin, and Martynov, concerning the terms sosna and zvoja, as well as the collective item bor.

Three items beginning with čel- (čeljadь, čeljustь, čelověkъ) were discussed in Schütz 1981, who takes the findings of the new Soviet Slavic etymological dictionary as his point of departure. Nouns with the suffix -ęt and denoting young animals were discussed by Tschižewskij (1977), who attributes an original connotation 'round object' to all of them. M. Rudnicki (1974), in an aside, claims CS origin for *korljь 'ruler,' according to him, originally meaning 'mediator.' He thus rejects the standard etymology deriving this item from the name of Charlemagne. Š. Ondruš (1975) argues for CS, and partly PIE, origin of two designations for dog in Czech, while L. Moszyński (1981) discusses the earliest evidence of *němьcь and *glušьcь.

Early designations for 'island' in georgraphic names in Northwest Poland, once located on the Slavic linguistic periphery, were identified by H. Górnowicz (1972).

The often adduced semantic group of kinship terms was discussed at some length by V. Šaur (1975). In this study devoted to the etymology of this semantic class, not only is previous relevant research surveyed, but far-reaching conclusions about the early societal structure of the Slavs and their forebears are drawn as well, partly on the evidence of some less common terms belonging here. The word for 'daughter' was again examined by H. Schmeja (1976). The author traces the Slavic reflex, along with the "Old European" (Oskian, Germanic, and Baltic), Armenian and, partly, Indo-Iranian (OPers) forms, to an underlying *dhukter, as opposed to other IE variants (*dhugater, *dhugdher, *dhughiter). On kinship terms, cf. also Gołąb 1982, mentioned previously in this section.

New or reconsidered etymologies of individual items, with particular attention paid to their meaning, were offered in a number of studies. Among them are: Gasparini 1970/72, Hamp 1970, 1973b, 1976a, and 1981, Rudnicki 1971, Wallfield 1971, Otrębska-Jabłońska 1972, Gribble 1973 (offering an attractive etymology for *bykъ 'bull'), Schuster-Šewc 1973b, Aitzetmüller 1974, and Kopečný 1974b (the last two reconsidering the etymology of otrokъ), Varbot 1974, Vaillant 1971 (rejecting the previously assumed connection between užina 'breakfast' and jugъ 'south') and 1975, Gołąb 1976, Klepikova 1976, Lunt 1977b (assuming sexual conotations in the PIE item underlying igra), Schröpfer 1977, Witkowski 1977, Šaur 1977, 1978, 1979, and 1980b, Dzendzelivs'kyj 1978, Budziszewska 1978, Szymański 1980, Martynov 1980, Stieber 1980, Schenker 1981, and Mur'janov 1981 (this last pair discussing the item iskrь 'near, close'), Oguibenine 1981 (discussing *vorgъ 'enemy' in semantic and conceptual terms), and Shapiro 1982a (throwing new, unexpected light on the name *nejęsytь; cf below, V.4.).

The etymologies of various verbal items were discussed in: Kopečný 1973 (commenting on the three meanings of the verb byti—existential, copular, and auxiliary), Zaręba 1973 (discussing verbs of perception), Watkins 1978 (commenting on two Slavic items denoting confession), Boryś 1980 (analyzing the relationship of CS *piti and *pojiti), Šaur 1980a (commenting on the origin of the verbs baviti and slaviti), and Huntley 1982 (on the semantic shades of OCS tešti : točiti deduced from textual evidence).

Adjectival synonymy of formations in -t and -st in Slavic and Baltic was discussed primarily in terms of diachronic lexicology by É. A. Balalykina (1980).

Synsemantic (grammatical) etyma were discussed in Wójcikowska 1978 (treating prepositions and adverbs signaling inclusion or exclusion and finding a north-south distribution reflecting a CS dialectal split), Förster 1979 (analyzing the origin of the prefix pod- in denominal formations), Budich 1977 (distinguishing between two kinds of Slavic eterъ), and Pavlov 1974 (commenting on the etymology of jako).

Primarily semantic considerations also underlie the comprehensive monograph by V. V. Ivanov and V. N. Toporov (1974), discussing lexical and phraseological reconstructions of CS texts. Here once again such items as *Perunъ* and *Velesъ*/*Volosъ* are discussed. Additionally, such fertility symbols as *Jarila* and *Kupala* are examined in light of the transformation of basic myths and corresponding rituals. Lexemes and idiomatic phrases pertinent to primitive apiculture among the Balts and the Slavs were investigated by R. Eckert (1981). Here such phrases (syntagms) as **laziti bъčely*, **laziti medъ*, **laziti ulьi* and **děditi bъčeli*, **děditi medъ* are reconstructed.

Problems of etymology and semantics were further discussed in Dukova 1979, Lépissier 1971, Mańczak 1975, Moskov 1975, Moszyński 1977a, and Oguibenine 1979, all of which are primarily concerned with lexical borrowing. Further contributions to semantics in etymological research are by Schuster-Šewc (1971a and 1976), Martynov (1972), Karaliūnas (1972), Pohl (1973), Kurz (1973), Stieber (1973c), Liukkonen (1973 and 1974), Wojtyła-Świerzowska (1974a and b), Nagy (1974), Vasil'ev (1975), Zaręba (1976), Kuryłowicz (1976/78), Moskov (1978 and 1980), Mel'ničuk (1978), Beleckij (1980), Mareš (1980b), Palmaitis (1981), Šaur (1981), Udolph (1982), Hamp (1982b), and Sławski (1982). These studies are discussed or referred to elsewhere in this survey.

V.4. Lexical Borrowings in Common Slavic.

Much work in reconstructing loanwords in CS has been done also during the last decade. Thus, Leeming (1978a) discusses some lexical loans in Early Slavic—both CS and OCS—heretofore not properly identified or understood. Among the items discussed are: **kъn'igy*, considered by the British scholar to be an Altaic loanword; **sъto*, in accordance with the majority of specialists regarded as a loan from Iranian; **tysǫtja*/*tysętja*, a lexeme shared with Germanic and Baltic and regarded by the author as probably derived from Germanic in Slavic; **tьma*, said to be a Turkic loan; **pьsati*, showing a semantic development shared only with Iranian and Old Prussian; **buky*, traditionally believed to have been borrowed from Germanic; **lěs-*, with parallels in Persian; **lup-* and derivatives, considered to be in alternation with **rob-* in the meaning of 'to rob,' and derivatives; as well as several other lexemes. The same linguist has also discussed these and some further items in three other papers, where he considered a possible Turkic, along with Iranian or Germanic, origin: Leeming 1973, mentioned above, see V.3.; Leeming 1974, analyzing OCS *kramola* 'sedition,' believed to reflect a Turkic verb; and Leeming 1976a, discussing some Slavic stellar names and their prehistoric origins, with Turkic, again, assumed to be a major source. The possibility of Slavic-Turkic bilingualism as an influence was also considered in Hamp 1975, reconstructing the protoform of Russian *devjanosto* (cf. V.2., above). Finally, Turkic loanwords found in all the Slavic languages were discussed in connection with some Slavic and Balkan etymologies proposed by Moskov (1975). Specifically, he analyzed the root *tun-* 'nothing, misfortune; cheap, worthless, etc.' and also attempted to formulate a comprehensive explanation for the relation of the vowels in the root *tyr-* : *těr-* : *tur-* : *tъr-*.

Some IE and, especially, non-Indo-European (but rather Proto-European) substratum items found in the vocabulary of several West Slavic languages were discussed in Polák 1973b. M. Shapiro (1982a) proposed a more complex etymology for Slavic *nejęsytь 'pelican' (and its reflexes in various Slavic languages), suggesting that the OCS hapax, attested in the *Psalterium Sinaiticum*, goes back to a solecism of the Septuagint, and thus ultimately reflects Hebrew. Early Semitic, especially Arabic, loans in Slavic also during the prehistoric period were considered in Račeva 1979.

The previous etymology of Early Slavic *ǫbolъ* 'gallery, covered aisle; well, cistern' as adapted from Greek was confirmed in Lépissier 1971, some claimed phonetic and other difficulties notwithstanding. Greek influence is also assumed by W. Budich (1977) for one of the two homophones expressed by Slavic *eterъ*, corresponding to Greek *héteros*, while the other word of the same appearance is an approximate synonym of OCS *někyi, jedinъ, drugyi*, or *inъ*. Baltic origin for dialectal Late CS *degъtь* (R *degot'* 'tar') is posited by S. B. Bernštejn (1980), who compares this item with Lith dial. *degùtis* rather than with standard Lith *degùtas*.

Possible Iranian origin was, as previously mentioned (cf. V.3.), considered for a number of lexical items belonging to the sphere of mythology and religion. In particular, this refers to the several recent discussions of the Slavic words *bogъ* and *divъ* (Georgiev 1972, Rudnyc'kyj 1974, Hamp 1974 and 1978, Gołąb 1975b, Polák 1977, Worth 1978, and Sławski 1979). The same items, in addition to a few others (*svętъ*; P *patrzyć* 'to look,' Cz *patřiti* 'to belong' < Iran /*pāϴrāi* 'to protect, preserve'), were also discussed by U. Dukova (1979). Another mythological term, potentially derived from Iranian, is the name of the god *Jazomir*. For this, B. Oguibenine (1979) assumes underlying Iran *MiϴOrayaz-*, with metathesis of the two components in its Slavic reflection; on this theonym, cf. also Birnbaum 1977a. The magnitude of the Iranian impact was assessed differently, as was mentioned before (cf. II.5.), in Gołąb 1973 and Mańczak 1974/75 on the basis of Slavic items beginning with *x*-. In a discussion of Slavic loanwords in Russian, H. D. Pohl (1975b) differentiates between three chronological layers, according to the time at which such items entered Slavic: 1) during the CS period (e.g., *sto, raj*); 2) in post-CS times (e.g., *čertog*); and 3) in the course of the history of the individual Slavic languages, among them Russian. In view of O. N. Trubačev's startling finding (reported in 1967, *Ètimologija 1965*, 3–81) that some Early Slavic loans from Iranian are attested exclusively in West Slavic, Pohl's attempted chronology assumes particular significance.

The lexical impact of Late (Vulgar) Latin or Early Romance on Early Slavic at the very beginning of literacy was, again, illustrated with the word for 'Jew' (*židъ*) in Birnbaum 1981b. While this item seems to have reached the Slavic world directly from the Romance area (probably through Northeast Italy or Dalmatia), OCS *misa* 'bowl' is assumed to have entered Slavic through Germanic, even though its source, too, was Late Latin (*mēnsa*). This is the view of M. Enrietti (1977/79), who suggests Old High German rather than Gothic as an intermediary, considering the geographic proximity of Moravia.

The two variants of the controversial Slavic word for 'church,' *cŕ̥ky* and *cir(ъ)ky*, are both considered to go back to Germanic sources by L. Moszyński (1977a). However, while Moszyński argues that the first of the two cited forms is a loan from Gothic in the Black Sea region (and unaffected by the second palatalization of velars), he believes that the second was adopted by the Slavs from the Bavarians in Carinthia. Using linguistic and historical evidence, the Polish linguist subsequently traces the paths of the two forms in Slavic territory and elucidates their phonetic modifications. A Germanic-Slavic lexical problem was further discussed, although in purely negative terms, in Rudnicki 1974, who, as mentioned above (V.3.), does not believe that CS *korljь is derived from *Karl*, i.e., the name of Charlemagne.

Taking semantic considerations into account, but arguing primarily on purely phonetic grounds, W. Mańczak (1975) maintains that Slavic *skotъ* 'cattle' is a loan from Gothic, rather than the other way around. This view, recently also advocated by Kiparsky (1975a), makes good sense — contrary to the opinion expressed by, among others, E. Stankiewicz and R. Jakobson (cf. Birnbaum 1979a, 304). Despite the suggestive title, the Slavic facet was barely touched upon and, at any rate, hardly given a new assessment in Mańczak 1983. Here the focus is instead on the place of Gothic within Early Germanic, both geographically and in terms of the classification of the Germanic languages. Mańczak's reasoning, based on superficially evaluated considerations of frequency, is far from convincing. The Germanic loanwords in CS, their various chronological layers, and particular sources, are, on the other hand, reassessed at some length in Birnbaum 1983a, with attention paid also to the recent findings by V. Kiparsky (1975a).

The question of whether a particular lexical item borrowed by CS from Early Germanic should be assigned to Proto-Germanic, Gothic, or Old High German (primarily Old Bavarian) is the topic of several papers by M. Enrietti; cf., in addition to Enrietti 1977/79, already mentioned, Enrietti 1973a, 1973b, and 1975/1976. In the first of these studies, while he assumes Proto-Germanic origin for *tynъ* 'fence' and Gothic as the source for *xlěb* 'bread,' he claims that *koldędzь 'well' is difficult to trace to a particular Germanic source. However, considering its spread in Slavic, Enrietti is inclined to assign it to Proto-Germanic rather than to East Germanic (specifically, Gothic). The criterion of areal diffusion is also used by the Italian linguist in discussing the origin of *xysъ/*xyzъ 'house.' While the latter form is said to be of Proto-Germanic origin, he believes the former to go back to Old High German. He thus does not admit the possibility of a Gothic origin, otherwise frequently assumed. Moreover, in his study of the two competing items meaning 'dish,' *bljudo* and *misa*, and their respective spread in Slavic, Enrietti concludes that the former is of Gothic, the latter of Old High German (and, as we have seen, ultimately Vulgar

Latin), origin.

Finally, F. Papp (1973) discussed Early Slavic loanwords in Hungarian, reflecting the substratum character of Slavic in that language. The author views the problem particularly in terms of common phonological and morphological features.

VI. SPECIAL PROBLEMS OF COMMON SLAVIC

VI.1. Common Slavic in Its Indo-European Setting; Common Slavic in Its Relationship to Particular Indo-European (and Other) Language Groups; The Problem of Balto-Slavic

The Slavic component in the dictionary of Nostratic, including several language families of Eurasia and Africa, by V. N. Illič-Svityč is the topic of a paper by R. V. Balatova (1977). Balatova surveys all the Slavic lexemes and morphemes appearing in the dictionary's tentative listing of items considered to belong to the common lexical stock of that tentatively posited macrofamily. In particular, she discusses some of the more problematic among the Slavic forms cited. Slavic as a whole, viewed in its East European setting, is treated in typological-historical terms in Polák 1973a. Considering the broader, Eurasian framework, the author points to parallels and possible ties with Finno-Ugric, among other language groups.

Slavic data are included in V. Pisani's programmatic essay on Indo-European in Europe (1974a), surveying the field and highlighting some controversial problems while reiterating the author's basic positions on these issues. As previously mentioned (III.2.), this paper includes an excursus on the Slavic genitive-accusative; another excursus treats isoglosses obtaining among Indo-European languages of Europe. A specific problem of PIE grammar, pertinent also to Slavic, was tackled in Puhvel 1973. Two partly competing suffixes (*-ias- and *-tero-) used for the formation of the comparative were discussed here together with two alternative syntactic means employed in its construction (case *vs.* particle use). The author demonstrates that neither of the two suffixes discussed was originally comparative in function but rather expressed an "equative" or "exaggerative" meaning. Both syntactic constructions are said to antedate the use of the suffixes; subsequently, they combined in different ways in various parts of IE.

The question of the earliest contacts between the Slavs and Iranians was, once again, discussed by O. N. Trubačev (1977). Referring to previous relevant contributions by Sobolevskij, Vasmer, Abaev, and others, the Soviet etymologist points to the importance of closely analyzing the onomastic and lexical data attested in the area in question. Some of these items are rightly considered difficult to evaluate given the Gothic wars, demographic shifts, and Turkic invasions. Stressing the potential importance of future findings in this region, the author assumes that the Slavs reached the Black Sea and the Sea of Azov by the fifth-sixth centuries AD. For a discussion of these issues in a broader factual and methodological context, see now also Trubačev 1982 (cf. VI.4.).

C. S. Stang took up an idea only briefly referred to in his 1942 book on the Slavic and Baltic verb in the monograph *Lexikalische Sonderübereinstimmungen zwischen dem Slavischen, Baltischen und Germanischen* (1972). In his last major work, Stang sought to supplement Trautmann's Balto-Slavic dictionary of 1923 by listing and examining, or reexamining, the shared vocabulary of Baltic, Slavic, and

Germanic as well as exclusive Baltic-Germanic and Slavic-Germanic lexical agreements. Excluding provable loanwords, Stangs's study covers, on the one hand, items which reflect the same phonological form and are restricted to Baltic, Slavic and/or Germanic (type Lith *liáudis* : ChSl *ljudьje* : OHG *liuti*) and, on the other hand, items which do not fully correspond to, but merely resemble, each other and are restricted to Baltic, Slavic and/or Germanic without presumably being borrowed among these language groups (type Lith *sidābras*, OPr *sirablan* : ChSl *sьrebro* : Goth *silubr*). Stang concludes that the majority of the lexemes shared by Baltic, Slavic, and Germanic are technological in meaning and usually designate simple instruments and objects made of wood. The author further echoes his earlier view about a prehistoric Balto-Slavo-Germanic *Sprachbund* within the northwestern portion of disintegrating PIE (cf., in particular, the -*m*- marker in the instr. sg. and dat. and instr. du. and pl., as well as various phenomena of derivation). The monograph also includes excursuses on the evolution of PIE *sk'* in Balto-Slavic and on the suffix -*e/oro* (with ablaut variants) in Baltic, Slavic, and Germanic. For an assessment, see Schmid 1975/76 and the reference in Toporov 1975c (87–8).

The ever-controversial problem of Balto-Slavic was further discussed during the last decade in work by many authors. Karaliūnas (1972) suggests that CS *pasti*, Lat *pāscō*, Toch A *pās*-, B *pāsk*- and Hitt *pahš*- have their equivalent in Lith *póseti* 'to worship (an idol)' and *pōseleti/púoseleti* 'to feed.' Schmalstieg (1974b) sketches some changes in the consonant systems of preliterate Baltic and Slavic, only to arrive at the fairly inconclusive suggestion "that it is possible that Baltic and Slavic shared a certain period of common development in the consonantal system" without however considering such an assumption "absolutely necessary." The American linguist thus leaves the question of a possible Balto-Slavic unity open. Otkupščikov (1974) comments generally on the significance of Lithuanian data for reconstructing CS. Nepokupnyj (1976), focusing on North Slavic and its relationship to Baltic, discusses: 1) general lexical-semantic phenomena shared by Baltic and North Slavic; 2) West Baltic lexical items in North Slavic; and 3) East Baltic lexical items in North Slavic. In the two latter sections, ethno- and anthroponymy as well as common nouns are discussed separately. The author covers both prehistoric (reconstructed) as well as historical (attested) data, and focuses his attention in particular on the crucial Poles'e area, recently examined also by N. I. Tolstoj. For a review of this work, see Řeháček 1979.

In two papers (1976, 1978), H. Mayer argues, among others things, that Slavic cannot simply be considered the continuation of an earlier Balto-Slavic linguistic entity which presumably is largely preserved or, at any rate, easily retrievable on the basis of Baltic data alone. He discusses in some detail various developments of vocalism, especially in auslaut position, in the two language groups to substantiate his point. In the later paper he takes issue, in particular, with Birnbaum's 1970 "modeling" approach to Balto-Slavic. He disregards, however, the fact that this approach was originally proposed by Ivanov and Toporov, and that Birnbaum merely considered it along with three other conceivable approaches to this intricate problem.

Mayer thus argues against the assumption of a Balto-Slavic linguistic unity and suggests that CS is derived directly from a Late IE dialect. He explains the striking similarities between Baltic and Slavic as due to the conservative nature of the two language groups, but stresses also some profound differences between them, particulary as they pertain to vocalism.

Reexamining three specific problems of Balto-Slavic phonology, Kortlandt (1979a) concludes that: 1) the change PIE *eu* > *ov* (before vowels) preceded the parallel shift *eu* > *jou* (before consonants); 2) the Balto-Slavic reflex of PIE *sk* is *š* (Lith *š*, Sl *s*) before *i* but *sk* (Lith *šk* after *i*) in other positions; and 3) the clusters *ngn*, *ndn* blocked the operation of "Winter's Law" (cf. above II.3.). Balto-Slavic was also one of the terms of comparison in a recent study by V. V. Martynov (1978), discussing problems of Balto-Slavo-Italic lexical agreements and parallels in light of recent research into this question, especially by Trubačev. The essay on Baltic by V. P. Mažiulis in Gadžieva *et al.* 1981 contains some reference to Balto-Slavic and Balto-Slavo-Germanic problems. It should further be noted that the generally very positive assessment of the linguistic legacy of Kuryłowicz and Stang in Ivanov and Toporov 1980 concerns, to a large extent, the former scholars' contributions to the Balto-Slavic problem.

Opening a new annual serial publication, *Balto-slavjanskie issledovanija 1980* contains a number of relevant articles. Contributions by O. N. Trubačev (1981) and V. V. Ivanov (1981c) are largely programmatic, but are both also germane to the reconstruction of CS. V. V. Martynov (1981) discusses such CS items as *běsъ* - *divъ*, *bl'usti* - *patriti*, *bъrtviti* - *gatati*, *do* - *pri* - *kъ*, *onъ* - *ovъ*, *slava* - *xvala*, and others. Based on typological considerations and the unusual character of the *s* > *š* shift (after *i u r k*), V. N. Čekman (1981) considers this sound change in the three language branches where it occurs to various extents (namely, Slavic, Baltic, and Indo-Iranian) to be genetically related (granted differences in detail, most of which are accounted for and explained). V. V. Sedov (1981) comments, from the archeological point of view, on the early Slavic expansion into Baltic territory (on the Upper Dnieper). Also pertinent here are the papers by Ageeva (1981), Vanagas (1981), Dambe (1981), and Katonova (1981).

Problems of CS in its IE setting and in its relationship to specific IE language groups as well as the issue of Balto-Slavic were also discussed or at least touched upon in a number of other publications with a different major focus. Specifically, these are Kiparsky 1975a, Schmalstieg 1976, Auty 1977, Panzer 1978a, and Aitzetmüller 1978 (discussing OCS and Russian); Schmalstieg 1973 (on IE phonology); Kiparsky 1973, Dybo 1974, 1979b, 1980, and 1981, Prinz 1978, Bubenik 1980, and Nikolaev and Starostin 1982 (all discussing some aspect of accentology); Mathiassen 1974, Pohl 1974, Stipa 1974, Schelesniker 1975, Samilov 1975, Martinet 1978, Lekomceva 1978 and 1980, Winter 1978, and Lunt 1979/80 (all primarily concerned with some problem of vocalism); Gołąb 1969, Klyčkov 1972, Steensland 1973, Čekman 1974a, and Kortlandt 1978 (on consonantism, especially velars); Kortlandt 1977 (on the treatment of PIE *u-* in Slavic and Baltic); Mažiulis

1973, Enrietti 1977, Žuravlev 1977/78, and Žuravlev and Mažiulis 1978 (on problems of inflection); Otrębski 1972, Eckert 1972a, 1972b, 1974, and 1979, Martynov 1973, and Sławski 1974 and 1974- (on derivation); Fisher 1977, Stepanov 1978, Kortlandt 1979d, Machek 1980, Palmaitis 1981, and, in particular, Ivanov 1978a and 1981a (on the verb); Press 1973 (on absolute case constructions); Windekens 1971, Eckert 1977, Gluhak 1978, and Kostov 1980 (on the inherited vocabulary of CS); Schelesniker 1972, Toporov 1975b, Desnickaja 1978, and Balalykina 1980 (on semantic problems of the CS lexicon); Papp 1973 (on Early Slavic loanwords in Hungarian); Pătruţ 1972, and Xaburgaev 1980 (on the methodology of reconstruction and the problem of the time limits of CS); Filin 1972 and 1980, Sós 1973, Arumaa 1977a and 1977b, Sedov 1978, Toporov 1980, and Trubačev 1982 (on onomastics, etymology, and some extralinguistic problems of the ethnogenesis and early migrations of the Slavs).

VI.2. Methodology of Reconstruction; Time Limits, Periodization, Chronology of Common Slavic

While G. A. Xaburgaev (1980) uses certain controversial issues of CS to illustrate the methodology of reconstruction, H. D. Pohl (1977/78), in a critical assessment of Slavic historical linguistics since 1945, dwells on both Slavic as a whole in its relationship to other IE languages and on CS itself (cf., esp., 1–30). H. Birnbaum (1973b) explores the two basic methodologies—the comparative method and internal reconstruction—as they apply, with some refinement, to the difficult reconstruction of the initial phase of CS or, to be exact, PS. The same scholar (Birnbaum 1977c) offers a general discussion of the methods of linguistic reconstruction (10–17), using CS (as well as Baltic) data. Specifically, syntactic reconstruction (30–41) is illustrated with both IE and particular Slavic data; Slavic material is also utilized in consideration of semantic reconstruction (41–51, where relevant kinship terminology and other subspheres of meaning are discussed). The monograph further contains a section on distant genetic relationship and typology, using Nostratic as a case in point (51–69). Inspired by some of the positive aspects of Georgiev's work on linguistic reconstruction, Birnbaum 1980 comments on, among other things, the future prospects for the reconstruction of CS and Balto-Slavic structure in the overall methodological framework established, anticipating, to be sure, the necessity of operating with a number of hypothetical assumptions also in the future.

V. K. Žuravlev and V. P. Neroznak (1981), in a paper concerned with the methodology of linguistic reconstruction and, in particular, the problems arising from the need of determining various stages in the evolution of a protolanguage, also discussed some specific problems of retrieving unattested Slavic evidence. The new Soviet reference work on historical comparative linguistics, edited by Gadžieva, Žuravlev and Neroznak (1981), surveys a variety of language families. It contains a fairly thorough discussion of the current state of the art and its attendant problems.

Here also are separate chapters on the Slavic (63–106) and Baltic (107–19) languages—the latter curiously titled "Balto-Slavic Languages," presumably because problems of Balto-Slavic pertinent to both these branches of IE are considered. The Slavic chapter, authored by V. K. Žuravlev, particularly stresses the salient characteristics of CS and discusses at some length various methods for its reconstruction. Moreover, problems of pertinent methodology take up a good portion of the comprehensive discussion in Trubačev 1982 (for details, cf. VI.4., below).

Considerations of chronology, but also the very unity and duration of CS, were the topic of two papers by I. Pǎtruţ (1972 and 1976). In the first of these, the Romanian Slavist discusses the earliest Slavic-Romance-Greek linguistic contacts and concludes, on the basis of Slavic loans in Greek (especially toponyms), Baltic, Finnic, and what he terms Danubian Latin, that the Slavic dialects were essentially CS up to the eighth century. He arrives at this conclusion on the strength of the evidence of such archaisms as the retention of $\breve{u}$, unshifted k (not affected by the progressive palatalization), $\breve{a}$ instead of $\breve{o}$ (appearing only later), ρ and even aN, as well as $tart/talt$ in Greek and Romanian. A second wave of Slavic influence, dating from the ninth and tenth centuries, already show clearly Bulgarian features. In the second paper, the author rejects the dialectal division of CS in the first half of the first millennium AD proposed by Šaxmatov and Bernštejn. Instead, Pǎtruţ claims that the phonological criteria adduced in favor of such a division are actually of a later date.

V. I. Georgiev (1973b) posits three periods for CS: 1) Early CS (PS), beginning in the second millennium BC and lasting through the eight/seventh centuries BC; 2) Middle CS, roughly from the eight/seventh centuries BC to the fourth/fifth centuries AD; and 3) Late CS, covering the fourth/fifth through eighth/ninth centuries AD. Characteristic of the second period, according to Georgiev, was the strong influence from Iranian and Gothic, while the third period saw the tripartition into the major CS dialect areas. A somewhat different chronology of CS was proposed by A. Lamprecht (1978). According to him, the disintegration of PIE occurred around 3000 BC, and the separation of the Balto-Slavic from the Germanic dialects sometime after 2000 BC, probably c. 1500 BC. The crystallization of the Slavic dialects from Late PIE (or Balto-Slavic) is said to have taken place approximately 500 BC. Early CS is considered phonologically still quite close to Baltic. The emergence of "classical CS" is dated to c. 400–800 AD, and the evolution of Late CS to about 800–1000 AD. The periods of "classical" and Late CS are further subdivided chronologically according to major sound shifts.

Problems of CS chronology were also discussed in Duridanov 1973 (on the chronological layers of nominal formations in Slavic and Baltic); Kortlandt 1975 and Kolesov 1979a (on accentology); Moszyński 1972c, Stipa 1974, Žuravlev 1974, Mareš 1971, Marvan 1973 and 1979 (on vocalism, specifically monophthongization, the origin of *akan'e*, and vowel contraction); Jacobsson 1973, 1974, and 1977 (on the progressive palatalization), Wukasch 1974, 1976a, and 1976b, Savignac 1975, and Lunt 1977a (on consonantism, notably the velar palatalizations); Kiparsky 1971b, Schuster-Šewc 1977b, and Moszyński 1979 (on the chronological stratification of individual languages, namely Russian, Sorbian, and OCS).

VI.3. Disintegration of Common Slavic; Common Slavic Dialects

CS as the point of departure for the evolution of the individual Slavic languages was discussed by F. Kopečný (1974a), who stressed, in particular, the development on various levels of linguistic structure. The underlying CS model is further peripherally touched upon in a contribution by E. Lekov (1978). Lekov discussed the main trends of Slavic linguistic evolution, as conditioned by internal and external (i.e., Slavic/non-Slavic) factors partly traceable to preliterate times. CS in its last, dialectally differentiated stage is indirectly implied in an attempt by F. V. Mareš (1980a) at a new grouping of the contemporary Slavic languages. The author envisages a fourfold division into: 1) SE Slavic, 2) SW Slavic, 3) NW Slavic, 4) NE Slavic, allowing for two binary splits—S vs. N and E vs. W. It goes without saying that some of the criteria on which the Czech-Austrian Slavist bases his "tetrachotomy" reach back to the Late CS period.

The Late CS stage of evolution serves as a point of departure also for a comprehensive and important discussion of "Conservatism and Innovatism of the Slavic Languages" presented by Z. Gołąb at the Eighth International Congress of Slavists held in Zagreb (Gołąb 1978). Surveying the conservative and innovative trends in the history of the recorded Slavic languages in terms of "lexical substance" and "grammatical substance," the author finds that the origin of some of these trends goes back to incipient tendencies ascertainable in the final phase of the Slavic protolanguage.

The earliest dialectal differentiation of CS—or rather the earliest recoverable differentiation of Late CS—was the subject of a study by L. Moszyński (1980). As indicated, it should be noted, however, that the author treats only post-fifth-century developments and does not even attempt to reconstruct any possible earlier dialectal differences of CS, now irretrievably lost (on this subject, cf. Birnbaum 1973b, with reference to work by V. K. Žuravlev).

Two specific phenomena of Late CS regional phonological evolution were considered by H. Andersen (1977). Here the Danish Slavist examines two complex sound changes with their roots in prehistoric times: 1) $e > o$ as attested in East Slavic, and 2) $g > \gamma$ as known from a East and West Slavic languages. The two shifts, often considered post-CS, are analyzed using techniques of historic dialectology and with consideration given to their interrelation as Late CS innovations. The author demonstrates that both these changes originated in phonological relations characteristic of a phase prior to the emergence of the major Early Slavic dialectal groups. He thus suggests that, although becoming evident only in the course of the historically recorded period, both shifts should be considered prehistoric innovations. Although only marginally concerned with CS, Timberlake 1981 discusses the reflexes of CS *dj* in Late CS dialects and individual Slavic languages, focusing on those in which there is a dual reflex within one dialect or language (as in Ukr ž vs. ǯ).

The author offers a sophisticated explanation for this seeming irregularity and comments on the problem of abrupt *vs.* gradual phonetic/phonemic change.

The general problems of the crystallization of the South Slavic linguistic branch from its Late CS origin and the subsequent dialectal divisions within South Slavic, were treated by I. Gălăbov (1975). The discussion is based on the reflexes of CS *tj*. The same overall problem, though using other criteria, was further considered by L. V. Kurkina (1981), who views the dialectal background in light of Kopitar's theory of a NW *vs.* SE split. Moreover, she takes into account the concept of the different evolution at the core *vs.* at the periphery of a compact linguistic area, a concept developed in recent years particularly by N. I. Tolstoj. In the course of her investigation, Kurkina reanalyzes a number of South Slavic lexical isoglosses. L. Moszyński (1979) discussed specific methodological problems for reconstructing Cyrillo-Methodian "Proto-Church Slavic" (in the sense introduced by Trubeckoj). This study can be considered relevant to CS and its reconstruction, given that the earliest form of OCS may be regarded as a first recording of a Late CS dialect. Even OCS, of course, can be reconstructed only on the basis of the extant written evidence, dating from about a century or more subsequent to the activities of Constantine and Methodius.

Some specific SE Bulgarian phonological phenomena were further surveyed in their broader Slavic context and against their CS background by I. Kočev (1978). Z. Stieber (1973c) discussed the Hungarian lexeme *rend* (< CS *rędъ*), retaining the same meaning, 'order,' as in South Slavic from where it was obviously borrowed.

F. Bezlaj (1977) relates the present Slavic languages directly to CS dialects, illustrating his point with the function of the prefix and preposition *ob*(-). He explains the lexical and semantic agreements found between OCS and Slovenian as originating in the times of the first settlement of the Proto-Slovenes in the East Alpine region (on this problem, cf. also Birnbaum 1977a and, in particular, recent work by O. Kronsteiner, reported on below). The author points to the complexity of various language strata during the CS period as particularly pronounced in certain key areas of contact with another, non-Slavic population; this applies, for example, to Slovenian in its relation to Italian and to OCS—in the Salonica region—in its relation to Greek.

The Slovene, and ultimately Late CS dialectal, substratum in the East Alpine region (and adjoining territories) has been the subject of several studies by the Austrian Slavist O. Kronsteiner. In his 1975 monograph on Alpine Slavic anthroponymy, the author considers problems of frequency, phonology (with special attention paid to the rendition of Slavic forms in Old High German, specifically Old Bavarian, orthography) and morphology, as well as the sociological and topological implications of his findings. The author's conclusions are as follows: 1) The term "Alpine Slavic" is applicable to the period up to the eleventh century only; after that, the Slavic data from south of the ridge of the Alps in Carinthia and Styria exhibit phonological features—vowels earlier, consonants later—distinctly identifiable as Old Slovenian. 2) Some isolated items (*sve*, *kъsьnъ*, the name *xъrvatъ* in toponyms) suggest the presence of Old Croatian splinter groups also in the Alpine region (but cf. Kronsteiner 1978). 3) Alpine Slavic displays phonological, morphological, and onomastic peculiarities unique to the area. 4) South Slavic traits cannot be found north of the Alpine ridge in onomastic material (as has been claimed earlier). 5) West Slavic linguistic traits—peculiar to Upper and Lower Austria—have penetrated across and south of the Alpine ridge (to Carinthia, Styria, and East Tyrolia), as is best shown by the *dl/l* distribution (cf. also Kronsteiner 1976 for details). 6) The name of Carinthian nobles (*Svętipъlkъ*, *Mojьmirъ*, *Gorazdъ*, *Prěslavъ*) prove that early ties with the nobility of Moravia existed in the area. The Alpine region was thus linguistically heterogenous and West Slavic elements played a larger role in it than previously thought. South Slavic was strictly limited to Carinthia and Styria, although there, too, a West Slavic dialect must have existed coterritorially with, and perhaps even before, South Slavic. For evaluations of Kronsteiner's monograph, see, e.g., Schelesniker 1976/77, Dickenmann 1978, and Schlimpert 1979.

Subsequent studies by Kronsteiner—all by-products or revisions of his 1975 work—deal with specific problems also addressed there. Kronsteiner 1976 examines the *dl/l* doublets, primarily in Slovenian, as a criterion for differentiating between West and South Slavic and for identifying the linguistic reality underlying the notion "Alpine Slavic." Kronsteiner 1977, tying in with the study just mentioned, reexamines the tripartition of the Slavic languages, and questions this division on the basis of the reflexes of the liquid metathesis in place names. Generally, the author suggests that the metathesis occurred only after the major Slavic migrations, during the period of the disintegration of CS, with peripheral zones preserving the earlier CS situation. An intermediate stage in the treatment of liquid groups was retained in Czech, Slovak, and the South Slavic languages, while only Polish (or rather all of Lekhitic West Slavic plus Sorbian) and East Slavic show further developments occurring since the tenth century. Superseding his earlier (1975) assumption of Old Croatian splinter groups in the Eastern Alps, Kronsteiner 1978 identifies the earliest attestation of Croats with the Avar military layer among the Alpine Slavs.

Problems of early South Slavic and West Slavic ties and their exploration were studied by Z. Stieber (1972b, on Slovenian-West Slavic data) and C. Vasiliev (1975, on Serbo-Croatian-West Slavic lexical agreements). The second of these studies is particularly interesting. Here Vasiliev concludes that: 1) certain items must have existed without ever having been recorded; 2) in Serbo-Croatian, loanwords from German, Romance, and Turkish have partly replaced earlier inherited items; and 3) certain lexemes, originally found in western Serbo-Croatian and shared with West Slavic, have yielded to eastern Serbo-Croatian items which spread as a result of internal migrations caused by the Turkish conquest.

The emergence of Slovak from its Late CS origins was studied by K. Horálek (1971). In addition to its prehistoric evolution, the recorded history of Slovak is also briefly discussed and certain parallels with Croatian linguistic separatism are drawn with regard to the establishment of modern standard Slovak. R. Krajčovič (1974) is concerned only with the prehistoric situation of Slovak. Here he discusses the CS dialectal base of Slovak in terms of the specific isogloss area from which Slovak evolved in the ninth/tenth centuries. In other words, the author does not consider Slovak merely an offshoot of Old Czech.

H. Schuster-Šewc (1979a) also proceeds from Late CS in discussing the position of the two Sorbian languages (or rather Proto-Sorbian) in the general framework of Slavic. He thus considers Proto-Sorbian, along with Proto-Polish, an autonomous "dialect complex" of CS and does not adhere to the theory according to which Sorbian forms a bridge, as it were, between Lekhitic and non-Lekhitic West Slavic; nor does he mention Trubačev's hypothesis, assuming the western settlement of the Sorbs to be a result of their secondary "occidentalization." A recent study by Schuster-Šewc (1982) again discusses Late CS dialectal divisions, positing various zones, among them one from which Czech, Slovak, Slovenian, and Serbo-Croatian are said to have evolved. Another such dialectal zone is thought to underlie Ukrainian, Belorussian, and Sorbian, and yet another is considered the base for Lekhitic and Macedo-Bulgarian. The East German linguist thus denies the erstwhile existence of a homogeneous, compact Common West Slavic linguistic entity. With support of archeological evidence, he considers the possibility that the Proto-Sorbs had migrated from an original territory east of the Carpathian Mountains, through the Moravian Gate (between the Carpathian and Sudeten Mountains), and into the Bohemian basin. From there they would subsequently have moved, following the Elbe River, into a region west of the Upper Oder and the Neisse (Nysa) Rivers. Here, the Sorbs are said to have clashed and mingled with Lekhitic tribes coming from the east. As a result, a mixing of dialectal features of different origin occurred, re-flected especially in phonology and lexicology. The structure of the present Sorbian languages therefore shows traces of the blending of two Late CS dialects, a south-eastern and a northwestern (or Lekhitic). As can be gathered from this brief account of Schuster-Šewc' recent contribution, his conception is now, though without any such specific reference, much closer to Trubačev's "occidentalization" hypothesis as regards the origin of Sorbian. The position of Proto-Sorbian was further discussed in light of onomastic data and, again, without any reference to Trubačev's relevant hypothesis, by E. Eichler (1981).

The question of Samo's semi-legendary first Slavic state (in the mid-seventh cen-tury, i.e., in Late CS times) has been thoroughly reassessed in a number of studies by the German Slavist H. Kunstmann (1979a, 1979b, 1980, 1981a, and 1981b). Kunstmann's work is based on a renewed study and reinterpretation of the relevant data—the medieval Latin chronicle texts mentioning Samo, as well as pertinent onomastic evidence. This has led Kunstmann to the view that the political entity headed by Samo (which latter Kunstmann believes to have been a title rather than a proper name) was not geographically as large as previously thought. Rather it was probably confined to a region located somewhere in present-day North Bavaria/East Franconia, around the Upper Main. The three articles by H. Jakob (1979, 1980, and 1981) are also related to this complex problem.

Pertinent to the emergence of the East Slavic group from among Late CS dialects is a study by P. S. Ureland (1979), assuming the existence of a prehistoric *Sprachbund* around the Baltic sometime between 800 and 1100 AD. The author finds support for his hypothesis in a comparison of certain morphosyntactic parallels obtaining between modern Swedish, Finnish, Latvian, and Russian, on the one hand, and, specifically, Runic Swedish (i.e., the earliest attested form of that language) and Old Russian, on the other. Particular shared features in the phrase structure and lexicon of Old Scandinavian, Slavic, and Baltic dialects are ascribed to the language of the bi- or multilingual Varangians, whose speech is said to have served as an innovative force (cf. earlier thoughts along those lines by A. Stender-Petersen, who had discussed a number of hybrid Slavic-Scandinavian coinages). Among the examples cited by Ureland are the Nordic names for the Dnieper rapids and other onomastic data, as well as some loanwords pointing to reciprocal borrowing between Slavic and Scandinavian. The emergence of Early East Slavic was further discussed by A. Lamprecht (1973), using phonological phenomena pertaining to vowel quantity and the correlation of consonantal palatalization (or the correlation of "softness") as illustration. Finally, a variety of problems relevant to the evolution from Late CS to Common East Slavic were recently reassessed in Shevelov 1982.

As previously mentioned (cf. I.4.), problems of Late CS and CS dialectology were also dealt with, or at least touched upon, in a number of recent texts on individual Slavic languages and their historical development. Among the more important ones, see, in particular, Lunt 1974, Schmalstieg 1976, Aitzetmüller 1978 (on OCS); Kiparsky 1975a, Auty 1977, Panzer 1978a, Issatschenko 1980 (on Russian); and Kuraszkiewicz 1972 (on Polish). Of work on CS accentology (cf. II.2.), Kortlandt 1976, Zaliznjak 1977, and Feldstein 1975 and 1978b are especially noteworthy. Among studies treating CS and Early Slavic vocalism (cf. II.3.), the following, in particular, should be mentioned here: Mareš 1971, Newman 1971, Marvan 1973 and 1979, Čekman 1975, and Martinet 1978. Research into consonantism (cf. II.4.) also has considered the period of disintegrating CS. Here, particularly, the studies by Cohen (1969), Channon (1972), Karaś (1973), Pianka (1974), Stieber (1974), Scatton (1978), and Zaliznjak (1982) come to mind.

Of morphological studies, some papers on derivation (cf. III.3.) pertain to the disintegration of CS and the emergence of dialectal groups: Grošelj 1972, Zaręba 1978, Handke 1979. Gołąb 1972, on a problem of syntax, treats both CS as a whole and a portion of its subsequent development, namely, North Slavic.

Several of the publications addressing some facet of CS lexicology (cf. V.1.) also have repercussions for CS dialectology and the final phase of the Slavic protolanguage. Among them may be mentioned Leeming 1971, Popowska-Taborska 1975, L'vov 1978, Schuster-Šewc 1979, Němec 1979b, as well as Boryś 1979 and 1982. Many studies focusing on semantic aspects of the CS vocubulary (cf. V.3.) discuss Late CS and its regional variations. Here, see, in particular, Górnowicz 1972, Konnova 1972, Otrębska-Jabłońska 1972, Schuster-Šewc 1973b, Trubačev 1974, Klepikova 1976, Mareš 1977, Dzendzelivs'kyj 1978, Wójcikowska 1978, Szymański 1980, and Šaur 1980b. Naturally, issues of CS dialectology are also considered in a number of studies on lexical borrowing in CS (cf. V.4.) even though in many instances CS is viewed here still as a homogeneous whole. Of relevant studies, at least the following deserve mention: Polák 1973b, Pohl 1975b, Moszyński 1977a, and Birnbaum 1981b. Of other studies relevant, at least secondarily, also to the disintegration and dialectal differentiation of CS, see especially Schuster-Šewc 1980 (cf. V.2), Marojević 1982 (cf. III.3. and 4.), and Polański 1982 (cf. II.3. and 5.).

Among studies surveying the relationship of Slavic to other branches of IE, specifically Baltic and Iranian, the book by A. P. Nepokupnyj (1976) on Baltic-North Russian linguistic contacts and O. N. Trubačev's paper on the linguistic periphery of early Slavdom and the Indo-Iranians in the Pontic region (1977) pertain to the disintegration of CS; cf. now also Trubačev 1982 (for details of this essay, cf. VI.4.). Of contributions discussing the time limits, periodization, and chronology of CS (cf. VI.2.), the two previously reported studies by I. Pătruţ (1972 and 1976), addressing, among other things, the question of early contacts between the Slavs and Greek and Romance populations in the Balkans deserve mention. Also relevant here are the papers by H. Birnbaum (1974 and 1979b) and R. Aitzetmüller (1975 and 1979a), reflecting these scholars' controversy regarding various issues of CS, among them the claimed time gap between the end of the CS period and the onset of Slavic literacy. Finally, G. A. Xaburgaev's essay touching on several controversial issues in the history of CS (1980) falls into this category. A number of further studies to be discussed or referred to below (VI.4.) also consider problems relating to disintegrating and dialectal CS.

VI.4. Problems Related to Common Slavic (Ethnogenesis, Prehistory, and Early History of the Slavs; Original Homeland and Early Migrations of the Slavs; Earliest Slavic Texts; Onomastic Evidence of Common Slavic and Early Slavic)

Several archeological studies published in the last years bear, in one way or another, on problems of CS. Thus, S. I. Penjak (1972) discusses the chronology of the settlement of Slavs of the Carpathian region. Here, the author concludes on the basis of finds from prehistoric times that the first Slavic groups appeared in that region during the first half of the first millenium AD. Objects clearly belonging to various Early Slavic cultures corroborate a mass settlement of Slavic tribes on the slopes of the Carpathians. This appears less surprising in light of J. Udolph's recent hypothesis placing the Slavic protohome in historical Galicia, broadly conceived. The early move of the Slavs into the East Carpathian region was further discussed in terms of archeological evidence by È. A. Symonovič (1978).

The study by Á. C. Sós, *Die slawische Bevölkerung Westungarns im 9. Jahrhundert* (1973), ascertains with the help of archeological and early historical data the Slavic substratum in present-day West Hungary (Transdanubia) during the ninth century AD. Surveying earlier relevant research, the author concludes (83) that the population of Transdanubia at that time was heterogeneous and, in addition to the predominantly Slavic population, included Avar, German (Bavarian) and Romance groups. The ethnic composition of the lower strata of the population seems to have varied from region to region, and it is clear that the controversial Avars were gradually Slavicized, allowing for local variations. It appears even possible that part of the non-Slavic population in this area survived as such up to the Hungarian land-taking (in the late ninth-early tenth centuries). The composition of the local Slavic population was heterogeneous, too. Thus, Slavic groups seem to have arrived during the ninth century both from the north and the south. Neither the available linguistic evidence nor the historical records permit any clear delineation of the various Slavic settlements of different provenance; but it is also not possible to infer that Slavs came to Transdanubia from only one direction. By contrast, the upper stratum of that society seems to have consisted of both Slavic and Frankish-Bavarian elements.

B. A. Rybakov's study (1978) purporting to outline "the historical fate of the Proto-Slavs" is a problematic and not overly compelling attempt at chronologizing the past of the prehistoric Slavs. The paper by the renowned Soviet historian introduces such highly hypothetical notions as the "linguistic forebears of the Slavs" (presumably from the fifth-third millennia BC), the "pre-Slavs" (*protoslavjane*, during the late third and early second millenia BC), and the "Proto-Slavs" (*praslavjane*, from the fifteenth century BC onward). The discussion of references to the Slavs and their ancestors found in ancient authors and the matching of the ethnonyms of the Primary Chronicle with specific cultural subtypes also invites critical comment. The well-known Soviet archeologist V. V. Sedov has contributed two studies, one (1978) reexamining Slavs and Iranians in ancient times, the other (1980) correlating Slavic hydronyms and archeological finds in areas with profuse Slavic evidence. Finally, H. Jakob (1981) focuses on ceramic finds in East Franconia in the context of his and H. Kunstmann's recent research on the historical reality behind Samo's legendary Slavic state (cf. above, VI.3.).

The perennial controversy about the ethnogenesis of the Slavs and the origin of the Slavic languages has again yielded some significant studies. Thus, the late F. P. Filin (1972) continued his inquiry into the origin of Slavic, viewing this phenomenon against its general IE background, including the issue of the emergence of the Indo-Europeans. Discussing further the relationship of Slavic to other IE language groups, the Soviet scholar also reassessed the contribution of other disciplines, such as paleobotany, paleozoology, paleoclimatology, and, of course, archeology. As for the controversial issue of the location of the Slavic protohome, Filin adhered to the southeastern hypothesis, placing the original homeland of the Slavs somewhere between the mid-Dnieper and the mid-Vistula. He considered the seventh-eighth centuries to be the upper limit for the disintegration of CS, rather than the tenth-early thirteenth centuries as sometimes claimed on the basis of the chronology of the *jer*-fall and related sound shifts. In a subsequent study (1980), the same linguist reiterated his view of the direct lineage of CS from Late PIE (i.e., without an intermediate

Balto-Slavic stage) and of Proto-Russian (or Early East Slavic) as uniformly stemming from CS (that is, without any admixture of other, notably West Slavic, elements). In particular, Filin in this study polemicizes with the ethno- and glotto-genetic theories propounded in recent years by G. A. Xaburgaev (cf. also Shevelov 1982). Three further studies—Zástěrová 1975, Popowska-Taborska 1981, and Bernštejn 1981—rather review current research germane to the ethnogenesis of the Slavs, urging closer cooperation among disciplines, but are not genuinely original contributions to the field.

Some Polish scholars continue to maintain that the original homeland of the Slavs should be sought in a relatively western region. Thus, M. Rudnicki (1977) reiterated some of his previous views and responded to some of the criticism leveled against his 1959/61 book *Prasłowiańszczyzna*. He still attempts to locate the Slavic protohome somewhere on the southern coast of the Baltic, between the Pregel River and the western boundary of Mecklenburg, or, in other words, roughly between Kaliningrad (Königsberg) and Lübeck. J. Nalepa (1973) also attempts to corroborate his previous view of the western, or northwestern, protohome of the Slavs. Still considering the original home of the Indo-Europeans to have been in Europe, somewhere around the mid-Danube (cf. similarly also Trubačev 1982, reported on below), the author assumes an early migration of a part of the IE population towards the north, following the recession of the continental ice (c. 4000 BC). He assumes a first tripartite division of that northern ethnic complex into a pre-Slavic, a pre-Baltic, and an unspecified third group, the latter distinguished by river names in -*apa* (cf. H. Krahe's and W. P. Schmid's "Old European" hydronymy). Nalepa considers the Elbe basin, the Baltic shore, and the Central European mountain ranges to mark the original boundaries of the pre-Balto-Slavic territory. He further attributes the original split into Balts and Slavs roughly along the Middle and Lower Vistula to unexplained causes, and holds that the emergence of East and South Slavic was a result of subsequent migrations of the early Slavs. He thus rejects the notion that a region roughly coinciding with the West Ukraine could have been the protohome of the Slavs, given its claimed Baltic and Iranian ethnicity as corroborated by hydronymic data. W. Mańczak's recent book, *Praojczyzna Słowian* (1981), also seems to support the overall view that the original homeland of the Slavs must have been situated along the Oder and Vistula rivers.

A different point of view was propounded some time ago by H. Birnbaum (1973a), who was inclined to place the Slavic protohome further to the southeast, possibly up to, or even beyond, the mid-Dnieper. It was claimed that such a view could be supported by new evidence of close Slavic-Iranian linguistic ties (particularly as set forth by Z. Gołąb). This assumption is not necessarily contradicted by the well-established early Slavic-Germanic contacts (cf. for details on the latter also Birnbaum 1983a). The protohome of the Slavs was viewed by W. P. Schmid (1975) as tantamount to a new area of settlement by a population only then clearly identifiable as Slavs (but coming from what subsequently were Baltic lands). Schmid bases his conception primarily on lexical and onomastic data. In particular, some common nouns and their cognates were reexamined here in terms of their spatial distribution as evidenced in "Old European" hydronymy. His former student, J. Udolph, in a paper (1979b), which is basically a by-product of his well researched dissertation (1979a, discussed below), highlights the major facets of his own view of the original homeland of the Slavs. Udolph places it somewhere in present-day southern Poland and the westernmost part of the Ukraine, i.e., historical Galicia in the broad sense. He also sketches the subsequent migrations of the Slavs, toward the Dnieper, down the Vistula and Oder Rivers, as well as across the Carpathians, here following two main routes.

Udolph's views concerning the Slavic protohome find general support in Gołąb 1983. The latter assumes the final dissolution of the PIE linguistic community to have taken place c. 3000–2500 BC, and that a transitional Balto-Slavic community existed up to c. 1000 BC, after which the Proto-Slavs proper (separate from the Proto-Balts) emerged. The starting point of the Pre-Slavs is said to be the Upper Don basin from where (beginning c. 2500 BC) they gradually moved southwest, along the parkland belt. This movement brought the Pre-Slavs, at this point moving together with the Pre-Balts, to the mid-Dnieper (the original Slavic name of the Dnieper is assumed to have been *Dunaj*—but cf. Trubačev 1982) and Volynia regions. Here the previously close contacts with the Pre-Balts loosened, thus crystallizing the Proto-Slavs (in the Kiev and Volynia regions). Early expansion by the Proto-Slavs further to the west occurred across the Western Bug and into the Vistula basin (*Vistula* = *Vistla*, here considered a river name of Slavic origin!), and was perhaps due to the blocking of any southeast expansion by the Scythian invasion of the Pontic area (c. 700 BC). Gołąb postulates early contacts and cultural-linguistic exchange with Late PIE groups, especially Pre-Aryans, later with Iranians and western (*centum*, "Central European", i.e., Italo-Celtic) groups, in which Proto-Balts did not participate. The author further considers a possible earlier pre-Armenian substratum (somewhere in the present Ukraine), and a later West IE (*centum*) substratum (in today's Poland). The argumentation is based primarily on linguistic considerations but, obviously, takes geographic facts into account as well. It excludes, however, archeological findings, which are independently called upon to corroborate or disprove the linguistic evidence. Nevertheless, according to Gołąb, it is the linguistic evidence which should be accorded primary significance in solving this difficult and complex problem.

Various aspects of the early Slavic migrations and of the regions reached by them were the topic of a number of other studies published in the last decade or so. Thus, O. N. Trubačev (1979a) identified the earliest attestation of the ethnonym for the Slavs in Iranian as rendered in a Greek source (Herodotus), and pointed to the pre-Slavic (Scythian, i.e., Iranian) source of some Early Slavic hydronyms. B. Strumins'ky (1979/80) again addressed the old question of whether the Antes were indeed Slavs, or more precisely, early Eastern Slavs. Based on "Antian" personal names found in historical sources (but not on the ethnonym *Antes* itself), the author concludes that they were probably Pontic (i.e., Black Sea) Goths, ancestors of the

Crimean Goths, attested as late as the mid-sixteenth century. This view is contrary to that expressed by S. Rospond, who, in a more traditional fashion, considered *Antes* to refer to a Slavic 'ethnic group'. The question of the Antes was further discussed by N. G. Samsonov (1973), who adheres to the standard view that the Antes were, in fact, the ancestors of the Eastern Slavs. For a critical evaluation of this last work, see Lunt 1975.

Focusing on the significance of the Avars for the expansion of the Slavs in the early Middle Ages, W. H. Fritzer (1979) points out that it was not only external factors—for example, the collapse of the state of the Huns in the mid-fifth century and the establishment of the Avar realm centered in Hungary in the 560s—that were crucial here, but internal demographic processes among the Slavs as well. The author demonstrates the full complexity and the spatial diversification of the Slavic-Avar symbiosis alternating between cooperation and confrontation. It is also suggested that the Avar advances toward the Frankish Empire (in the 580s and '90s) were not intended to extend Avar dominion toward the west, and therefore did not cause the settlement of the Slavs east of the Saale River in Germany. Rather, the author claims that the Sorbs were settled there by the Franks to protect the empire's eastern flank after the withdrawal of a number of Germanic groups. I. A. Duridanov (1978) discussed the Slavic settlement of Lower Moesia and the Haemus region of the Balkan Peninsula on the basis of toponymic data. Only indirectly related to the outer limits of the Slavic expansion is a paper by V. N. Toporov (1980), discussing the ethnonym *galint* (reflected in OR *goljadь*) as signaling the periphery of the Baltic settlement.

A few recent studies add further to our knowledge about the westward expansion of the Slavs. Among them is a monograph by G. Osten (1978), which comments on traces of Slavic settlement in the region of the farthest westward advance of the Slavs, namely, west and south of the Lower Elbe (for a review, see Carsten 1980). The westward migration into Central Europe, assuming the Slavic protohome to have been located in the forest zone of Eastern Europe, was studied from an archeological vantage point by K. Godłowski (1979). J. Werner (1981) offered some archeologically founded remarks on the northwestern portion of the Slavic settlement area in the fourth-sixth centuries AD.

General problems of Slavic toponymy and hydronymy, including methodological questions as well as substantive issues, were discussed in a number of studies by S. Rospond (1974/76, 1975, and 1979). The first of these is an ambitious attempt at a comprehensive description of Slavic toponymic stratigraphy (shortly to appear also in a German version) and synthesizes much of the Polish scholar's previous work in the field. Here the author focuses on formational problems (including their chronology); cf. also his study on the suffix -*ynja* in toponymy (Rospond 1978). Rich in factual data, some of Rospond's etymologies and findings, tending to maximize the genuinely Slavic share, remain nonetheless quite controversial. The subsequent study reexamines primarily a number of CS and Early Slavic phonological developments on the basis of onomastic data, and the most recent contribution focuses on topographic terminology as reflected in geographic names.

The evolution of formational types of Slavic toponyms, partly tracing them back to CS sources, is also the topic of a paper by I. Lutterer (1971). E. Eichler (1972) offers a general discussion of the main areal divisions of Slavic in light of onomastics. Among other things, the East German scholar suggests that the great number of East Slavic-West Slavic agreements (even larger than hitherto known, as will be shown in future topo- and hydronymic research) merely represent a shared CS inheritance. A number of Early Slavic lexical relics mirrored in Slavic toponymy and hydronymy were also discussed by E. Dickenmann (1980a), and J. Udolph (1980) elucidated some previously obscure etymologies on the basis of hydro- and toponymic evidence.

Onomastic data also provide Udolph (1981a) with a clue in disentangling the complex stratigraphy of the Lower Vistula valley and delta area. The German scholar was able to ascertain that no Finno-Ugric substratum, as has been occasionally claimed, can be identified in the region; that the earliest local toponymy reflects the "Old European" hydronymy, applicable also to the name of the Vistula itself; and that this "Old European" layer was subsequently gradually superseded by a Baltic substratum which in turn was overlaid by roughly simultaneous Germanic (German) and Slavic (Polish and Pomeranian) settlements. Udolph thus refutes the view held by many Polish researchers that the area investigated was part, or even formed the core, of the Slavic protohome (cf. above). Udolph's (1981b) study on the landtaking of the Eastern Slavs, in light of onomastic evidence, first discusses some near-synonymous lexemes and subsequently arrives at a new understanding of the chronological details of the East Slavic expansion: 1) circumvention of the Pripet Marshes; 2) after reaching the Belorussian hills, a northward migration toward Lakes Peipus and Il'men'; 3) bifurcation of the migratory movement north of Lake Il'men', partly towards the north (Karelia) and partly towards the east (Upper Volga basin and adjoining regions); 4) continued eastward migration along the Volga; 5) branching expansion in northern and southern directions, mostly following the larger rivers.

A recent study by Udolph (1982) of Slavic designations for 'salmon' identifies *losos'* as the most significant among them. He sees in the diffusion of this name of the salmon no contradiction to his general hypothesis concerning the earliest settlement of the Slavs on the northern slopes of the Carpathians (between Zakopane and the Bukovina) and adjoining territories north and northeast thereof. Evidence for this view is seen in the river-name *Lososina*, derived from the Slavic word for 'salmon,' and found in the region of the Dunajec, a tributary to the Upper Vistula (cf. below, on Udolph 1979a).

In Udolph 1981c, the author establishes that in North Slavic toponymy and hydronymy there are attested names derivable from common nouns now found only in South Slavic. He argues that these geographic names must have originated in a language which possessed the items subsequently yielding the South Slavic common nouns. This language can be assumed to have been (Late) CS. The occurrence of the names in question shows a high degree of density in the Ukraine and southern

Poland. Further research will have to corroborate the surmise that this area is therefore identical with the protohome of the Slavs. In this context the onomastic evidence examined, based on common nouns no longer attested (or productive) in East and West Slavic, can be considered crucial for solving the thorny question.

Two studies by H. Jakob (1979 and 1980) make a contribution towards identifying some place names connected with the military exploits of the semi-legendary ruler Samo (cf. also above, VI.3.). R. Katičić (1980) discusses the earliest Slavic evidence in the northern Italian region of Friul, adding to the elucidation of the earliest Slavic-Romance (or Slavic-Late Latin) linguistic contacts. J. Zaimov (1976a) approaches Bulgarian toponymic data as mirroring Early Slavic (CS and OCS) lexical items. Further, A. A. Beleckij (1980) reviews some major problems of Slavic toponymy in Greece during the early period spanning the sixth/seventh through fifteenth centuries. In particular, he considers a number of names containing terrain designations. While the study just mentioned is broad in scope, both as regards space and time, P. Malingoudis (1981) focuses instead on the terrain designations in a microregion of Greece—*Mani* in the Peloponnesus—providing us with an in-depth analysis. He is thus able to add substantially to, and partly correct, some of the relevant findings reported in M. Vasmer's classic *Die Slaven in Griechenland*. His study sheds new light on the Slavic settlement in southern Greece and the subsequent re-Hellenization of the area. Only marginally pertinent to the Slavic ethnonymy of Greece is Z. Stieber's note on the Polish village name *Mlądz* (located near Warsaw), which he associates with the Slavic tribe of the *Milingi* in Greece, mentioned in the mid-tenth century by Constantine Porphyrogenitus (Stieber 1972a). The author tentatively suggests that a Late CS ethnic group, reconstructed as *Mьlędzi*, underlies both the Slavic tribal name in Greece and the Polish toponym (< sg. *mьlędzь*).

J. Udolph's *Studien zu den slavischen Gewässernamen und Gewässerbezeichnungen* (1979a) is a major contribution to Slavic hydronymy with significant repercussions also for the prehistory of the Slavs. The material is here divided into common names attested in all three groups of Slavic, and hydronyms derived from them. The same principle of organization is then repeated for attestations in East and West Slavic, East and South Slavic, and West and South Slavic, respectively. Finally, common nouns attested in only one of the three branches of Slavic are analyzed. Further sections treat word and name formation; the problem of Illyrian, Thracian, and Dacian hydro- and toponyms; as well as the significance of the data examined for the early history of Slavic and of the Slavs. As mentioned previously, Udolph places the protohome of the Slavs on the northern foothills of the Carpathians (from the Tatra in the west to the Bukovina in the east), dating the settlement in that original homeland to before 500 AD. (The essentially similar views in Gołąb 1983 regarding the location of the Slavic protohome were discussed above.) Subsequently, Udolph sketches the Slavic migrations towards the east, west, and south (for some details discussed in Udolph 1981b, cf. also above) and discusses the Slavic evidence as it relates to "Old European" hydronomy. The German scholar is skeptical with regard to the assumed existence of a Balto-Slavic ethnic and linguistic unity, opting rather—along lines once proposed by A. Meillet—for an early parallel development and mutual influence. With his former teacher, W. P. Schmid, he sees the original Baltic area as central to "Old European," the latter viewed as a major component of Late PIE. For assessments of Udolph's cogent findings, see Eichler 1980, Dickenmann 1980b, Bräuer 1981, Leeming 1982, and Schelesniker 1982. Specific problems of Slavic and Baltic (as well as Finno-Ugric) hydronymy were further discussed by P. Arumaa (1977a and 1977b), concerned with, among other things, derivational problems.

Anthroponymic evidence was recently discussed by, among others, G. Schlimpert (1978), investigating Slavic personal names recorded in medieval German sources; for some evaluations, see Šrámek 1979 and Wenzel 1979. Anthroponymic material was also scrutinized by H. Birnbaum (1975), discussing dialectal Late CS names attested in distorted form in two Old Bavarian-Latin texts. The same author (Birnbaum 1977a) takes *Jasomir*, contained in the Austrian term *Jasomirgott*, as the point of departure for a further discussion of the original diffusion of the ancestors of the modern Slovenes. He comments here also on some pertinent issues of Late CS dialectology.

Finally, in vindicating the *Kiev Folia* (generally considered the earliest continuous Slavic text, but recently again questioned as to its authenticity) Birnbaum (1981a) speculates further on the possible protographs of this highly archaic text. He concludes that the extant text, whatever its precise provenance, is best viewed as a hybrid reflection of several Late CS dialects.

Several studies treated earlier in this report bear also on the issues considered in the present section. Concerning CS consonantism as it is reflected in onomastic data, see Rospond 1977 (cf. II.4.). Onomastic evidence is also relevant to two papers, Taszycki 1972 and Pohl 1973, primarily concerned with deriviation (cf. III.3.). Of lexicological studies, a number of contributions are relevant here: Gołąb 1977 (cf. V.1.); Rudnicki 1971, Górnowicz 1972, Maher 1973 and 1974, Trubačev 1974, Gołąb 1975a, and 1982, Mareš 1977, and Shapiro 1982a (all dealing with lexical semantics; cf. V.3.). Finally, several publications treated in previous sections of this chapter but of interest also here should be mentioned: Trubačev 1977 (cf. VI.1.); Kronsteiner 1976, 1977 and 1978, Kunstmann 1979a, 1979b, 1980, 1981a and 1981b, Eichler 1981, and Kurkina 1981 (all concerned with the disintegration of CS or its dialects; cf. VI.3.).

In concluding this bibliographic survey of the 1970s and early 1980s, reference ought to be made to an important recent contribution pertinent to a number of controversial issues discussed in this last section. In a necessarily sketchy and somewhat speculative study, O. N. Trubačev (1982) offers an extremely wide-ranging and fresh look at a whole set of problems germane to the prehistory of the Slavs. In his paper, the author treats the ethnogenesis of the Slavs, their original homeland (including previous views expressed on the subject), and the prehistoric contacts between emerging and early Slavs and other ethnolinguistic groups. He bases his discussion on linguistic—essentially, etymological and onomastic—evidence. In so doing, Trubačev is highly critical of certain concepts and approaches, including some of the recently advanced suggestions by W. P. Schmid and J. Udolph. Trubačev's essay is so rich in terms of data as well as new or revived ideas and interpretations that only a summary of its chief tenets can be provided here.

From a methodological point of view, Trubačev objects to the very notion of protohome (or original homeland, R *prarodina*, G *Urheimat*, not to mention cradle). He points out that, in most instances, this is merely a makeshift term for identifying—or searching for—the area of the earliest ascertainable settlement of a given ethnolinguistic group. To be sure, the Soviet scholar himself subsequently uses such terms as *praindoevropejskij areal* or *praslavjanskoe lingvoètničeskoe prostranstvo*, not substantially different from 'IE protohome' or 'original homeland of the Slavs.' What is more, he also occasionally resorts to the notion of *prarodina*, in spite of his own initial objection to that term. He further points out that any attempt to identify the name *Dunaj* with the Dnieper (as was proposed by K. Moszyński and more recently by Z. Gołąb; see above) is doomed, as is any attempt to equate the name of th Danube with, or to derive it from, a common noun meaning 'puddle,' 'sea' (PIE *dhou-nā*). At the outset Trubačev recalls the East Slavic tradition, echoed in the Primary Chronicle, that the Slavs originated in the (mid-)Danube region. If accepted at face value, this would make their subsequent advent in the North Balkans a mere *Reconquista* of sorts. This point is subsequently elaborated on.

In his criticism of the protohome notion Trubačev also introduces the related but nevertheless different concept of land-taking (experienced, e.g., by Hungarians and Icelanders). He scrutinizes the idea that restricted space in an original area of settlement by a specific population might lead to resettlement. This explanation is rejected in favor of a more dynamic concept, allowing for early convergence, substratum phenomena, and interpenetration (as, incidentally, previously suggested by N. S. Trubeckoj, B. V. Gornung, V. K. Žuravlev, H. Birnbaum, and others). Also, Trubačev rightly remarks that the notion of early prehistoric linguistic homogeneity *vs.* subsequent dialectal differentiation is a fiction. As a rule, such perception derives from the fact that only relatively late preliterate dialectal features of a reconstructed protolanguage can actually be retrieved (again, a methodological consideration previously voiced, with regard to CS, by Žuravlev and Birnbaum, among others). This is consistent with the realization that prehistoric linguistic evolution does not necessarily imply only, or even primarily, divergence, that is, a development from uniformity to manifoldness (as implied by the metaphor of the genealogical tree). Rather, linguistic evolution is usually additionally characterized by convergence, suggesting a merger of many into fewer languages or dialects.

Concerned with problems of methodology, the Soviet linguist then discusses how we ought to conceive of CS—as a living language once spoken in the past or a mere abstract, consistent ("non-contradictory") linguistic model? He opts, naturally, for the former. Trubačev also criticizes the "method of exclusion," i.e., any attempt to identify areas of alleged "pure" topo- and hydronymy, without consideration of any sub-, ad-, or superstrata normally present. Such "pure" zones (at one time assumed, in the case of Slavic, for the region of the Pripet Marshes) do not in fact exist. Additionally, Trubačev offers some persuasive remarks concerning the density of onomastic data of a particular linguistic type as well as regarding the mobility, caused by the dynamics of ethnic migrations, of early areas of settlement. Thus, for example, the northern sub-Carpathian territory, tentatively delineated by Udolph, can, according to Trubačev, at most be considered one of the regions settled by the earliest Slavs, but not the unqualified entirety of their protohome.

Trubačev subsequently proceeds to examine the relationship of Slavic and Baltic, the agreements and differences between the two language groups, and their various interpretations. In particular, the notion of Slavic being somehow derived from Baltic or a (western) portion thereof is reexamined and discarded. Among differences in the phonological evolution of the two branches of IE, Trubačev notes both the thorough reshaping of orignial ablaut alternations in Baltic without an equivalent modification in Slavic, more conservative in this respect, and the different treatment of PIE *k'* (> Baltic *š*, CS *c* > *s*). The Soviet linguist obviously does not consider the possiblity of CS *s* here going back to *š* (as attested in Baltic and some other IE language families). Rather, he assumes a pre-Slavic transitional stage *c* (= *ts*) with further deaffrication to *s*. For the verb, the Soviet linguist considers Slavic more archaic than Baltic (cf. now esp. Ivanov 1981a), as, in general, he is not inclined to assign to Baltic a markedly more archaic character than that assumed for Slavic.

Whereas in late prehistoric times the Balts can be found in the Upper Dnieper region, Trubačev posits relatively close ties between pre- or Proto-Baltic and Early IE of the East Balkan (Daco-Thracian) area for a considerably earlier period (3rd millennium BC) without any participation of pre-Slavic or PS. As for the emergence of a distinctly CS (PS) linguistic type, Trubačev is less concerned with, or able to indicate, even an approximate time span for that process since he is anxious to view CS as directly derived from PIE (i.e., not via an intermediate Balto-Slavic stage). In its earliest phase, the Soviet scholar localizes PS somewhere in Central Europe, and more precisely on the mid-Danube. He argues, on the basis of linguistic evidence, that it had relatively close contacts with Italic (as deducible from Latin evidence) and, probably somewhat later, also with Germanic, but not with Baltic. Subsequently, the Slavs seem to have spread east- and northwards, establishing contact with the Illyrians (later found in the West Balkans). Although few, the well-identified *centum* elements in Slavic (cf. CS *korva* or *kārvā* 'cow') point to ties with Celtic tribes (cf. Celt *carvos*, *caravos* 'stag').

The early Balts seem to have participated initially in the trade link along the famed "amber route." Clearly, the Baltic element played a major role in the "Old European" hydronymy, posited by H. Krahe and subsequently elaborated upon by W. P. Schmid and J. Udolph, in particular. It was not, however, its only original or necessarily even most central component (as was proposed by Schmid and accepted by Udolph). Probably only in the second half of the first millennium BC were closer ties established between Balts and Slavs, resulting in many secondary conformities in phonology, grammatical structure, and vocabulary. As Trubačev hastens to point out, however, Slavic was also part of the "Old European" hydronymy as evinced, particularly, by a number of hydronyms that Slavic shared with other IE languages.

Concerning the origins of the Proto-Indo-Europeans as a whole, Trubačev is inclined to seek them, relying mostly on earlier scholarship but supported by some strong new arguments, in Europe—though obviously not in northern Europe, covered by glaciers right up to the end of the Ice Age. This view contrasts with the view, embraced, especially in recent years, by linguists (e.g., T. V. Gamkrelidze, V. V. Ivanov, W. Lehmann) and archeologists (e.g., M. Gimbutas), that these origins were in Asia (or easternmost Europe). What is rather generally accepted, however, is the secondary Indo-Europeanization of Anatolia, despite the fact of early, Hittite evidence. For methodological reasons stated at the outset, Trubačev does not wish to point to any specific subregion in Europe as the actual center of the earliest IE settlement. He nonetheless believes the core of this area to have been somewhere in the mid-Danube basin, with adjacent territories in the Balkans, on the one hand, and the right-bank Ukraine, on the other. In the same general core area on the Danube, then, the Soviet scholar also locates the earliest ascertainable homeland of the Proto-Slavs.

From this original region the Slavs would have spread to the northwest (forming the predecessors of the Western Slavs), the northeast (yielding the Eastern Slavs, and in both instances crossing the Carpathian Mountains), and south (crystallizing into the Southern Slavs, implying only relatively short-distance migrations). This, of course, is the most revolutionizing aspect of Trubačev's whole conception, putting the point of origin for the Slavs right back where the Primary Chronicle claimed it to have been. He thus rules out the possibility of a western ("autochthonic") first homeland in present-day Poland—where the Slavs instead are, according to this view, arrivals from the south!—and also severly limits the possibility of locating the Slavic protohome further to the east or even southeast (essentially between the Western Bug, Dniester and mid-Dnieper).

Referring to his earlier (equally unorthodox, if less wide-ranging) hypothesis that the Sorbs and their language(s) were secondarily "occidentalized," Trubačev now proposes that the bulk of the Sorbian population came to their present—or rather, previous, more widespread—territories (between the Saale and Nysa/Neisse Rivers) from the south (cf. the recent view of Schuster-Šewc 1982, accounted for above, VI.3.). Commenting on the Slavic onomastic evidence of the mid-Danubian region, the Soviet linguist notices the relative and gradual increase in its anthroponymy and, thereafter, also ethnonymy. The Slavic anthroponymy and ethnonymy being of relatively late date in this area, Trubačev now suggests that the self-designation *Slověne* did not yet exist during the Slavs' presence on the banks of the Danube. The *Sclaveni* referred to by writers of the Byzantine period are mentioned, as are the more peripheral *Veneti/Venedi* and *Antes/Anti*. Trubačev then tries to show, on the basis of a number of topo- and hydronyms, that pre-Hungarian Pannonia, including however also Transylvania, had a much denser Slavic population than previously thought.

It seems, according to Trubačev, that it was Celtic tribes, spreading during approximately the middle of the first millennium BC into these territories and as far as the western Ukraine, that ulitmately pushed the Slavs northwards (and probably also westwards) into what came to be Polish—or more generally Lekhitic—lands along the Vistula and other rivers farther to the west and northwest. It was presumably at this time that Slavic absorbed some of its few but striking *centum*-marked lexemes (cf. above). The Celts, attested by their ethnonym *Volcae* (etymologically meaning 'wolves;' cf. CS *vьlkъ* and also the SC anthroponym *Vuk*), seem also to hide behind Herodotus' enigmatic *Neuroi*, frequently identified with the earliest Slavs. Evidence for this is said to be the Celtic tribe *Nervii* in Gaul; but cf. also the name *Galicia*, with cognates encountered both north of the Carpathians and in northern Spain, and related to *Gaul*, Lat *Gallia*, and *Galatia*. Trubačev then dwells on the contacts between the Slavs of the right-bank Ukraine and the Iranians (having shown in a previous study that some significant Iranian loanwords of Slavic are restricted to West Slavic) as well as between these Slavs and elements of the Indo-Aryan (Old Indic) ethnolinguistic group, forming part of Greater Scythia. Thus the Slavic theonym *Svarogъ* may have a direct counterpart only in Skt *svargá-* 'sky, heaven.' Possibly of Old Indic, rather than Iranian, origin is further the ethnonym *sьrbi* (later a designation for both the *Sorbians* and the *Serbs*), while Iranian provenience remains the most likely for *xъrvati* ('Croats'); but cf. also Gołąb 1982.

Trubačev concludes with a note on the earliest towns of the Slavs, which, as we now know thanks to archeological finds, can be dated back to the sixth century, if not earlier, rather than only to the tenth century AD. Thus it can be shown, for example, that *Kiev*—or rather its predecessor—in addition to having been known under that name (*Kyevъ*), also had a second name, *Sǫvodъ* (*Samvatás* in Constantine Porphyrogenitus; cf. the extant hydronym *Suvid*). This second name originally denoted the confluence of the Dnieper and the Desna Rivers, but was soon lost as a toponym.

Trubačev's important contribution to the prehistory of the Slavs is founded on a comprehensive, yet imaginative reexamination of the available linguistic data and existing hypotheses. This rather condensed account of the Soviet linguist's recent work was given here as a telling example of the many exciting avenues open to future research even at the present stage of our knowledge and methodological sophistication.

SELECTIVE BIBLIOGRAPHY

Note: Of the titles listed below, those either discussed or referred to in the text of this bibliographic survey are marked by a double asterisk (∗∗) or single asterisk (∗), respectively. All entries are listed in alphabetical order. For purposes of content identification, each entry is classified using the same numerical system as the Table of Contents. The primary discussion of an entry is to be found in the text in the section corresponding to the first number listed to the right of that entry. To the extent possible, the specific order of the symbols quoted with each title reflects an order of decreasing general significance or particular relevance to the subject matter dealt with; however, no more than four such symbols are listed for any single title.

TABLE OF ABBREVIATIONS

AnzfslPh	*Anzeiger für slavische Philologie*
BSLP	*Bulletin de la Société de linguistique de Paris*
FL	*Folia Linguistica*
FLH	*Folia Linguistica Historica*
FS	*Folia Slavica*
IF	*Indogermanische Forschungen*
IJSLP	*International Journal of Slavic Linguistics and Poetics*
IRSL	*International Review of Slavic Linguistics*
JF	*Južnoslovenski filolog*
JIES	*The Journal of Indo-European Studies*
KZ	*Zeitschrift für vergleichende Sprachforschung auf dem Gebiete der indogermanischen Sprachen. Begründet von A. Kuhn* ("Kuhn's Zeitschrift")
MSS	*Melbourne Slavonic Studies*
PF	*Prace filologiczne*
RES	*Revue des études slaves*
RicSlav	*Ricerche slavistiche*
RL	*Russian Linguistics*
RS	*Rocznik slawistyczny*
ScSl	*Scando-Slavica*
SEEJ	*The Slavic and East European Journal*
SEER	*The Slavonic and East European Review*
SlavRev	*Slavistična Revija*
SlOcc	*Slavia Occidentalis*
SlOr	*Slavia Orientalis*
Studia filol. pol. i słow.	*Studia z filologii polskiej i słowiańskiej*
VJa	*Voprosy jazykoznanija*
WdSl	*Die Welt der Slaven*
WSlAlm	*Wiener Slawisticher Almanach*
WSlJb	*Wiener Slawistiches Jahrbuch*
ZbFL	*Zbornik Matice srpske za filologiju i lingvistiku*

ZfO	*Zeitschrift für Ostforschung*
ZfPhon	*Zeitschrift für Phonetik, Sprachwissenschaft und Kommunikationsforschung*
ZfSl	*Zeitschrift für Slawistik*
ZfslPh	*Zeitschrift für slavische Philologie*

Ageeva, R. A.

1981   *   "Problemy mežregional'nogo issledovanija toponomii   VI.1
baltijskogo proisxožednija na vostočnoslavjanskoj   VI.4
territorii," *Balto-slavjanskie issledovanija 1980*, 140–50.

Aitzetmüller, R.

1974   **   "Nochmals *otrokъ*," *AnzfslPh* 7, 155–8.   V.3

1975   **   "Das 'Urslavische' und einige seiner Probleme,"   VI.2
AnzfslPh 8, 163–8.   VI.3
     II.3

1977a   *   Review of *Słownik prasłowiański*. Tom I: A-B by F.   V.1
Sławski, *AnzfslPh* 9, 445–55.

1977b   *   Review of *Urslavische Grammatik. Einführung in das*   I.1
vergleichende Studium der slavischen Sprachen. II. Band
Konsonantismus by P. Arumaa, *AnzfslPh* 9, 455–61.

1978   *   *Altbulgarische Grammatik als Einführung in die slavische*   I.4
Sprachwissenschaft (Freiburg im Breisgau: U. W.   VI.3
Weiher).   VI.1

1979a   **   "Zum Vorangehenden," *AnzfslPh* 10/11, 211.   VI.2
     VI.3
     II.3

1979b   *   Review of *Nahtigalov zbornik, AnzfslPh* 10/11, 262–7.

American Contributions …

1973   *American Contributions to the Seventh International Congress of*
Slavists, Warsaw, August 21–27,1973. Volume I: *Linguistics and*
Poetics, L. Matejka, ed. (The Hague and Paris: Mouton).

1978   *American Contributions to the Eighth International Congress of*
Slavists, Zagreb and Ljubljana, September 3–9, 1978. Volume I:
Linguistics and Poetics, H. Birnbaum, ed. (Columbus, OH: Slavica).

Andersen, H.

1972   **   "Diphthongization," *Language* 48, 11–50.   II.3
     II.4
     II.5

1977   *   "On Some Central Innovations in the Common Slavic   VI.3
Period," *Nahtigalov zbornik*, 1–13.   II.3
     II.4

Antiquitates Indogermanicae …

1974   *Antiquitates Indogermanicae. Studien zur indogermanischen*
Altertumskunde und zur Sprach- und Kulturgeschichte der indoger-
manischen Völker. Gedenkschrift für Hermann Güntert, M.

Mayrhofer *et al.*, eds. (Innsbruck: Institut für Sprachwissenschaft der Universität Innsbruck).

Arumaa, P.

1976   ✶✶ *Urslavische Grammatik. Einführung in das*   I.1
vergleichende Studium der slavischen Sprachen II. Band:
Konsonantismus (Heidelberg: Winter).   II.4

1977a   ✶ "Zu den slavischen und baltischen Gewässernamen,"   VI.4
Commentationes Linguisticae, 1–16.   VI.1

1977b   ✶ "Zu baltisch-slavischen und finnisch-ugrischen   VI.4
Gewässernamen mit *ks.* Ein Beitrag zur historischen   VI.1
Demographie des europäischen Ostens," *Annales Societatis
Litterarum Estonicae in Suecia* 7 (1974–76; Stockholm),
89–112.

Auty, R.

1977   ✶✶ "The Russian Language," *Companion to*   I.4
Russian Studies 2: *An Introduction to Russian*   VI.3
Language and Literature, R. Auty and D. Obolensky,   VI.1
eds. (Cambridge: Cambridge University Press), 1–40.

Avksent'eva, A. G.

1976   ✶ "Palatal'naja korreljacija i mena *tl*, *dl* > *kl*, *gl*   II.4
v slavjanskix jazykax," *Istorija russkogo jazyka.
Drevnerusskij period*, V. V. Kolesov, ed. (Leningrad:
Izd-vo Leningradskogo Universiteta), 5–18.

Balalykina, È. A.

1980   ✶✶ "Sinonimija ad"ektivnyx obrazovanij s suffiksal'nymi   V.3
t, *st* v slavjanskix i baltijskix jazykax," *S10r* 29, 21–6.   III.3
   III.2
   VI.1

Balto-slavjanskie …

1974   *Balto-slavjanskie issledovanija*, T. M. Sudnik, ed. (Moscow: Nauka).

1980   *Balto-slavjanskie ètnojazykovye kontakty*, T. M. Sudnik, ed. (Moscow: Nauka).

1981   *Balto-slavjanskie issledovanija 1980*, V. V. Ivanov, ed. (Moscow: Nauka).

1982   *Balto-slavjanskie issledovanija 1981*, V. V. Ivanov, ed. (Moscow: Nauka).

Balto-slavjanskij sbornik

1972   *Balto-slavjanskij sbornik*, V. N. Toporov, ed. (Moscow: Nauka).

Bartula, C.

1972   ∗ "Elementy prasłowiańskie zdania złożonego w   IV.3
języku staro-cerkiewno-słowiańskim," *Z polskich studiów slawistycznych*, 5–11.

Basaj, M.

1971   ∗ "Syntaktyczne tendencje rozwojowe liczebników   IV.2
słowiańskich," *Studia filol. pol. i słow.* 10, 155–62.   III.4

Becker, L. A.

1981   ∗ Review of *Studies in Slavic Morphophonemics and*   II.2
Accentology by E. Stankiewicz, *SEEJ* 25.2, 105–8.

Beleckij, A. A.

1980   ∗∗ "Slavjanskaja toponimija Grecii," *Perspektivy*   VI.4
razvitija slavjanskoj onomastiki, A. V.   VI.3
Superanskaja and N. V. Podol'skaja, eds. (Moscow: V.3
Nauka), 266–73.   II.3

Bereiche der Slavistik

1975   *Bereiche der Slavistik. Festschrift zu Ehren von Josef Hamm*, F. V. Mareš *et al.*, eds. (Vienna: Österreichische Akademie der Wissenschaften)

Bernštejn, S. B.

1974   ∗∗ *Očerk sravnitel'noj grammatiki slavjanskix jazykov.* I.2
Čeredovanija. Imennye osnovy (Moscow: Nauka).   III.3
                                                    II.6
                                                    II.3

1977   ∗∗ "K voprosu ob ierarxii zakonov praslavjanskogo   II.5
perioda," *Nahtigalov zbornik*, 15–25.

1980   ∗∗ "K ètimologii praslavjanskogo *degъtь* 'pix axungia'," V.4
V čest Georgiev, 206–12.

1981   ∗ "O nekotoryx aspektax problemy ètnogeneza slavjan," VI.4
Studia filol. pol. i słow. 20, 53–8.

Bezlaj, F.

1971   ∗ "Einige Fälle des *-o-* : *-eu-* Ablauts im Slavischen," II.3
Linguistica (Ljubljana) 11, 23–32.

1976-	* *Etimološki slovar slovenskega jezika.* Prva knjiga, *A-J* (Ljubljana: Mladinska knjiga).	V.1
1977	** "Slovenščina in stara cerkevna slovenščina," *Nahtigalov zbornik*, 27–35.	VI.3 III.3 IV.3

Bielfeldt, H. H.

1970/72	* "Die Rekonstruktion eines slawischen Wortes aus deutschen Zeugnissen (*Döns* usw.)," *RicSlav* 17–19, 35–43.	V.2

Birnbaum, H.

1973a	* "The Original Homeland of the Slavs and the Problem of Early Slavic Linguistic Contacts," *JIES* 1, 407–21.	VI.4
1973b	* "O możliwości odtworzenia pierwotnego stanu języka słowiańskiego za pomocą rekonstrukcji wewnętrznej i metody porównawczej. (Kilka uwag o stosunku różnych podejść,)" *American Contributions ... Seventh ...*, 33–58.	VI.2
1974	** "Über unterschiedliche Konzeptionen der slavischen Ursprache und ihrer mundartlichen Gliederung," *AnzfslPh* 7, 146–52.	VI.2 VI.3 II.3
1975	** "Slavisches Namengut aus dem frühmittelalterlichen bayerischen Raum: Das Zeugnis des Salzburger Verbrüderungsbuches und das Placitum von Buchenau," *WSlJb* 21, 34–42.	VI.4 VI.3
1977a	** Der österreichische Jasomirgott und die frühere Verbreitung der Alpenslaven (Urslovenen)," *AnzfslPh* 9, 33–48.	VI.4 VI.3
1977b	* "Roman Jakobson's Contribution to Slavic Accentology," *Roman Jakobson: Echoes*, 29–37.	II.2
1977c	** *Linguistic Reconstruction: Its Potentials and Limitations in New Perspective (JIES*, Monograph 2).	VI.2
1978a	** "The Sphere of Love in Slavic," *American Contributions ... Eighth ...*, 155–79. Reprinted in author's *Essays in Early Slavic Civilization*, 9–25; see below, Birnbaum 1981b.	V.3
1978b	** "Kilka uwag o braku śladów drugiej palatalizacji tylno-językowych na północno-wschodniej peryferii zwartego słowiańskiego obszaru językowego," *S10r* 27.2, 185–9.	II.4
1978c	* Review of *Altbulgarische Grammatik als Einführung in die slavische Sprachwissenschaft* by R. Aitzetmüller, *Language* 56, 698.	I.4

1979a　*　*Common Slavic: Progress and Problems in Its Reconstruction* (Columbus, OH: Slavica). Reprint, with corrections, of 1975 ed.

1979b　** "Weiteres zu den 'Urslaven' und ihrer (Aus-)Sprache," *AnzfslPh* 10/11, 201–10.
　　　　　　　　　　　　　　　　　　　　　　VI.2
　　　　　　　　　　　　　　　　　　　　　　VI.3
　　　　　　　　　　　　　　　　　　　　　　II.3

1980　** "On Protolanguages, Diachrony, and 'Preprotolanguages' (Toward a Typology of Linguistic Reconstruction)," *V čest Georgiev*, 121–9.
　　　　　　　　　　　　　　　　　　　　　　VI.4
　　　　　　　　　　　　　　　　　　　　　　VI.2

1981a　** "Wie alt ist das altertümlichste slavische Sprachdenkmal? Weitere Erwägungen zur Herkunft der Kiever Blätter und zu ihrem Platz in der Literatur des slavischen Mittelalters," *WdSl* 26, 225–58.
　　　　　　　　　　　　　　　　　　　　　　VI.4
　　　　　　　　　　　　　　　　　　　　　　VI.3

1981b　* "On the Slavic Word for Jew: Origin and Meaning," *Essays in Early Slavic Civilization / Studien zur Frühkultur der Slaven* by H. Birnbaum (Munich: Fink), 25–35.
　　　　　　　　　　　　　　　　　　　　　　V.4
　　　　　　　　　　　　　　　　　　　　　　VI.3

1981c　* Review of *A Historical Phonology of the Polish Language* by Z. Stieber, *IJSLP* 23, 181–7.
　　　　　　　　　　　　　　　　　　　　　　II.1

1981d　* Review of *Urslavische Grammatik. Einführung in das vergleichenden Studium der slavischen Sprachen.* II. Band. *Konsonantismus* by P. Arumaa, *IJSLP* 24, 153–65.
　　　　　　　　　　　　　　　　　　　　　　I.1

1981e　* Review of *Grammaire comparée des langues slaves.* Tome IV: *La formation des noms* by A. Vaillant, *IJSLP* 24, 166–74.
　　　　　　　　　　　　　　　　　　　　　　I.2

1983a　** "W sprawie prasłowiańskich zapożyczeń z wczesnogermańskiego, zwłaszcza z gockiego (Na marginesie artykułu Witolda Mańczaka)," *IJSLP* 27, 25–44.
　　　　　　　　　　　　　　　　　　　　　　V.4

1983b　* Review of *Slavic Accentuation: A Study in Relative Chronology* by F. H. H. Kortlandt, *IJSLP* 27, 175–80.
　　　　　　　　　　　　　　　　　　　　　　II.2

1983c　* Review of *Grammaire comparée des langues slaves.* Tome V: *La syntaxe* by A. Vaillant, *IJSLP* 28, 181–5.
　　　　　　　　　　　　　　　　　　　　　　I.2

Boryś, W.

1975　** *Prefiksacja imenna w językach słowiańskich* (Wrocław-Warsaw-Gdańsk: Ossolineum) (*Monografie slawistyczne* 32).
　　　　　　　　　　　　　　　　　　　　　　III.3
　　　　　　　　　　　　　　　　　　　　　　III.4

1976   ** "Prasłowiańskie *osьkola, *sьčava,   III.3
       sьčavъ i pokrewne," *RS* 37, 47–63.   III.4

1978   * "Dwa archaizmy leksykalne w gwarach   V.2
       serbskochorwackich (sztok. *trĕmesla*, czak.
       šćūt)," *RS* 38, 37–45.

1979   * "Przyczynki do geografii wyrazów słowiańskich,"   V.1
       S10cc 36, 23–30.   VI.3

1980   ** "O rozwoju znaczenia psł. *piti, *pojiti,"   V.3
       RS 40, 39–42.

1981   * "Prasłowiańskie przymiotniki dewerbalne z apofonią   II.3
       o : ь (dial. * dropъ, *stromъ, *tromъ),"   III.3
       RS 41, 35–41.   III.4

1982   * "Prilozi proučavanju ostataka arhaičnog slavenskog   V.1
       (praslavenskog) leksika u kajkavštini," *Hrvatski*   VI.3
       dijalektološki zbornik. Knjiga 6 (Zagreb: JAZU), 69–76.

Bošković, R.

1976   ** "Neka pitanja imeničke mocije i praslovenske   III.3
       derivacije," *ZbFL* 19.2, 7–11.   III.4

Bräuer, H.

1981   * Review of *Studien zu den slavischen Gewässernamen*   VI.4
       und Gewässerbezeichnungen. Ein Beitrag zur Frage nach
       der Urheimat der Slaven by J. Udolph, *ZfslPh* 42, 203–8.

Browning, T.

1982   ** "On the Origin of Morphophonemic Alternations   II.6
       V∼VL' in Slavic," *SEEJ* 26, 460–71.   II.4

Bubenik, V.

1980   ** "Some Issues in Balto-Slavic Accentology,"   II.2
       Linguistics 18, 997–1017.   VI.1

Budich, W.

1977   ** "Zweimal slavisch *eterъ*," *WdSl* 22, N. F. 1.2,   V.3
       242–4.   V.2
            V.4

Budziszewska, W.

1974   * "O pochodzeniu nazwy *modrzęw* 'larix',"   V.2
       RS 35, 21–3.

1978   * "Pochodzenie ros. dial. *znozdь, znozda*,"   V.3
       RS 39., 47–9.   V.2

Bujukliev, I.

1977   ∗ "Razvoj na otnositelnite izrečenija s văveždašči   IV.3
vrăzki ot ∗k^w- osnova i sădbata na *iže*
v slavjanskite ezici," *Zakonomernosti* ..., 83–120.

Bulatova, R. V.

1977   ∗∗ "Slavjanskij material v 'Nostračiteskom slovare'   VL1
V.M. Illič-Svityča," *Konferencija*..., 74–9.

1979   ∗∗ "Raboty sovetskix issledovatelej po slavjanskoj   II.2
istoričeskoj akcentologii na materiale drevnix pamjatnikov
pis'mennosti," *ZbFL* 22.1, 73–85.

Cantarini, A.

1973/74 ∗ Review of *Gramatyka historyczna języka*   I.4
polskiego by W. Kuraszkiewicz, *RicSlav* 20–21, 395.

1977/79 ∗ Review of *Histoire de l'accentuation slave*   II.2
by P. Garde, *RicSlav* 24–26, 242–5.

Carsten, F. L.

1980   ∗ Review of *Slawische Siedlungspuren im Raum um*   VI.4
Uelzen, Bad Bevensen und Lünenburg by G. Osten, *SEER*
58, 595–6.

Channon, R.

1972   ∗∗ *On the Place of the Progressive Palatalization*   II.4
of Velars in the Relative Chronology of Slavic   VI.2
(The Hague and Paris: Mouton).

Cohen, D.

1969   ∗∗ "Why the Slavic 'Second Palatalization' Comes   II.4
First," *Papers from the 5th Regional Meeting*,   VI.2
(Chicago: Chicago Linguistic Society), 306–13.

Commentationes Linguisticae

1977   *Commentationes Linguisticae et Philologicae Ernesto*
Dickenmann, lustrum claudenti quintum decimum,
F. Scholz *et al.*, eds. (Heidelberg: Winter).

Comrie, B.

1975a ∗∗ "Common (?) Slavonic ∗*sedmъ*," *SEER*   II.4
53, 323–9.   III.4

1975b ∗ Review of *Slavic Accentuation: A Study in Relative* II.2
Chronology by F. H. H. Kortlandt, *SEER* 53, 634–5.

1978   ∗∗ "Morphological Classification of Cases in the   III.2
Slavonic Languages," *SEER* 56, 177–91.   IV.2

Čekman, V. N. (Czekman)

1973   * "Genezis i ėvolucija palatal'nogo rjada v   II.4
            praslavjanskom jazyke," (Minsk: Nauka i texnika).   II.6

1974a   ** "O refleksax indoevropejskix *k, *g v   II.4
            balto-slavjanskom jazykovom areale,"   VI.1
            Balto-slavjanskie issledovanija, 116–35.

1974b   * "O 'prasłowiańskim' rozwoju *gn (kn)   II.4
            > *$gń$ ($kń$)," *Studia filol. pol. i słow.*
            13, 115–23.

1975   ** "Akanie, istota zjawiska i jego pochodzenie,"   II.3
            S10r 24, 283–305.   VI.3

1979   ** *Issledovanija po istoričeskoj fonetike*   II.1
            praslavjanskogo jazyka. Tipologija i rekonstrukcija
            (Minsk: Nauka i texnika).

1981   ** "Drevnejšaja balto-slavo-indoiranskaja izoglossa   VI.1
            (*s_{i-k} > *$š$)," *Balto-slavjanskie*   II.4
            issledovanija 1980, 27–37.

Československé přednášky VII

1973   *Československé přednášky pro VII mezinárodní*
            sjezd slavistů ve Varšavě. Lingvistika (Prague: Academia).

Dambe, V.

1981   * "Slavjanskie sledy latvijskoj gidronimii i   VI.1
            mikrotoponimii," *Balto-slavjanskie issledovanija*   VI.4
            1980, 157–62.

Darden, B. J.

1972   ** "Rule Ordering in Baltic and Slavic Nominal   II.2
            Accentuation," *SEEJ* 16, 74–83.

1979   * "Nominal Accent Classes in Lithuanian as Compared   II.2
            to Slavic and Indo-European," *The Elements* (Chicago: III.2
            Chicago Linguistic Society), 330–38.   VI.1

1982   ** "Reflexes of I. E. Barytones among Balto-Slavic   II.2
            and Slavic Substantives," *Studies for Stankiewicz*,   III.2
            99–107.   VI.1

Degtjarev, V. I.

1981   ** "Proisxoždenie imen *pluralia tantum* v   III.4
            slavjanskix jazykax," *VJa* 1982.1, 65–77.   IV.2
                                                III.2
                                                III.3

Dejanova, M.

1977 * "Kăm văprosa za razvitieto na deepričastieto v   IV.2
         slavjanskite ezici," *Zakonomernosti* ..., 55–81.   III.4

Desnickaja, A. V.

1978 ** "O rannix balkano-vostočnoslavjanskix leksičeskix   V.3
         svjazjax," *VJa* 1978.2, 42–51.   V.2
                                                                  VI.1

Dickenmann, E.

1978 * Review of *Die alpenslawischen Personennamen* by   VI.3
         O. Kronsteiner, *WSlAlm* 2, 289–93.

1980a * "Über einige Relikte in slavischen geographischen   VI.4
         Namen," *Jubiläumsschrift zum fünfzigjährigen Bestehen*   V.2
         des Slavisch-Baltischen Seminars der Westfälsischen
         Wilhelms-Universität Münster, G. Ressel, H. Rösel and
         F. Scholz, eds. (Munich: Aschendorff) (= *Studia Slavica*
         et Baltica, Band 1), 35–56.

1980b * Review of *Studien zu den slavischen Gewässernamen*   VI.4
         und Gewässerbezeichnungen. Ein Beitrag zur
         Frage nach der Urheimat der Slaven by J. Udolph,
         Onoma 24, 279.

Dingley, J.

1979 * Review of *A Historical Phonology of the Belorussian*   II.1
         Language by P. Wexler, *SEER* 57, 414–15.

Dostál A.

1977 * Review of *An Introduction to Old Church Slavic*   I.4
         by W. R. Schmalstieg, *SEEJ* 21, 553–4.

Dukova, U.

1979 ** "Zur Frage des iranischen Einflusses auf die   V.4
         slawische mythologische Lexik," *ZfSl* 24, 11–16.   V.3

Duridanov, I. A.

1973 ** "Kăm stratigrafijata na imennite tipove v   III.4
         slavjanskite i baltijskite ezici," *Slavjanska*   VI.2
         filologija VII, 27–36.   V.2

1978 ** "Zaselvaneto na slavjanite v Dolna Mizija i   VI.4
         Xemimont po dannite na toponimijata," *Slavjanska*   VI.3
         filologija VII, 353–60.

Dybo, V. A.

1971 * "K voprosu ob udarenii proizvodnyx prilagatel'nyx   II.2
         v praslavjanskom (prilagatel'nye s suffiksom -ęi),   III.4

ZbFL 14.1, 7–24. III.2
III.5

1972 * "Akcentnye tipy prezensa glagolov s ъ, ь II.2
v korne v praslavjanskom," *VJa* 1972.4, 68–79. III.5
III.2

1974 * "Afganskoe udarenie i ego značenie dlja II.2
indoevropejskoj i balto-slavjanskoj akcentologii," VI.1
Balto-slavjanskie issledovanija, 67–105.

1975 * "Zakon Vasil'eva-Dolobko v drevnerusskom (na II.2
materiale Čudovskogo Novogo Zaveta)," *IJSLP* 18, 1–81.

1977 * "Imennoe udarenie v srednebolgarskom i zakon II.2
Vasil'eva-Dolobko," *Slavjanskoe i balkanskoe* III.4
jazykoznanie. Antičnaja balkanistika i III.2
sravnitel'naja grammatika, S. Bernštejn *et al.*, eds.
(Moscow: Nauka), 189–272.

1979a ** "Rekonstrukcija sistemy akcentnyx paradigm v II.2
praslavjanskom (konspekt)," *ZbFL* 22, 37–71. II.6
III.2

1979b ** "Balto-slavjanskaja akcentnaja sistema s tipologičeskoj II.2
točki zrenija i problema rekonstrukcii indoevropejskogo VI.1
akcenta. (Akcentologičeskij status konečnoudarnyx form
a.p. *c* v praslavjanskom)," *Balcanica: Lingvističeskie*
issledovanija, T. V. Civ'jan, ed. (Moscow: Nauka) 85–101.

1980 ** "Balto-slavjanskaja akcentnaja sistema s II.2
tipologičeskoj točki zrenija i problema rekonstrukcii VI.1
indoevropejskogo akcenta. I. Balto-slavjanskii prototip
praslavjanskoj akcentnoj sistemy," *Balto-slavjanskie*
ètnojazykovye kontakty, 91–150.

1981 ** *Slavjanskaja akcentologija. Opyt rekonstrukcii* II.2
sistemy akcentnyx paradigm v praslavjanskom (Moscow: II.6
Nauka).

1982 ** "Praslavjanskoe raspredelenie akcentnyx tipov v II.2
prezense tematičeskix glagolov s kornjami na nešumnye III.5
(materialy k rekonstrukcii)," *Balto-slavjanskie* III.2
issledovanija 1981, 205–61.

Dzenzelivs'kyj, J. O.

1978 * "Refleksi prasl. dial. *zerdmę*, *o/b/zerdъ*, V.3
zordъ, *o/b/zordъ* ta in.," *Slavia* 47, 267–78. VI.3

Eckert, R. (Ėkkert)

1972a   ** "O nekotoryx rasxoždenijax meždu imennymi osnovami   III.3
na -*i* v baltijskix i slavjanskix jazykax,"   III.4
Balto-slavjanskij sbornik, 206–16.   VI.1
   V.2

1972b   * "Zum Problem der baltisch-slawischen   III.3
Sprachbeziehungen (am Material der Nominalstämme   III.4
auf -*i*)," *ZfSl* 17, 605–15.   VI.1
   V.2

1974   ** "Studien zur Geschichte der nominalen Stammbildung   III.5
im Slawischen," *ZfSl* 19, 489–506.   III.4
   VI.1
   III.5

1975   * Review of *Očerk sravnitel' noj grammatiki*   I.2
slavjanskix jazykov. Čeredovanija. Imennye osnovy by
S. B. Bernštejn, *ZfSl* 20, 816–24.

1977   * "Die balto-slawischen Wortentsprechungen,"   V.2
ZfSl 22, 579–90.   VI.1

1979   ** "Zu einigen Reflexen der indoeuropäischen Heteroklita   III.3
auf -*l*-//-*n*- in den slawischen und baltischen   III.2
Sprachen," *ZfSl* 24, 17–23.   V.2
   VI.1

1981   ** *Untersuchungen zur historischen Phraseologie und*   V.3
Lexikologie des Slawischen und Baltischen   IV.3
(*Systemfragmente aus der Terminologie der Waldimkerei*)
(Berlin: Akademie der Wissenschaft der DDR).

Eichler, E.

1972   ** "Zur Gliederung slawischer Sprachräume im Lichte   VI.4
der Onomastik," *ZfSl* 17, 616–25.   VI.3

1980   * Review of *Studien zu den slavischen Gewässernamen*   VI.4
und Gewässerbezeichnungen. Ein Beitrag zur Frage nach
der Urheimat der Slaven by J. Udolph, *ZfSl* 25, 759–65.

1981   * "Die sprachgeschichtliche Stellung des Altsorbischen   VI.3
im Lichte der Onomastik," *Studia filol. pol. i słow.*   VI.4
20, 83–91.

Elson, M. J.

1976   * Review of *Slavic Accentuation: A Study in*   II.2
Relative Chronology by F. H. H. Kortlandt, *SEEJ*
20, 80–1.

Enrietti, M.

1973a   ** "Di alcune parole germaniche in slavo," *Accademia*   V.4
*Nazionale dei Lincei, Rendiconti della classe di scienze
morali, storiche e filologiche*, Serie 8, v. 28.1–2, 17–49.

1973b   ** "Slavi *xysŭ/xyzŭ* 'casa', 'capanna'," *Accademia*   V.4
*Nazionale dei Lincei, Rendiconti della classe di
scienze morali, storiche e filologiche*, Serie 8, v. 28.5–6,
729–39.

1975/76 ** "Slavi *bljudo* e *misa* 'piatto' 'scodella',"   V.4
Scritti in onore di Giuliano Bonfante, I (Brescia:
Paideia), 225–36.

1977   ** "Le desinenze slave di prima persona plurale   III.2
dei verba," *Accademia Nazionale dei Lincei, Rendiconti*   VI.1
della classe di scienze morali, storiche e filologiche,   III.5
Serie 8, v. 32.5–6, 471–80.

1977/79 ** "Ancora sulla slavo *misa*," *RicSlav*   V.4
24–26, 5–10.

Erhart, A.

1974   * Review of *Die Distribution der urindogermanischen*   II.4
sogenannten Gutturale by L. Steensland, *Slavia* 43, 68–9.

1975   * Review of *Studien zum slavischen und*   II.3
indoeuropäischen Langvokalismus by T. Mathiassen,
Slavia 44, 314–15.

Erhart, A. & R. Večerka

1981   ** *Úvod do etymologie* (Prague: Státní Pedagogické   V.1
Nak1.).

Ėtimologija

1972   * *Ėtimologija 1970* (Moscow: Nauka).   V.1

1973   * *Ėtimologija 1971* (Moscow: Nauka).   V.1

1974   * *Ėtimologija 1972* (Moscow: Nauka).   V.1

1975   * *Ėtimologija 1973* (Moscow: Nauka).   V.1

1976   * *Ėtimologija 1974* (Moscow: Nauka).   V.1

1977   * *Ėtimologija 1975* (Moscow: Nauka).   V.1

1978   * *Ėtimologija 1976* (Moscow: Nauka).   V.1

1979   * *Ėtimologija 1977* (Moscow: Nauka).   V.1

1980   * *Ėtimologija 1978* (Moscow: Nauka).   V.1

1981   * *Ėtimologija 1979* (Moscow: Nauka).   V.1

1982   * *Ėtimologija 1980* (Moscow: Nauka).   V.1

Eucharisterion

1979/80   *Eucharisterion: Essays presented to Omeljan Pritsak on his Sixtieth Birthday by his Colleagues and Students* (2 vols.), I. Ševčenko and F. E. Sysyn, eds. (Cambridge, MA: Ukrainian Research Institute) (= *Harvard Ukrainian Studies* 3/4).

Feinberg, L. E.

1978   ** "Thematic Vowel Alternation in Common Slavic   III.2
Declension," *FS* 2, 107–21.   III.4
     II.5
     II.3

Feldstein, R. F.

1975   ** "The Prosodic Evolution of West Slavic in the Context   II.2
of the Neo-Acute Stress," *Glossa* 9, 63–77.   VI.3

1976   ** "Another Look at Slavic Diphthongs," *Lingua*   II.3
38, 313–34.

1978a   ** "On the Paradigmatic Representation of Common   II.2
Slavic Prosody," *Linguistics* (special issue),   III.2
101–18.

1978b   ** "On Compensatory and Neo-Acute Lengthening in   II.2
the Dialects of Slavic," *IRSL* 3, 355–98.   II.3
     VI.3

Fermeglia, G.

1977   * "Contributi alla conoscenza del lessico slavo,"   V.2
*Accademia Nazionale dei Lincei, Rendiconti
della classe di scienze morali, storiche e
filologiche*, Serie 8, v. 32, 199–204.

Ferrell, J.

1974/75 ** "The History of the Slavic Imperfect Tense with   III.2
Particular Reference to the Developments in Old Church   III.5
Slavic, Slovene and East Slavic," *WdSl* 19–20, 37–63.   III.3

Filin, F. P.

1972   ** "K probleme proisxoždenija slavjanskix jazykov,"   VI.4
VJa 1972.5, 3–11. Reprinted in *Slavjanskoe jazykoznanie*   VI.1
jazykoznanie VII, 378–89.   VI.3

1980   ** "O proisxoždenii praslavjanskogo jazyka i   VI.4
vostočnoslavjanskix jazykov," *VJa* 1980.4, 36–50.   VI.1
     VI.3

Fisher, R. L.

    1977   ** "IE *po-* in Slavic and Iranian,"   III.5
                  KZ 91, 219–30.   III.3
                                                      VI.1

Förster, W.

    1979   ** "Betrachtungen zur Semantik des Präfixes   V.3
                  pod- in denominalen Bildungen des Slawischen,"   III.3
                  ZfSl 24, 28–33.

Friedrich, P.

    1975   * *Proto-Indo-European Syntax: The*   IV
                  Order of Meaningful Elements (= *JIES*, Monograph 1).   I.3

Fritze, W. H.

    1979   ** "Zur Bedeutung der Awaren für die slawische   VI.4
                  Ausdehnungsbewegung im frühen Mittelalter," *ZfO*
                  28, 498–545.

Gadžieva, I. Z., V. K. Žuravlev & V. P. Neroznak, eds.

    1981   ** *Sravnitel' no-istoričeskoe izučenie jazykov*   VI.2
                  raznyx semej. Sovremennoe sostojanie i problemy   VI.1
                  (Moscow: Nauka).   I.2
                                                      I.3

Galton, H.

    1978   ** "Interrelations Between the Open Syllable and   II.5
                  the Phonological System (as illustrated in Slavic),"
                  Makedonski jazik 29, 111–16.

    1979   ** "Syllabic Division and the Intonation of   II.5
                  Common Slavic," *Current Issues in Linguistic*   II.2
                  Theory 9 (= *Current Issues in the Phonetic Sciences*,
                  H. & P. Hollien, eds.) (Amsterdam: Benjamins), 261–5.

    1980a   * "Teleologische Sprachbetrachtung (an slavischem   II.5
                  Material)," *FL* 14, 83–102.

    1980b   ** "Über den Sinn der slavischen offenen   II.5
                  Silbe," *Current Issues in Linguistic Theory* 11 (= *Festschrift*
                  for Oswald Szemerényi on the Occasion of this 65th
                  Birthday, B. Brogyanyi, ed.) (Amsterdam: Benjamins),
                  265–81.

    1980c   * "The Spread of the Correlation of Palatalization   II.5
                  (A Teleological Approach)," *ZfPhon* 33, 575–8.

    1981   * "Bemerkungen zur slavischen Palatalisierungskorrelation,"   II.4
                  ZfslPh 42, 8–13.

Garde, P.

1973   ** "Le paradigme accentuel oxyton est-il slave commun?"   II.2
        RES 49, 159–71. Reprinted in *Communications de la
        délégation française, VIIe Congrès international des
        slavistes* (Paris: Institut d'études slaves), 159–71.

1976a ** *Histoire de l' accentuation slave* (2 vols.)   II.2
        (Paris: Institut d'études slaves) (= *Collection de*   II.2
        l'Institut d' études slaves 7.1–2).

1976b ** "Neutralization of Tone in Common Slavic,"   II.2
        Slavic Linguistics and Language Teaching, T. F. Magner,
        ed. (Cambridge, MA: Slavica), 1–19.

Gasparini, E.

1970/72 * "Semantica slava: *Desná, šurin*,"   V.3
        RicSlav 17–19, 191–203.

Gasparov, B. & P. Sigalov

1974   ** *Sravnitel' naja grammatika slavjanskix jazykov.*   I.2
        Posobie dlja studentov (2 vols.) (Tartu: Tartuskij
        Gosudarstvennyj Universitet).

Gălăbov, I.

1973   ** "Urslavische Auslautsprobleme," *WSlJb* 18, 5–17.   II.5

1975   ** "Ausgliederungsprozesse des Späturslavischen und die   VI.3
        südslavischen Sprachen," *WSlJb* 21, 61–71.   II.4

Georgiev, V.

1971- * *Bălgarski etimologičen rečnik*; Tom 1,   V.1
        A-Z; Tom 2, I-krepja, V. Georgiev, ed. (Sofia: BAN).

1972   ** "Slavischer Wortschatz und Mythologie,"   V.3
        AnzfslPh 6, 20–6.   V.4
                                V.2

1973a ** "Pričinite za văznikvaneto na roditelen-vinitelen   III.2
        padež v slavjanskite ezici," *Slavističen sbornik*   III.4
        (*po slučaj VII Meždunaroden kongres na slavistite văv
        Varšava*) (Sofia: BAN), 9–18.

1973b ** "Tri perioda razvitija praslavjanskogo jazyka,"   VI.2
        Slavjanska filologija VII, 5–16.

1974   ** "Starobălgarski *rozga—razgǫ*," *V*   V.2
        pamet na prof. d-r. St. Stojkov. Ezikovedski   II.3
        izsledvanija, L. Andrejčin *et al.*, eds.   II.2
        (Sofia: BAN), 567–9.

1976   ** "Die Herkunft des slavischen Imperfekts,"   III.2

WdSl 21, 48–51.   III.3
                                                                 III.5

1978   ✱✱ "Principi na slavjanskata diaxronna morfologija,"   III.1
           Slavjanska filologija VIII, 5–16.

1981   ✱✱ *Introduction to the History of the Indo-European*   I.3
           Languages (Sofia: BAN).

Gesemann, W.

1975   ✱✱ "Zur Funktion des *j* in der urslavischen   II.5
           Synharmonie," *Xenia Slavica*, 43–8.   II.4

Gluhak, A.

1978   ✱✱ "O jednoj indoevropsko-uralskoj paraleli,"   V.2
           ZbFL 21.1, 219.   VI.1

Godłowski, K.

1979   ✱ "Die Frage der slawischen Einwanderung ins östliche   VI.4
           Miteleuropa," *ZfO* 28, 416–47.

Gołąb, Z.

1969   ✱✱ "Kentum Elements in Slavic (A Summary),"   II.4
           Papers from the Fifth Regional Meeting, (Chicago: VI.1
           Chicago Linguistic Society), 330–6.

1972   ✱✱ "The Relative Clauses in Slavic: Common Slavic   IV
           and North Slavic," *The Chicago Which Hunt*:   VI.3
           Papers from the Relative Clause Festival, P. M. Peranteau
           et al., eds. (Chicago: Chicago Linguistic Society), 30–9.

1973   ✱✱ "The Initial *x*- in Common Slavic: A Contribution   II.5
           to Prehistorical Slavic-Iranian Contacts," *American* II.4
           Contributions ... Seventh ..., 129–56.   V.4

1975a   ✱✱ "*Veneti*/*Venedi* - the Oldest Name of the   V.3
           Slavs," *JIES* 3, 321–36.   VI.4

1975b   ✱✱ "Linguistic Traces of Primitive Religious Dualism   V.3
           in Slavic," *For Wiktor Weintraub: Essays in*   V.4
           Polish Literature, Language, and History Presented on
           the Occasion of His 65th Birthday, V. Ehrlich *et al.*,
           eds. (The Hague and Paris: Mouton), 151–9.

1976   ✱ "Scs. *srьdobol'a* 'krewny' - ślad   V.3
           indoeuropejskiej terminologii społecznej w   V.2
           słowiańskim?" *Rocznik naukowodydaktyczny WSP w*
           Krakowie 2.58 (= *Prace językoznawcze* 3), 21–7.

1977   ✱✱ "Stratyfikacja słownictwa prasłowiańskiego   V.1
           a zagadnienie etnogenezy Słowian," *RS* 38, 15–30.   VI.4

1978	** "Conservatism and Innovatism in the Development of the Slavic Languages," *American Contributions ... Eighth ...*, 337–78.	VI.3 V.1 III.1
1982	** "About the Connection between Kinship Terms and Some Ethnica in Slavic (The Case of *Sĭrbi* and *Slověne*), *Studies for Stankiewicz*, 165–71.	V.3 VI.4
1983	** "The Ethnogenesis of the Slavs in the Light of Linguistics," *American Contributions to the Ninth International Congress of Slavists*, Vol. 1, *Linguistics*, M. Flier, ed. (Columbus, OH: Slavica), 131–46.	VI.4

Górnowicz, H.

| 1972 | * "Związane z wyspami zanikłe apelatywa prasłowiańskie zachowane w nazwach geograficznych północno-zachodniej Polski", *Z polskich studiów slawistycznych*, 143–54. | V.3 VI.3 VI.4 |

Gribble, C. E.

| 1973 | ** "Slavic *bykъ* 'Bull'," *Linguistics* 113, 53–61. | V.3 |
| 1980 | * Review of *Grammaire comparée des langues slaves*. Tome V: *La syntaxe* by A. Vaillant, *SEEJ* 24, 317–18. | I.2 |

Grošelj, M

| 1972 | * "O proponi -*in*," *SlavRev* 20, 41–2. | III.3 III.4 VI.3 |

Halle, M.

| 1971 | ** "Remarks on Slavic Accentology," *Linguistic Inquiry* 2, 1–19. Reprinted in *Slavic Forum: Essays in Linguistics and Literature*, M. S. Flier, ed. (The Hague and Paris: Mouton), 17–41. | II.2 |

Halle, M. & P. Kiparsky

| 1981 | * Review article of *Histoire de l'accentuation slave* by P. Garde, *Language* 57, 150–81. | II.2 |

Hamilton, Jr., W. S.

| 1974 | ** "Deep and Surface Changes in Four Slavic Noun Systems," *Linguistics* 127, 27–73. | III.4 III.2 |

Hamp, E. P.

| 1970 | * "Pęstь," *ZbFL* 13.2, 292–3. | V.3 V.2 |
| 1971a | * "Notes on *Słownik etymologiczny języka* | V.1 |

	polskiego III,3," *RS* 32, 67–72.	V.2
		V.1
1971b	∗∗ "Russ. Slovene *oméla*, OCS. S-Cr. *imela*," *ZbFL* 14.1, 253–5.	V.2
		II.3
1973a	∗∗ "(For Roman, Who is Always) Number One," *IJSLP* 16, 1–6.	V.2
		III.4
1973	∗ "Fish," *JIES* 1, 507–11.	V.3
		V.2
1974	∗ "An Archaism in Slavic," *ZbFL*. 17.1, 241–4.	V.3
		V.4
		V.2
1975	∗∗ "Devjanosto '90'," *RL* 2, 219–22.	V.2
		V.4
		III.4
1976a	∗∗ "Slavic *ískra*," *ZbFL*. 14.2, 193.	V.3
		V.2
		IV
1976b	∗∗ "On Slavic *ev < eu̯*," *ZbFL*. 14.2, 13–14.	II.3
1977	∗ "Ad Słownik etymologiczny języka polskiego IV 5 (20)," *RS* 38, 83–4.	V.1
1978	∗ "On *deiu̯o-* in Slavic," *FS* 2, 141–3.	V.3
		V.4
		V.2
1981	∗ "Łyżka," *RS* 41, 63.	V.3
		V.2
1982a	∗ "Two uncertain IE roots," *FLH* 3, 127–30.	II.3
		II.4
		VI.1
1982b	∗∗ "On Some Colour Terms in Baltic and Slavic," *Studies for Stankiewicz*, 187–92.	V.2
		V.3
		VI.1
Handke, K.		
1979	∗∗ "Urslawische Muster der westslawischen Nominalkomposita," *ZfSl* 24, 44–50.	III.3
		VI.3
Harvie, J. A.		
1978	∗∗ "Dative Absolutism in Perspective," *MSS* 13, 40–50.	IV
Holzer, G.		
1980	∗∗ "Die urslavischen Auslautsgesetze," *WSlJb* 26, 7–27.	II.5

Honowska, M.

1976   * Review of *An Introduction to Old Church*   I.4
            Slavic by W. R. Schmalstieg, *RS* 40, 57–62.

Horálek, K.

1971   ** "Postavení slovenštiny," *Slavia*   VI.3
            40, 537–50.

Huntley, D.

1975   * Review of *Old Church Slavonic Grammar*   I.4
            (sixth ed.) by H. G. Lunt, *SEEJ* 19, 357–61.

1976   * Review of *An Introduction to Old Church*   I.4
            Slavic by W. R. Schmalstieg, *Language* 54, 450–2.

1978   ** "Phonological models in Slavic palatalizations,"   II.4
            Recent Developments in Historical Phonology, J.
            Fisiak, ed. (The Hague: Mouton), 209–12.

1982   * "Old Church Slavonic *tešti - točiti*,"   V.3
            Studies for Stankiewicz, 193–9.   III.5
                                                          II.3

Hüttl-Folter, G.

1980   * Review of *A Historical Phonology of the*   II.1
            Ukrainian Language by G. Y. Shevelov, *WSlJb* 26, 236–7.

Issatschenko, A.

1980   ** *Geschichte der russischen Sprache*. 1. Bd.:   I.4
            Von den Anfängen bis zum Ende des 17. Jahrhunderts VI.3
            (Heidelberg: Winter).

Istorija, kul'tura …

1978   *Istorija, kul'tura, ètnografija i fol'klor slavjanskix*
            narodov. VIII Meždunarodnyj s″ezd slavistov.
            Zagreb-Ljubljana, sentjabr' 1978g. Doklady
            sovetskoj delegacii, V.A. D'jakov *et al.*, eds.
            (Moscow: Nauka).

Ivanov, V. V.

1973   ** "Tipologija razvitija slavjanskix i indoevropejskix   III.3
            predlogov i poslelogov," *Strukturno-tipologičeskie*   IV
            issledovanija, 51–60.

1975   ** "Proisxoždenie semantičeskogo polja slavjanskix   V.3
            slov, oboznačajuščix dar i obmen," *Slavjanskoe i*   V.2
            balkanskoe jazykoznanie. Problemy interferencii, 50–78.

1978a   * *Otraženie v baltijskom i slavjanskom dvux serij*   III.5
            indoevropejskix glagol'nyx form, Avtoref. dis. na soisk. III.2

uč. st. dokt. filol. nauk (Vilnius: Vil'njusskij gos. III.3
universitet im. V. Kapsukasa VI.1

1978b ** "O sledax indoevropejskix kompleksov ėnklitik IV
v slavjanskom," *Studia linguistica*, 191–201. II.2

1981a ** *Slavjanskij, baltijskij i rannebalkanskij* III.5
glagol. Indoevropejskie istoki (Moscow: III.2
Nauka). III.3
 VI.1

1981b * "Morfonologičeskie čeredovanija v indoevropejskom II.6
glagole," *Slavjanskoe i balkanskoe jazykoznanie.* II.3
Problemy morfonologii, 32–52. III.5

1981c ** "K prostranstvenno-vremennoj interpretacii VI.1
balto-slavjanskogo dialektnogo kontinuuma,"
Balto-slavjanskie issledovanija 1980, 6–10.

Ivanov, V. V. & V. N. Toporov

1973 ** "Ėtimologičeskoe issledovanie semantičeski V.3
ograničennyx grupp leksiki v svjazi s problemoj IV
rekonstrukcii praslavjanskix tekstov," *Slavjanskoe
jazykoznanie VII*, 153–69.

1974 ** *Issledovanija v oblasti slavjanskix drevnostej.* V.3
Leksičeskie i frazeologičeskie voprosy rekonstrukcii V.2
tekstov (Moscow: Nauka). IV

1978 ** "O jazyke drevnego slavjanskogo prava (k analizu V.3
neskol'kix ključevyx terminov)," *Slavjanskoe jazykoznanie
VIII*, 221–40.

1980 * "Nasledie Kuriloviča i Stanga," VI.1
Balto-slavjanskie ėtnojazykovye kontakty, 286–90. II.2
 III.5

Jacobsson, G.

1973 ** "Odwieczny problem palatalizacji postępowej II.4
tylnojęzykowych w językach słowiańskich," VI.2
*Göteborg Contributions to the Seventh International
Congress of Slavists in Warsaw, August 21–27, 1973*, G.
Jacobsson, ed. (= *Slavica Gothoburgensia* 6), 49–74.

1974 ** "Some Problems Connected with the Third II.4
Palatalization in Slavic," *ScSl* 20, 187–95. VI.2

1977 ** "Die progressive Velarpalatalisierung im II.4
Slavischen phonologisch betrachtet," *WSlJb* 23, 70–5. VI.2

Jakob, H.

1979   *   "'Die Burg' in der Maintal-Aue bei Kemmern/Ofr.   VI.4
Refugium und Kultstätte der Mainwenden," *WdSl* 24,   VI.3
N. F. 3.2, 248–69.

1980   *   "War Burk das historische *Wogastisburc*, und wo lag   VI.4
das *oppidum Berleich*? Eine historisch-geographische   VI.3
Standort-Analyse," *WdSl* 25, N. F. 4.1, 39–67.

1981   *   "Frühslavische Keramikfunde in Ostfranken,"   VI.4
WdSl 26, N. F. 5.1, 154–69.   VI.3

Jeffers, R. J.

1975   **   "Remarks on Indo-European Infinitives,"   III.5
Language 51, 133–48.   III.3

Jelitte, H.

1980/81   *   Review of *Altbulgarische Grammatik als*   I.4
Einführung in die slavische Sprachwissenschaft by R.
Aitzetmüller, *Kratylos* 25, 166–71.

Jeżowa, M.

1975   *   *Sufiks* -ika *w językach słowiańskich*   III.3
(Wrocław: Ossolineum) (= *Monografie slawistyczne* 34).

Johnson, D. J. L.

1980   **   "Dybo's Law and Metatony in the Present Tense of   II.2
the Slavonic Verb," *SEER* 58, 481–99.   III.2
   III.5

Junković, Z.

1977   *   "La metatonie et le ton complexe en slave commun,"   II.2
RES 50, 601–13.

Kantor, M. & R. N. Smith

1975   *   "A Sketch of the Major Developments in Russian   II.1
Historical Phonology," *FL* 7, 389–400.   I.4

Karaliūnas, S. S. (Karaljunas)

1972   **   "K baltijskomu sootvetstviju slavjanskogo   VI.1
pasti," *Balto-slavjanskij sbornik* (Moscow: III.5
Nauka), 281–8.   V.3

Karaś, M.

1973   *   "Protetyczne *s*- w językach słowiańskich,"   II.4
JF 30, 135–41.   VI.3

Katičić, R.

1980   ** "Slavica Foroiuliensia," *WSlJb* 26, 28–32.   VI.4
    VI.3

Katonova, E. M.

1981   * "Dannye gidronimii o balto-slavjanskix kontaktax   VI.1
na severe Belorussii," *Balto-slavjanskie issledovanija*   VI.4
1980, 177–84.

Keipert, H.

1977   * Die Adjektive auf -*telьnъ*. Studien zu einem   III.3
kirchenslavischen Wortbildungstyp. 1. Teil. (Wiesbaden: III.4
Harrassowitz) (=*Veröffentlichungen der Abteilung*
für slavische Sprachen und Literaturen des Osteuropa-
Instituts [Slavisches Seminar] an der Freien Universität Berlin 45).

Kiparsky, P.

1973   ** "The Inflectional Accent in Indo-European,"   II.2
Language 49, 794–849.   III.2
    VI.1

Kiparsky, V.

1971a   ** "Zum gegenwartsprachigen Stand der etymologischen   V.1
Untersuchungen," *PF* 21, 265–75.

1971b   * "On the Stratification of the Russian Vocabulary,"   V.1
Oxford Slavonic Papers N. S. 4, 1–11.

1972   * "O sud'be -*ь*- v suffiksax -*ьsk* i -*ьstvo*,"   III.3
VJa 1972.2, 77–82.   II.3

1974   * Review of *Istorija russkogo udarenija. Imennaja*   II.2
akcentuacija v drevnerusskom jazyke by V. V. Kolesov,
ZfslPh 37, 427–31.

1975a   ** *Russische historiche Grammatik*. Band III: I.4
Entwicklung des Wortschatzes (Heidelberg: Winter).   V.1
    VI.1
    VI.3

1975b   * Review of *Sravnitel' naja grammatika slavjanskix*   I.2
jazykov. Posobie dlja studentov by B. Gasparov and P.
Sigalov, *ZfslPh* 38, 375–77.

1977   * Review of *Histoire de l' accentuation slave* by P.   II.2
Garde, *RL* 3, 313–16.

Klepikova, G. P.

1976   * "Die Entsprechungen von urslaw. *kъbьlъ im   V.3
Bulgarischen und in anderen slawischen Sprachen,"   III.3

    ZfSl 21, 839–46.   VI.3

Klyčkov, G. S.

1972   * "K probleme vyvedenija slavjanskogo konsonantizma iz   II.4
          indoevropejskogo arxetipa," *Studia filol. pol. i słow.*   VI.1
          11, 201–12.

Koch, C.

1976/78 * "Slavische *v*- Präsentien," *WdSl* 21, 121–42.   III.5
                                                                  III.3

Kočev, I.

1978   * "Obščoslavjanskoto značenie na njakoi fonetični   VI.3
          javlenija v jugoistočnite bălgarski govori,"   II.3
          Slavjanska filologija VIII, 127–33.   II.4

Kolesov, V. V.

1972 ** *Istorija russkogo udarenija. Imennaja akcentuacija*   II.2
          v drevnerusskom jazyke (Leningrad: Izd-vo   III.2
          Leningradskogo Universiteta).   III.4

1973   * "Praslavjanskaja fonema (=/ǫ/) v rannix   II.3
          preobrazovanijax slavjanskix vokaličeskix sistem,"
          Slavjanskoe jazykoznanie VII, 170–95.

1975 ** "Udarenie prefiksal'nyx imen v drevnerusskom i   II.2
          praslavjanskom," *Studia Slavica* 21, 17–44.   II.6

1979a ** "Otnositel'naja xronologija prosodičeskix   II.2
          izmenenij v praslavjanskom," *Issledovanija v oblasti*   VI.2
          sravnitel' noj akcentologii indoevropejskix jazykov, S. D.
          Kancel'son, ed. (Leningrad: Nauka), 111–42.

1979b * "Udarenie proizvodnyx imen s neproduktivnymi   II.2
          suffiksami v slavjanskom i drevnerusskom," *Slavia*   III.3
          48, 124–34.   III.4

1980a ** *Istoričeskaja fonetika russkogo jazyka*   II.1
          (Moscow: Vysšaja škola).   I.4

1980b * "Udarenie proizvodnyx imen s suffiksom *-išč* v   II.2
          istorii russkogo jazyka," *SlOr* 29, 121–9.   III.3
                                                                     III.4

Koneski, B.

1981   * "Za *tj (**kt'*) > *št*, *dj > *žd*,"   II.4
          Studia filol. pol. i słow. 20, 103–5.

Konferencija ...

1977   *Konferencija: Nostratičeskie jazyki i nostratičeskoe jazykoznanie.*
          Tezisy dokladov, V. V. Ivanov *et al.*, eds. (Moscow: Nauka).

Konnova, V. F.

1972   * "Neskol'ko leksiko-semantičeskix izogloss na   V.3
            slavjanskoj jazykovoj territorii," *VJa* 1975, 82–96.   VI.3

Kopečný, F.

1973   * "*Byti* — verbum existentiae (VE), kopula (VC) a   V.3
            pomocné sloveso (VA), přecházející v morfém v p. č.
            slk.," *Slavia* 42, 135–48.

1973-   ** *Etymologický slovník slovanských jazyků.*   V.1
            Slova gramatická a zájmena. Svazek 1: *Předložky.*
            Koncové partikule. Svazek 2: *Spojky, částice, zájmena*
            adverbia (Prague: Academia, 1973, 1980).

1974a   * "Problematika praslovanštiny a její rozvoj do   VI.3
            jednotlivých slovanských jazyků (I–1)," *Slavia* 43, 60–4.

1974b   ** "Noch ein Wort zu slav. *otrokъ*," *AnzfslPh*   V.3
            7, 153–4.

1979   * "Zu den Bedingungen einer etymologischen   V.1
            Rekonstruktion," *ZfSl* 24, 70–6.

Kortlandt, F. H. H.

1975   ** *Slavic Accentuation: A Study in Relative*   II.2
            Chronology (Lisse: de Ridder).   III.2
                                                  VI.2

1976   ** "The Slovene Neo-Circumflex," *SEER* 54, 1–10.   II.2
                                                  VI.3

1977   ** "Initial *u* in Baltic and Slavic," *KZ*   II.5
            91, 37–40.   II.2
                                                  III.3
                                                  VI.1

1978a   * "On the history of Slavic accentuation," *KZ* 92,   II.2
            269–81.

1978b   ** "I.-E. palatovelars before resonants in   II.4
            Balto-Slavic," *Recent Developments in Historical*   VI.1
            Phonology, J. Fisiak, ed. (The Hague: Mouton), 237–43.

1978c   ** "On the History of the Genitive Plural in Slavic,   III.2
            Baltic, Germanic, and Indo-European," *Lingua* 45,   II.2
            281–300.

1978d   * Review of *Histoire de l'accentuation slave* by P.   II.2
            Garde, *Lingua* 44, 67–91.

1978e   * Review of *Grammaire comparée des langues slaves.*   I.2
            Tome V. *La syntaxe* by A. Vaillant, *Lingua* 48, 393–4.

| 1979a | ** "Three problems of Balto-Slavic Phonology," *ZbFL* 22.2, 57–63. | VI.1 II.3 II.4 |

1979a ** "Three problems of Balto-Slavic Phonology," VI.1
ZbFL 22.2, 57–63. II.3
II.4

1979b ** "Sur l'accentuation des noms postverbaux en slave," II.2
Dutch Contributions to the Eighth International III.4
Congress of Slavists, J. M. Meijer, ed. (Amsterdam:
Benjamins), 325–8.

1979c ** "On the History of the Slavic Nasal Vowels," II.3
IF 84, 259–72. II.5

1979d ** "Toward a Reconstruction of the Balto-Slavic Verbal III.5
System," *Lingua* 49, 51–70. VI.1

1980 * Review of *Studies in Slavic Morphophonemics and* II.2
Accentolology by E. Stankiewicz, *Lingua* 52, 198–200.

1982a * Review of *Prehistoric Slavic Contraction* by J. II.3
Marvan, *Lingua* 56, 98–100.

1982b * "A rejoinder," *Lingua* 56, 182–3. II.2

1982c ** "IE *pt* in Slavic," *FLH* 3, 25–8. II.4
II.5

Kostov, K.
1980 ** "Randbemerkungen zum Problem der V.2
lateinisch-slawischen lexikalischen VI.1
Übereinstimmungen," *V čest Georgiev*, 312–7.

Kølln, H.
1977 * "Verben mit Infinitiv auf -*ěti* und Präsensstamm III.5
auf -*e/o-*," *ScSl* 23, 103–13. III.3

Kragalott, J.
1977 * "On Developments of the -*ęt*- Declension in III.2
Slavic," *FS* 1, 212–23. III.4

Krajčovič, R.
1973 ** "K teorii protikladu fortis-lenis v praslovančine a II.4
slovanských jazykoch," *Československé přednášky VII*,
41–9.

1974 ** "Problém praslovenskej genézy slovenčiny," VI.3
Slavia 43, 368–77.

1975 ** *A Historical Phonology of the Slovak Language* II.1
(Heidelberg: Winter). I.4

Kronsteiner, O.
1975 ** *Die alpenslawischen Personennamen* (Vienna: VI.3
Österreichische Gesellschaft für Namenforschung). VI.4

1976	** "Die Bedeutung der Lautgruppe _dl/l_ für die sprachliche Klassifizierung des Alpenslawischen," _Opuscula Slavica_, 217–25.	VI.3 VI.4
1977	** "Ist die Einteilung der slawischen Sprachen in ein Ost-, West- und Südslawisch gerechtfertigt?" _Österreichische Namenforschung_ 5.2, 17–28.	VI.3 VI.4
1978	** "Gab es unter den Alpenslawen eine kroatische ethnische Gruppe?" _WSlJb_ 24, 137–57.	VI.3 VI.4

Kučera, H.

1975	** "Havlík's Rule in Generative Phonology," _Bereiche der Slavistik_, 137–93.	II.3

Kunstmann, H.

1979a	* "Was besagt der Name _Samo_, und wo liegt _Wogastisburg?_" _WdSl_ 24, N. F. 3.1, 1–21.	VI.3 VI.4
1979b	* "Die Pontius-Pilatus-Sage von Hausen-Forchheim und _Wogastiburg_," _WdSl_ 24, N. F. 3.2, 225–47.	VI.3 VI.4
1980	* "Samo, Dervanus und der Slovenenfürst Wallucus," _WdSl_ 25, N. F. 4.1, 171–7.	VI.3 VI.4
1981a	* "Wo lag das Zentrum von Samos Reich," _WdSl_ 26, N. F. 5.1, 67–101.	VI.3 VI.4
1981b	* "Der oberfränkische Ortsname _Banz_," _WdSl_ 26, N. F. 5.1, 62–6.	VI.3 VI.4

Kuraszkiewicz, W.

1972	** _Gramatyka historyczna języka polskiego_ (Warsaw: Państwowe zakłady wydawnictw szkolnych).	I.4 VI.3

Kurkina, L. V.

1981	** "Nekotorye voprosy formirovanija južnyx slavjan v svjazi s pannonskoj teoriej E. Kopitara," _VJa_ 1981.3, 85–97.	VI.3 VI.4 V.1

Kuryłowicz, J.

1970/72	** "Gli aggettivi in -_l_- e il perfetto slavo," _RicSlav_ 17–19, 323–8.	III.3 III.2 III.5 III.4
1973	* "Les itératifs en -_eie/o_- en slave et en baltique," _JF_ 30, 143–7.	III.5 III.3
1976/78	* "Der doppelte Status der russischen Perfektiva auf -_nut'_," _WdSl_ 21.2, 91–7.	III.5 III.3 V.3

1977a	**	*Problèmes de linguistique indo-européene* (Wrocław: Ossolineum) (= *Prace językoznawcze* 90).	I.3 III.5 III.2 II.2
1977b	*	Review of *Histoire de l'accentuation slave* by P. Garde, *BSLP* 72.2, 283–9.	II.2

Kurz, J.

1971	**	"O rekompozici složených sloves v slovanštině," *Slavia* 40, 511–24.	III.3 III.5
1973	*	"K problematice existence a významu slav. zájmena *jь, ja, je*," *JF* 30, 149–53.	III.4 V.3

Lamprecht, A.

1973	*	"Pozdní praslovanština a její vývoj na východoslovanském území. Vývoj vokalické kvantitý a měkkostní korelace," *Československé přednášky VII*, 29–39.	VI.3 II.3 II.4
1978	**	"Praslovanština a její chronologické členění," *Českoskovenské přednášky pro VIII. mezinárodní sjezd slavistů v Zahřebu. Lingvistika*, B. Havránek *et al.*, eds. (Prague: Academia), 141–50.	VI.2

Laskowski, R.

1975	*	Review of *A Historical Phonology of the Slovak Language* by R. Krajčovič, *RS* 39, 58–64.	II.1

Leeming, H.

1971	*	"Origins of Slavonic Literacy: The Lexical Evidence," *SEER* 49, 327–38.	V.1 VI.3
1973	**	"Spostrzeżenia nad terminologią dotyczącą pisma w języku prasłowiańskim," *RS* 34, 23–6.	V.3 V.4 V.2
1974	**	"The Etymology of Old Church Slavonic *kramola*," *SEER* 52, 128–31.	V.4
1976a	*	"The Mysterious Origin of Some Slavonic Names for the Pleiades," *MSS* 11, 5–17.	V.4
1976b	*	Review of *Studien zum slavischen und indoeuropäischen Langvokalismus* by T. Mathiassen, *SEER* 54, 593–4.	II.3
1978a	**	"Some Unidentified Loan-Words in Common Slavonic and Old Church Slavonic," *SEER* 56, 161–76.	V.4
1978b	*	"A Slavonic metal-name," *RS*	V.2

39, 7–17.

1980	* Review of *Urslavische Grammatik. Einführung in das vergleichende Studium der slavischen Sprachen* II. Band: *Konsonantismus* by P. Arumaa, *SEER* 58, 422–4.	I.1

1981a   * Review of *Prehistoric Slavic Contraction* by J. Marvan, *SEER* 59, 413.   II.3

1981b   * Review of *Der genetische Aufbau des Russischen* by B. Panzer, *SEER* 59, 15–16.   I.4

1982   * Review of *Studien zu den slavischen Gewässernamen und Gewässerbezeichnungen. Ein Beitrag zur Frage nach der Urheimat der Slaven* by J. Udolph, *SEER* 60, 87.   VI.4

Leili, P.

1975   * Review of *On the Place of the Progressive Palatalization of Velars in the Relative Chronology of Slavic* by R. Channon, *Studia Slavica* 21, 439–41.   II.4

Lekomceva, M. I.

1978   ** "Zum Problem des baltischen Substrats des Akan'je," *ZfSl* 23, 628–34.   II.3 VI.1

1980   ** "Problema baltijskogo substrata akan'ja," *Balto-slavjanskie ètnojazykovye kontakty*, 157–68.   II.3 VI.1

Lekov, I.

1978   * "Modelăt na obščestvenata i vătrešnosistemnata obuslovenost v razvoja na slavjanskata ezikova grupa," *Slavjanska filologija VIII*, 17–43.   VI.3

Leszczyński, Z.

1977   * "Warunki trwałości *str zdr* < *sr zr*," *RS* 38, 85–92.   II.4 II.5

Lépissier, J.

1971   * "Slave *ǫbolŭ* 'allé couverte, galerie' et 'puits, citerne'," *Symbolae in honorem Shevelov*, 257–60.   V.4 V.3

Lindert, B.

1978   ** "Nazwy zabudowań mieszkalnych w językach słowiańskich pochodzące z epoki prasłowiańskiej," *Z polskich studiów slawistycznych*, Seria 5: *Językoznawsto* (Warsaw: PWN), 81–94.   V.3

Liukkonen, K.

1973   ** "Das Götterdvandva im Slavischen: Versuch einer Erklärung des sog. Genitiv-Akkusativs," *ScSl*   III.2 III.4

19, 249–53.   V.3

1974 ** "Der Ursprung des štokavischen Gen. Pl. auf   III.2
-ā," *ScSl* 20, 159–64.   III.4
    V.3

Lunt, H. G.

1974 ** *Old Church Slavonic Grammar*. Sixth edition,   I.4
completely revised and extended with an epilogue   VI.3
Toward a Generaltive Phonology of Old Church Slavonic
(The Hague and Paris: Mouton).

1975 * Review of *Drevnerusskij jazyk* by N. G. Samsonov,   VI.4
SEEJ 19, 361–3.

1976 * Review of *Russische historische Grammatik*. Band   I.4
III: *Entwicklung des Wortschatzes* by V. Kiparsky, *SEEJ*
20, 503–5.

1977 ** "Praslavjanskaja progressivnaja palatalizacija,"   II.4
Nahtigalov zbornik, 167–81.   VI.2

1977b ** "Slavic *jьgra 'dance, game, play'"   V.3
Papers in Slavic Philology, 172–8.   V.2

1978/80 ** "On *Akanje* and Linguistic Theory,"   II.3
Eucharisterion, 595–608.   VI.1

Lutterer, I.

1971 ** "Zur Entwicklung der Bildungstypen slawischer   VI.4
Ortsnamen," *Forschungen zur slawischen und*   III.3
deutschen Namenkunde, T. Witkowski, ed. (Berlin:
Akademie-Verlag), 8–13.

L'vov, A. S.

1978 ** "Obščeslavjanskoe i dialektnoe v leksike pamjatnikov   V.1
staroslavjanskoj pis'mennosti," *Slavjanskoe*   VI.3
jazykoznanie VIII, 265–84.

Machek, V.

1980 ** "Die slawischen und baltischen Entsprechungen der   III.5
lateinischen Intensivverba auf -*tāre* und -*sāre*,"   III.3
ZfSl 25, 53–61.   VI.1

Maher, J. P.

1973 * "The Linguistic Paleontology of some Pre-Christian   V.3
Burial Terms in Slavic Lexicon," *JIES* 1, 105–110.   VI.4

1974 * "The Ethnonym of the Slavs — Common Slavic   V.3
*Slověne," *JIES* 2, 143–55.   V.2
    VI.4

Malingoudis, P.

1981   ✳✳ *Studien zu den slavischen Ortsnamen Griechenlands.*   VI.4
I. *Slavische Flurnamen aus der messenischen Mani*   VI.3
(Wiesbaden: Steiner).

Malkova, O. V.

1981   ✳✳ "O principe delenija reducirovannyx glasnyx na   II.3
sil'nye i slabye v pozdnem praslavjanskom i v drevnix
slavjanskix jazykax," *VJa* 1981.1, 98–111.

Mańczak, W.

1974/75 ✳✳ "Czy prasłowiańskie wyrazy na *✳ch-* są   II.5
pochodzenia irańskiego?" *IJSLP* 21, 7–12.   II.4
   V.4

1975   ✳✳ "Scs *skotъ*, goc. *skatts* a łac. *pecū*,   V.4
pecūnia," *RS* 36, 67–71.   V.3

1977a   ✳✳ *Słowiańska fonetyka historyczna a frekwencja*   II.1
(Cracow: Uniwersytet Jagielloński).   II.5

1977b   ✳ "Rozwój *✳jedinъ* w językach słowiańskich,"   II.5
PF 27, 309–20.   II.3

1981   ✳ *Praojczyzna Słowian* (Wrocław: Ossolineum).   VI.4

1983   ✳✳ "Czas i miejsce zapożyczeń germańskich w   V.4
prasłowiańskim," *IJSLP* 27, 15–23.

Mareš, F. V.

1971   ✳✳ "Kontrakce vokálů v slovanských jazycích,"   II.3
Slavia 40, 525–36.   VI.2
   VI.3

1977   ✳✳ "Die Metalle bei den alten Slaven im Lichte des   V.3
Wortschatzes," *RS* 38, 31–3.   VI.3
   VI.4

1978   ✳✳ "Das slavische Konjugationssystem des Präsens in   III.2
diachroner Sicht," *WSlJb* 24, 175–209.   III.5

1980a   ✳✳ "Die Tetrachotomie und doppelte Dichotomie der   VI.3
slavischen Sprachen," *WSlJb* 26, 33–45.

1980b   ✳✳ "Aksl. *velii —velikъ*," *V čest*   III.3
Georgiev, 513–16.   V.3
   III.4
   IV

Marojević, R.

1982   ✳ Praslovenska adiectiva possessiva tipa   III.3
Tvorimiřičь (od patronima tipa *Tvorimiřičь*),   III.4

njihova sudbina i tragovi u slovenskim jezicima," *JF*   VI.3
38, 89–109.

Martinet, A.

1978   ** "Des *jers* slaves aux voyelles caduques du   II.3
japonais," *Studia linguistica*, 263–6.   VI.1
                                         VI.3

Martynov, V. V.

1972   *   "Slavjanskie ětimologičskie versii," *Russkoe*   V.1
i slavjanskoe jazykoznanie, 185–92.   V.3

1973   ** "Praslavjanskaja i balto-slavjanskaja suffiksal'naja   III.4
derivacija imen," *VII Meždunarodny s″ezd slavistov.*   III.3
Doklady (Minsk: Nauka i texnika).   VI.1

1978   ** "Balto-slavjano-italijskie izoglossy. Leksičeskaja   VI.1
sinonimija" (Minsk: [full bibliographical data not   V.2
available]).

1980   *   "Slavjanskoe nazvanie kleti," *SlOr* 29, 161–4.   V.3
                                         V.2

1981   ** "Balto-slavjano-iranskie jazykovye otnošenija i   VI.1
glottogenez slavjan," *Balto-slavjanskie issledovanija*   V.2
1980, 16–26.   V.4

Marvan, J. (I.)

1973   *   "Russkoe stjažnie i slavjanskaja doistoričeskaja   II.3
kontrakcija," *MSS* 8, 5–9.   VI.2
                                         VI.3

1979   ** *Prehistoric Slavic Contraction*, trans. by W. Gray   II.3
(University Park, PA, and London: Pennsylvania State   VI.2
University Press).   VI.3

Mathiassen, T.

1973   *   "Die verbalen Nasalsuffixe im morphologischen System   III.5
des Urslavischen," *ScSl* 19, 245–7.   III.3

1974   ** *Studien zum slavischen und indoeuropäischen*   II.3
Langvokalismus (Oslo-Bergen-Tromsø: III.3
Universitetsforlaget).   VI.1

1975   ** "Nochmals die 2. P. sg. des athematischen Imperativs   III.2
im Slavischen," *ScSl* 21, 113–18.   III.5
                                         II.5
                                         II.3

1978   ** *Zametki o paradigme slavjanskoj sravnitel'noj*   III.3
stepeni, osobenno o formax im. p. ed. č. m. r.   III.4

(= *Meddelelser* 16, Universitet i Oslo).   III.2

Mayer, H.
1976   ** "Kann das Baltische als das Muster für das   VI.1
        Slavische gelten?" *ZfslPh* 39, 32–42.
1978   ** "Die Divergenz des Baltischen und des Slavischen,"   VI.1
        ZfslPh 40, 52–62.

Mažiulis, V.
1973   ** "Proisxoždenie balto-slavjanskix tematičeskix form   III.2
        instr. pl.," *RS* 34, 17–21.   III.4
                                                                  VI.1

Mel'ničuk, A. S.
1978   * "Ètimologičeskie razyskanija. 3. Obščeslavjanskoe   V.2
        větiti," *Vostočnoslavjanskoe i obščee*   V.3
        jazykoznanie, 103–14.

Micklesen, L. R.
1973   ** "The Common Slavic Verbal System," *American*   III.5
        Contributions … Seventh …, 241–73.

1977   * Review of *Urslavische Grammatik. Einführung in*   I.1
        das vergleichende Studium der slavischen Sprachen. II.
        Band: *Konsonantismus* by P. Arumaa, *SEEJ* 21, 433–4.

1982   ** "The Accentology of Slavic Verbs in -*i*-,"   II.2
        Studies for Stankiewicz, 267–79.   III.5

Moskov, M. (Moskow)
1975   ** "Slavjanski i balkanski etimologii," *Godišnik*   V.4
        na Sofijskija Universitet, Fakultet po slavjanski   V.3
        filologii, 68.3, 299–350.   II.3

1978   * "Ein besonderes Präfixsystem in den slavischen   III.3
        Sprachen," *Slavistische Studien VIII*, 345–60.   III.4
                                                                  V.2
                                                                  V.3

1980   * "Slavjanski dumi s predstavki," *V čest*   III.3
        Georgiev, 341–7.   III.4
                                                                  V.2
                                                                  V.3

Moszyński, L. (Mošinskij)
1972a   ** "Rozwój systemu fonologicznego od wspólnoty   II.1
        językowej prasłowiańskiej do języka Cyryla i
        Metodego," *Z polskich studiów slawistycznych*, 293–304.

1972b	*	"Przyczynek do historii drugiej palatalizacji grupy spółgłoskowej *sk*," *Studia filol. pol. i słow.* 12, 255–68.	II.4
1972c	*	"O vremeni monoftongizacii praslavjanskix diftongov," *VJa* 1972.4, 53–67.	II.3 VI.2
1977a	**	"Najstarsze zasięgi słowiańskich form obocznych *cŕky* // *cir(ъ)ky*," *Nahtigalov zbornik*, 281–92.	V.4 V.3 VI.3
1977b	*	"Dwa nowe słowniki etymologiczne języka prasłowiańskiego," *RS* 38, 105–15.	V.1
1979	**	"Metody rekonstrukcji języka pra-cerkiewno-słowiańskiego," *WSlJb* 25, 48–55.	VI.3 VI.2
1980	**	"Najstarsze zróżnicowanie dialektyczne Prasłowiańszczyzny," *SlOr* 29, 195–200.	VI.3
1981	*	"Zagadnienie leksykalizacji formacji słowotwórczych *němьcь* i *glušьcь*," *Studia filol. pol. i słow.* 20, 165–76.	V.3 III.3

Mur'janov, M. F.

1981	**	"O staroslavjanskom *iskrь* i ego proizvodnyx," *VJa* 1981.2, 115–23.	V.3 V.2

Nagy, G.

1974	**	"Perkūnas and Perunъ," *Antiquitates Indogermanicae*, 113–31.	V.2 V.3

Nahtigalov zbornik

1977		*Slovansko jezikoslovje. Nahtigalov zbornik. Prispevki z mednarodnega simpozija v Ljubljani, 30 junija - 2. julija 1977*, F. Jakopin, ed. (Ljubljana: Univerza v Ljubljani, Filozofska fakulteta).

Nalepa, J.

1973	**	"Miejsce uformowania się Prasłowiańszczyzny," *Slavica Lundensia* 1, 55–114.	VI.4

Naylor, K. E.

1972	**	"On Some Developments of the Dual in Slavic," *IJSLP* 15, 1–8.	III.2
1980	*	Review of *A Historical Phonology of the Belorussian Language* by P. Wexler, *SEEJ* 24, 198–200.	II.1

Nepokupnyj, A. P.

1976	**	*Balto-severnoslavjanskie jazykovye svjazi* (Kiev: Naukova dumka).	VI.1 VI.3

Neweklowsky, G.

1979   * Review of *Histoire de l'accentuation slave* by   II.2
          P. Garde, *WSlJb* 25, 149–53.

Newman, L.

1971   * "On Reconstructing a Third *jat'* in the Northern   II.3
          Dialects of Common Slavic," *Slavia* 40, 325–41.   VI.3

1973   * Review of *On the Place of the Progressive*   II.4
          Palatalization of Velars in the Relative Chronology of
          Slavic by R. Channon, *SEEJ* 17, 252–4.

Němec, I.

1979a ** "O slovanské expresívní předponě *la-*   III.3
          (Františku Kopečnemu k sedmdesátým narozeninám),"   III.5
          Slavia 48, 120–3.

1979b * "Kritéria jinoslovanského původu slov v   V.1
          slovanské etymologii," *Slavia* 48, 329–31.   VI.3

Nikolaev, S. L. & S. S. Starostin

1982   ** "Paradigmatičeskie klassy indoevropejskogo   III.5
          glagola," *Balto-slavjanskie issledovanija 1981*,   II.2
          261–343.   VI.1

Oguibenine, B.

1979   ** "Le dieu Jazomir," *WSlAlm* 4, 433–8.   V.4
                                                  V.3

1981   ** "Un modèle conceptuel pour l'étymologie du slave   V.3
          commun *vorgŭ* 'ennemi'," *IJSLP* 23, 13–23.

Ondruš, Š.

1975   ** "Praslovanský původ českých pomenovaní psa   V.3
          'věžník' a 'vyžle'," *Slavia* 44, 337–40.   V.2

1977a * Review of *Słownik prasłowiański*. Tom 2   V.1
          (C-D) by F. Sławski, ed., *Slavia* 46, 417–24.

1977b * Review of *Ètimologičeskij slovar' slavjanskix*   V.1
          jazykov. Praslavjanskij leksičeskij fond, vyp. 3 by O. N.
          Trubačev, ed., *Slavia* 46, 417–24.

Opuscula Polono-Slavica

1979   *Opuscula Polono-Slavica. Munera linguistica*
          Stanislao Urbańczyk dedicata. J. Sarafewicz *et al.*, eds.
          (Wrocław: Ossolineum).

Opuscula Slavica

1976   *Opuscula Slavica et linguistica. Festschrift*

für Alexander Issatschenko, H. D. Pohl and N. Salnikow,
eds. (Klagenfurt: J. Heyn).

Ossadnik, E. M.

1979 * Review of *Historisch-etymologisches Wörterbuch*   V.1
        der ober- und niedersorbischen Sprache. 1: A- bohot by H.
        Schuster-Šewc, *WSlJb* 25, 153–4.

Osten, G.

1978 * *Slawische Siedlungsspuren im Raum um Uelzen, Bad*   VI.4
        Bevensen und Lünenburg (Uelzen: Selbstverlag des   VI.3
        Museums- und Heimatvereins des Kreises Uelzen)
        (= *Uelzener Beiträge*, Heft 7).

Otkupščicov, J. V.

1974 * "Litovskij jazyk i praslavjanskie rekonstrukcii,"   VI.1
        Baltistica 10, 7–20.

Otrębska-Jabłońska, A. (Otrembskaja-Jablonskaja)

1972 * "Ob odnom arxaičeskom zemledel'českom termine,"   V.3
        Russkoe i slavjanskoe jazykoznanie, 200–4.   V.2
                                                                    VI.3

Otrębski, J. (Otrembskij)

1972 ** "Iz oblasti slavjanskogo i baltijskogo   III.2
        slovoobrazovanija (st.-slav. *měsęcь* i lit.   III.4
        měnuo)," *Balto-slavjanskij sbornik*, 186–92.   VI.1

Palmaitis, M. L (Palmajtis)

1981 ** "Ot grečeskoj sistemy k slavjanskoj. K tipologii   III.5
        vida," *VJa* 1981.4, 45–54.   V.3
                                                                    VI.1

Panzer, B.

1978a ** *Der genetische Aufbau des Russischen*   I.4
        (Heidelberg: Winter).   VI.3
                                                                    VI.1

1978b ** "Struktur und Entwicklung des slavischen   III.5
        Verbalstammklassensystems," *Referate und Beiträge zum VIII.*
        Internationalen Slavistenkongress (Munich: Sagner), 95–126.
        95–126.

Papers in Slavic Philology

1977   *Papers in Slavic Philology*, 1. *In Honor of James*
        Ferrell, B. A. Stolz, ed. (Ann Arbor: Department of Slavic
        Languages and Literatures, University of Michigan).

Papp, F.

1973   ∗∗ "O nekotoryx obščix čertax slavjanskix   V.4
         zaimstvovanij v vengerskom jazyke," *Studia Slavica*   VI.1
         19, 225–34.

Pavlov, B. N.

1974   ∗∗ "Ob ėtimologičeskoj prirode slavjanskogo   V.3
         jako," *ZfSl* 19, 736–40.   V.2

Pătrut, I.

1972   ∗∗ "Pierwsze kontakty językowe   VI.2
         słowiańsko-romańsko-greckie a okres trwania   VI.1
         języka prasłowiańskiego," *RS* 33, 7–19.   VI.3

1976   ∗∗ "O edinstve i prodolžitel'nosti obščeslavjanskogo   VI.1
         jazyka," *RS* 37, 3–9.   VI.3

Penjak, S. I.

1972   ∗∗ "K voprosu o vremeni zaselenija slavjanami   VI.4
         Karpatskogo bassejna," *Issledovanija po istorii*   VI.3
         slavjanskix i balkanskix narodov. Ėpoxa
         srednevekov'ja. Kievskaja Rus' i ee slavjanskie sosedi,
         V. D. Koroljak *et al.*, eds. (Moscow: Nauka), 68–77.

Pennington, A. E.
1980   ∗ Review of *Grammaire comparée des langues slaves.*   I.2
         Tome V: *La syntaxe* by A. Vaillant, *SEER* 58, 101–2.

Perfecky, G. A.

1981   ∗ Review of *A Historical Phonology of the Ukrainian*   II.1
         Language by G. Y. Shevelov, *SEEJ* 25, 134–6.

Pianka, W.

1974   ∗ "Fonem /ˢt'/ w języku staro-cerkiewno-   II.4
         słowiańskim na tle słowiańskich   VI.3
         procesów palatalizacyjnych," *Studia filol. pol. i słow.*
         13, 197–211.

Pisani, V.

1974a ∗∗ *Indogermanisch und Europa* (Munich: Fink).   VI.1
                                                                        III.2

1974b ∗∗ "Zu russ. *devjanosto* 'neunzig'," *Studia*   V.2
         indoeuropejskie, 171–3.

Pizłówna, B.

1972   ∗∗ "Element prasłowiański w słownictwie   I.4
         współczesnego języka serbsko-chorwackiego,"   V.1
         Studia filol. pol. i słow. 12, 285–300.

Plevačová, H.

1974   ** "Na okraj slovanského *ner-*, *nor-* 'nořiti',"   V.2
         Slavia 43, 357–61.   II.3

Pohl, H. D.

1973   ** "Verbale Rektionskomposita mit regierendem   III.3
         Vorderglied im Slavischen und in anderen   III.5
         indogermanischen Sprachen," *WSlJb* 18, 190–202.   VI.4
         V.3

1974   ** "Reflexe der indogermanischen Laryngale im   II.3
         Slavischen," *WSlJb* 20, 144–51.   II.2
         II.4
         VI.1

1975a   ** "Das slavische Imperfekt auf *-ěax-* und *-aax-*,"   III.3
         ZfslPh 38, 349–60.   III.5
         III.2

1975b   ** "Slova iranskogo proisxoždenija v russkom jazyke,"   V.4
         RL 2, 81–90.   VI.1
         VI.3

1977   ** *Die Nominalkomposition im Alt- und Gemeinslavischen.*   III.3
         Ein Beitrag zur slavischen, indogermamischen und   III.4
         allgemeinen Wortbildung (Klagenfurt: Klagenfurter
         Sprachwissenschaftliche Gesellschaft). (=*Klagenfurter*
         Beiträge zur Sprachwissenschaft, Beiheft 1).

1977/78 * "Historische slavische Sprachwissenschaft seti 1945,"   VI.2
         Kratylos 22, 1–39.

1980   ** "Slavisch *st* aus älterem **pt*," *Die Sprache*   II.4
         21.1, 62–3.   II.5

Polański, K.

1971-   * *Słownik etymologiczny języka Drzewian*   V.1
         połabskich. Zesz. 2: D'üzd-l'otü (1971), zesz.
         3: L'ǫdü-Perě (1973), zesz. 4: Perět-Ŕottʿə(Wrocław:
         Ossolineum).

1979   ** "Uwagi o rozwoju prasłowiańskiej deklinacji   III.2
         atematycznej," *Opuscula Polono-Slavica*, 291–5.   III.4
         III.3

1982   ** "Some Remarks on the Development of Jers in   II.5
         Polabian," *Studies for Stankiewicz*, 379–81.   II.3
         VI.3

Polák, V.

1973a   ∗∗ "Konsolidace slovanského jazykového typu v   VI.1
širších východoevropských souvislostech," *Slavia* 42,
125–34.

1973b   ∗ "Několik poznámek k problematice substrátových   V.4
slov v jazycích západoslovanských," *Slavia* 42,   VI.3
267–77.

1977   ∗∗ "Etymologické přispěvky k slov. démonologii,"   V.3
Slavia 46, 283–91.   V.2
     V.4

1980   ∗ "Metodologie etymologického rozboru v slovanských   V.1
jazycích," *Slavia* 49, 321–37.

Popowska-Taborska, H.

1975   ∗∗ "Z problematyki badawczej nawiązań leksykalnych   V.1
(na materiale kaszubsko-południowosłowiańskim),"   VI.3
RS 36, 3–16.

1981   ∗ "Współczesne prace językoznawcze nad   VI.4
etnogenezą Słowian oraz zarysowujące się
perspektywy badawcze," *RS* 41, 23–34.

Press, J. I.

1973   ∗∗ "The Syntax of Absolute Constructions in Slavonic and   IV
Baltic, with Reference to Finno-Ugrian," *SEER* 51,   VI.1
11–21.

1977   ∗ "The Place of the Vowel *y* in the Development of   II.3
the Slavonic Languages," *SEER* 55, 470–90.

Priestly, T. M. S.

1978   ∗∗ "Affective Sound-Change in Early Slavic," *Canadian*   II.5
Contributions to the VIII International Congress of Slavists,
Z. Folejewski *et al.*, eds. (Ottawa: Canadian Association of
Slavists), 143–66.

Prinz, J.

1977   ∗∗ "Die Entwicklung des slavischen Auslauts bis zum   II.5
Wirksamwerden des Gesetzes der offenen Silben,"
Commentationes Linguisticae, 259–74.

1978   ∗∗ "Der Reflex der vier baltischen Intonationstypen   II.2
der litauischen Nominalflexion in den ältesten   VI.1
erschliessbaren slavischen Intonationsverhältnissen,"
Slavistische Studien VIII, 403–15.

Puhvel, J.

1973 ** "Nature and Means of Comparison in   VI.1
        Proto-Indo-European Grammar," *JIES* 1, 145–54.

Račeva, M.

1979 * K ėtimologičeskoj problematike rannix zaimstvovanij   V.4
        semitskogo proisxoždenija v slavjanskix jazykax," *ZfSl*
        24, 105–14.

Raecke, J.

1979 ** "Urslavische Monophthongierung und 'Gesetz der offenen   II.5
        Silbe' (Zur Frage der 'Begründung' von Lautwandel),"   II.3
        Slavistische Linguistik 1978, J. Raecke and C. Sappok, eds.
        (Munich: Sagner) (= *Slavistische Beiträge* 133), 170–201.

Reinhart, J. M.

1974 * Review of *Historisch-etymologisches Wörterbuch der*   V.1
        ober- und niedersorbischen Sprache (*Probeheft*) by H.
        Schuster-Šewc, *WSlJb* 20, 205–6.

1976 * Review of *Grammaire comparée des langues slaves.*   I.2
        Tome IV: *La formation des noms* by A. Vaillant, *WSlJb*
        22, 125–9.

Robinson, D. F.

1977 ** "A Note on 'Thematic' and 'Athematic' in the   III.2
        Baltic Verb," *FS* 1, 224–7.   III.5

Roman Jakobson: Echoes

1977   *Roman Jakobson: Echoes of His Scholarship*, D. Armstrong
        and C. H. van Schooneveld, eds. (Lisse: Peter de Ridder).

Rospond, S.

1974/76 ** *Stratygrafia słowiańskich nazw miejscowych*   VI.4
        (*Próbny atlas toponomastyczny*) (3 vols, vol. 3 = *Mapy*)
        (Wrocław: Ossolineum).   German edition in prep.
        (Heidelberg: Winter).

1975 ** "O historycznej fonologii ogólnosłowiańskiej w   II.1
        świetle onomastyki," *Bereiche der Slavistik*, 261–75.   VI.4

1977 * "Zastępstwo ps. *tj dj* > *št žd* w   II.4
        nazewnictwie pd.-słowiańskim," *Commentationes*   VI.4
        Linguisticae, 311–20.

1978 * "Uwagi o toponimach z suf. *-ynja*, czes. *-yně*,"   VI.4
        Slavia 47, 371–5.   III.3
                                                                   III.4

1979 ** "Terminologia topograficzna w nazewnictwie   VI.4

geograficznym," *Opuscula Polono-Slavica*, 305–12.

Rudnicki, M.

| 1971 | * "O wyrazie *glaz* 'bursztyn'," *SlOcc* 28/29, 221–4. | V.3 V.2 VI.4 |

| 1972 | ** "O prakolebce Słowian," *Z polskich studiów slawistycznych*, 321–31. | VI.4 |

| 1974 | ** "Resztki językowe wróżdy i pokory," *SlOcc* 31, 97–105. | V.3 V.2 V.4 |

Rudnyc'kyj, J. B.

| 1971 | ** "Do peredistoriji praslov'janskoho vyzvuku," *Symbolae in honorem Shevelov*, 360–65. | II.5 |

| 1974 | ** "Slavic Terms for 'god'," *Antiquitates Indogermanicae*, 111–12. | V.3 V.2 V.4 |

Russkoe i slavjanskoe jazykoznanie

| 1972 | *Russkoe i slavjanskoe jazykoznanie. K 70-letiju člena-korrespondenta AN-SSSR R. I. Avanesova*, F. P. Filin *et al.*, eds. (Moscow: Nauka). | |

Rybakov, B. A.

| 1978 | ** "Istoričeskie sud'by praslavjan," *Istorija, kul'tura ...*, 182–96. | VI.4 |

Řeháček, L.

| 1979 | * Review of *Balto-severnoslavjanskie jazykovye svjazi* by A. P. Nepokupnyj, *Slavia* 48, 283–8. | VI.1 |

Sadnik, L. & R. Aitzetmüller

| 1975 | ** *Vergleichendes Wörterbuch der slavischen Sprachen* Band I: A-B (Lfgg. 1–7: 1963–75) (Wiesbaden: Harrassowitz). | V.1 |

Samilov, M

| 1975 | ** "Zero-Grade Laryngeals as *o* in Slavic," *Xenia Slavica*, 179–84. | II.3 II.2 VI.1 |

Samsonov, N. G.

| 1973 | ** *Drevnerusskij jazyk* (Moscow: Vysšaja škola). | VI.4 VI.3 I.4 |

Savignac, D.

  1975   * "Common Slavic *vьx- in Northern Old Russian,"   II.4
              IJSLP 19, 41–52.   VI.2

Scatton, E. A.

  1978   * "Old Church Slavonic *tj/dj* ~ *št/žd*,"   II.4
              Linguistics 208, 13–21.   VI.3

Schelesniker, H.

  1972   * "*Slověne* und *slověnskъ*," *AnzfslPh* 6,   V.3
              119–23.   V.2
                                                    VI.1

  1975   ** "Turanische Einflüsse im urslavischen Sprachsystem,"   II.3
              WSlJb 21, 237–41.   VI.1

  1975/77 * Review of *Slavic Accentuation: A Study in*   II.2
              Relative Chronology by F. H. H. Kortlandt, *Kratylos* 20,
              141–6.

  1976   ** "Der slavische Genitiv auf -*y*/-*ę* und der   II.5
              awestische Lokativ auf -*ąm*," *Opuscula Slavica*, 383–91.   III.2
                                                         III.4

  1976/77 * Review of *Die alpenslawischen Personennamen* by   VI.3
              O. Kronsteiner, *Kratylos* 21, 207–8.

  1982   * Review of *Studien zu den slavischen Gewässernamen*   VI.4
              und Gewässerbezeichnungen. Ein Beitrag zur Frage nach
              der Urheimat der Slaven by J. Udolph, *AnzfslPh* 13, 77–86.

Schenker, A. M. (Šenker)

  1981   ** "Drevnecerkovnoslavjanskoe *iskrъ* 'blizko' i   V.3
              ego proizvodnye," *VJa* 1981.2, 110–14.   V.2

Schlimpert, G.

  1978   ** *Slawische Personennamen in mittelalterlichen*   VI.4
              Quellen zur deutschen Geschichte (Berlin:
              Akademie-Verlag).

  1979   * Review of *Die alpenslawischen Personennamen* by O.   VI.3
              Kronsteiner, *ZfSl* 24, 577–8.

Schmalstieg, W. R.

  1971   ** "The Slavic First Person Singular," *Symbolae*   II.5
              in honorem Shevelov, 375–6.   III.2
                                                        III.5

  1972   ** "Die Entwicklung der *ā*-Deklination im   III.2
              Slavischen," *ZfslPh* 36, 130–46.   III.4
                                                        II.5

1973   * "New Thoughts on Indo-European Phonology," *KZ*   II.1
        87, 99–157.   VI.1

1974a ** "Some Morphological Implications of the   III.2
        Indo-European Passage of *-oN* to *ō*," *KZ* 88,   II.5
        187–98.

1974b ** "A Question without a Clear Answer: One Aspect of   VI.1
        the Relations between Baltic and Slavic," *Lietuvių*   II.4
        Katalikų Mokslo Akademija Suvažiavimo Darbų 8,
        [Rome] 1974.

1976   ** *An Introduction to Old Church Slavic* (Cambridge,   I.4
        MA: Slavica).   VI.3
                                                                VI.1

Schmeja, H.

1976   ** "Zum idg. Wort für Tochter," *Opuscula Slavica*,   V.3
        393–400.

Schmid, W. P.

1975/76 * Review of *Lexikalische Sonderübereinstimmungen*   VI.1
        zwischen dem Slavischen, Baltischen und Germanischen by
        C. S. Stang, *IF* 80, 325–7.

1979   * "Urheimat und Ausbreitung der Slawen," *ZfO* 28,   VI.4
        405–15.

Schmidt, K. H.

1977   ** "Zum Problem des Genitivs der *o*-Stämme im   III.2
        Baltischen und Slavischen," *Commentationes Linguisticae*,
        335–44.

Schröpfer, J.

1977   * "De Nominis Vi Ac Nominibus," *Korrespondenzen*:   V.3
        Festschrift für Dietrich Gerhardt aus Anlass des 65.   V.2
        Geburtstages, A. Engel-Braunschmidt and A. Schmücker,
        eds. (= *Marburger Abhandlungen zur Geschichte und*
        Kultur Osteuropas. Bd. 14). (Giessen: W. Schmitz).

Schuster-Šewc, H.

1971a ** "Ergänzungen zur Etymologie von slaw.   III.3
        kъniga 'Buch'," *ZfSl* 16, 47–51.   III.4
                                                                V.3

1971b * "Slawische Etymologien," *ZfSl* 16, 369–76.   V.1

1973a * *Historisch-etymologisches Wörterbuch der ober-*   V.1
        und niedersorbischen Sprache (*Probeheft*) (Bauzen:
        Domowina).

1973b * "Zur Frage der südslawischen *Perunika*-Namen,"   V.3
       JF 30, 213–21.   V.2
                                                            VI.3

1975a * Review of *Ètimologičeskij slovar' slavjanskix*   V.1
       jazykov. Praslavjanskij leksičeskij fond, vyp. 1 by O. N.
       Trubačev, ed., *ZfSl* 20, 824–33.

1975b ** *Slawische Wortstudien. Sammelband des*   V.1
       internationalen Symposiums zur etymologischen und
       historischen Erforschung des slawischen Wortschatzes.
       Leipzig, 11–13.10. 1972, H. Schuster-Šewc, ed.
       (Bauzen: Domowina).

1976   * "Rozważania etymologiczne (Dolnołużyckie   V.2
       jěsny 'prędki, szybki', 'wcześnie'; *jěśćiś*   V.3
       'błyszczeć, świecić' i pochodne," *SlOcc* 33, 75–81.

1977a ** "Die Sprache der Lausitzer Sorben und ihre Stellung   VI.3
       im Rahmen der slawischen Sprachen," *ZfPhon* 30, 10–27.

1977b ** "Historia języków łużyckich i sprawa jej   VI.3
       periodizacji," *PF* 27, 389–99.   VI.2

1978- * *Historisch-etymologisches Wörterbuch der ober- und*   V.1
       niedersorbischen Sprache. 1: A-bohot (Bauzen: I.4
       Domowina).

1979   ** "Zur Bedeutung der sorbischen Lexik für die slawische   V.1
       historisch-etymologische Wortforschung," *ZfSl*   VI.3
       24, 120–31.

1980   ** "Etimologija i istorija južnoslovenske reči   V.2
       vatra," Naučni sastanak slavista u Vukove dane.   VI.3
       Referati i saopštenja 8 (Belgrade: Međunarodni   II.5
       slavistički centar), 345–9.   V.4

1982   ** "Die Ausgliederung der westslawischen Sprachen   VI.3
       aus dem Urslawischen mit besonderer Berücksichtigung   VI.2
       des Sorbischen," *Lětopis Instituta za serbski*   V.1
       ludospyt A 29/2, 113–40.

Schütz, J.

1981   ** "Methodisches zu eimen neuen Wörterbuch   V.3
       (*čeljadъ, čeljadъ, čelověkъ*)," *ZfslPh*   V.2
       42, 14–19.

Sedov, V. V.

1978   * "Slavjane i irancy v drevnosti," *Istorija*,   VI.4
       kul'tura…, 227–40.   VI.1

1980   * "Nekotorye arealy arxaičeskix slavjanskix gidronimov   VI.4

i arxeologija," *Perspektivy razvitija slavjanskoj onomastiki*, A. V. Superanskaja and N. V. Podol'skaja, eds. (Moscow: Nauka), 141–7.

1981   ** "Načal'nyj ėtap slavjanskogo rasselenija v oblasti   VI.4
dneprovskix baltov," *Balto-slavjanskoe issledovanija*   VI.1
1980, 45–52.

Shapiro, M.

1982a   ** "Slavic *nejęsytь* 'pelican':   V.3
Perpetuation of a Septuagintal Solecism," *SEER* 60,   V.2
161–71.   V.4
                             VI.4

1982b   ** "Neglected Evidence of Dioscurism (Divine Twinning)   V.3
in the Old Slavic Pantheon," *JIES* 10, 137–65.

Shevelov, G. Y.

1976   ** "On the Problem of the Participation of *y* and   II.3
i in the Loss of the *jers*," *JF* 32, 121–41.

1979   ** *A Historical Phonology of the Ukrainian Language*   II.1
(Heidelberg: Winter).   I.4

1980   * Review of *Some Reflexes of the Indo-European*   II.2
Laryngeals in the Slav Prosodic Paradigms by R. Slonek,
SEEJ 24, 456–7.

1982   ** "Meždu praslavjanskim i russkim," *RL* 6,   VI.3
353–76.   VI.4

Skupskij, B. I.

1978   ** "Voprosy istočnikov rekonstrukcii sintaksisa   IV
pervonačal'nogo slavjanskogo perevoda evangelija,"
WSlJb 25, 107–24.

Slavistische Studien VIII

1978   *Slavistische Studien zum VIII. Internationalen*
Slavistenkongress in Zagreb 1978, J. Holthusen, W.
Kasack, and R. Olesch, eds. (Cologne-Vienna-Graz:
Böhlau).

Slavjanska filologija

1973   *Slavjanska filologija. Dokladi i statii za VII*
Meždunaroden kongress na slavistite. Tom 12.
Ezikoznanie, V.I. Georgiev *et al.*, eds. (Sofia: BAN).

1978   *Slavjanska filologija. Dokladi i statii za VIII*
Meždunaroden kongress na slavistite. Tom 15.
Ezikoznanie, V.I. Georgiev *et al.*, eds. (Sofia: BAN).

Slavjanskoe i balkanskoe jazykoznanie

1975   *Slavjanskoe i balkanskoe jazykoznanie. Problemy interferencii i jazykovyx kontaktov*, S.B. Bernštejn *et al.*, eds. (Moscow: Nauka).

1981   *Slavjanskoe i balkanskoe jazykoznanie. Problemy morfonologii*, S. B. Bernštejn *et al.*, eds. (Moscow: Nauka).

Slavjanskoe jazykoznanie

1973   *Slavjanskoe jazykoznanie. VII Meždunarodnyj s″ezd slavistov. Varšava, avgust 1973g. Doklady sovetskoj delegacii*, S. B. Bernštejn *et al.*, eds. (Moscow: Nauka).

1978   *Slavjanskoe jazykoznanie. VIII Meždunarodnyj s″ezd slavistov.* Zagreb-Ljubljana, sentjabr, 1978g. *Doklady sovetskoj delegacii*, V.I. Borkovskij *et al.*, eds. (Moscow: Nauka).

Slonek, R.

1972   ** "The Accentological Works of V. A. Dybo and the   II.2
Reflexes of Indo-European Laryngeals in Slav," *MSS* 7,   II.3
84–9.

1979   * *Some Reflexes of the Indo-European Laryngeals in the*   II.2
Slav Prosodic Paradigms (Amsterdam: Hakkert).

Slupski, A.

1971   ** "Slavisch 'Zauberer, Hexe' und Verwandtes,"   V.3
ZfslPh 35, 302–20.

Sławski, F.

1954-   * *Słownik etymologiczny języka polskiego* (Cracow: V.1
Towarzystwo miłośników języka polskiego).

1974   * "O słowiańskich formacjach na *-do, -da,*   III.3
-dь," *Studia indoeuropejskie*, 213–16.   III.4
   VI.1

1974-   ** *Słownik prasłowiański.* F. Sławski, ed.   V.1
Tom 1: A-B (1974), Tom 2: C-D (1976), Tom 3: D   III.3
(1979), Tom 4: D (1981) (Wrocław: Ossolineum).

1976   * "Das urslavische Suffix *-tъ*," *WSlJb* 22, 74–7.   III.4

1979   ** "Z mitologii słowiańskiej," *Opuscula*   V.3
Polono-Slavica, 369–71.   V.2
   V.4

1980   * "Prasłowiański suffiks *-ęt-,*" *V čest Georgiev*,   III.3
386–92.   III.4

1982   ** "Common Slavic *drugъ* and its Derivatives   V.2

(Methodological Observations)," *Studies for*	V.3
Stankiewicz, 423–7.	III.3

Sós, Á. C.

1973	** *Die slawische Bevölkerung Westungarns im 9.*	VI.4
	Jahrhundert (Munich: C. H. Beck'sche	VI.3
	Verlagsbuchhandlung) (= *Münchner Beiträge zur Vor-*	VI.1
	und Frühgeschichte 22).	

Stang, C. S.

1972	** *Lexikalische Sonderübereinstimmungen zwischen dem*	VI.1
	Slavischen, Baltischen und Germanischen (Oslo-Bergen-	
	Tromsø: Universitetsforlaget).	

Stanislav, J.

1973	** *Dejiny slovenského jazyka* (vols. 4, 5) (Bratislava: SAV).	I.4
		IV

Stankiewicz, E.

1973	** "The Historical Phonology of Common Slavic,"	II.1
	IJSLP 16, 179–92.	

1979	** *Studies in Slavic Morphophonemics and Accentology*	II.2
	(Ann Arbor: Department of Slavic Languages and	II.6
	Literatures, University of Michigan).	

1982	* "A reply to the review of my book 'Studies in Slavic	II.2
	Morphophonemics and Accentology'," *Lingua* 56, 179–81.	

Steensland, L.

1973	** *Die Distribution der urindogermanischen sogenannten*	II.4
	Gutturale (Uppsala: Almqvist & Wiksell) (= *Studia*	VI.1
	Slavica Upsaliensia 12).	

1974/75	* "Ein Beitrag zur Diskussion anlässlich R. Channons	II.4
	On the Place of the Progressive Palatalization of Velars in	
	Relative Chronology of Slavic," *IJSLP* 21, 90–106.	

Stepanov, J. S.

1978	** "Slavjanskij glagol'nyj vid i baltijskaja diateza	III.5
	(problema obščego genezisa i rekonstrukcii),"	III.3
	Slavjanskoe jazykoznanie VIII, 335–63.	III.2
		VI.1

Stieber, Z.

1970/72	** "Jeszcze o prasłowiańskim supinum,"	III.2
	RicSlav 17–19, 505–6.	III.5

1972a	* "O nazwie wsi *Mlądz* pod Warszawą," *WSlJb*	VI.4
	17, 287–8.	

1972b * "O drevnix slovensko-zapadnoslavjanskix jazykovyx   VI.3
svjazjax," *Russkoe i slavjanskoe jazykoznanie*, 309–10.

1973a ** *Zarys gramatyki porównawczej języków*   I.2
słowiańskich. Cz. II, zesz. 2: *Fleksja werbalna*   III.5
(Warsaw: PWN).   III.2

1973b ** *A Historical Phonology of the Polish Language*   II.1
(Heidelberg: Winter).   I.4

1973c ** "Izoglosa południosłowiańsko-węgierska,"   VI.3
JF 30, 211.   V.3

1974   * "Jeszcze o scs. *šť* z psł. *tj* i *kť*,"   II.4
Studia filol. pol. i słow. 13, 235–6.   VI.3

1976   * "Jeszcze o rzekomym prasłowiańskim *o*,"   II.3
Studia filol. pol. i słow. 15, 285–8.   VI.2

1980   * "Jeszcze o scs. *vyja*," *V čest Georgiev*, 318.   V.3
                                                               V.2
                                                               III.3

Stipa, G. J.

1974   ** "Ist das russische Akanje durch Substratwirkung   II.3
entstanden?" *ZfslPh* 37, 325–42.   VI.1
                                                               VI.2

Stolz, B. A.

1980   * Review of *Der genetische Aufbau des Russischen* by B. I.4
Panzer, *SEEJ* 24, 194–6.

Stone, G.

1980   * Review of *Historisch-etymologisches Wörterbuch der* V.1
ober- und niedersorbischen Sprachen. 1: A-bohot by H.
Schuster-Šewc, *SEER* 58, 270–2.

Strukturno-tipologičeskoe issledovanija

1973   *Strukurno-tipologičeskie issledovanija v oblasti
grammatiki slavjanskix jazykov*, A. A. Zaliznjak, ed.
(Moscow: Nauka).

Strumins'skyj, B.

1979/80 ** "Were the Antes Eastern Slavs," *Eucharisterion*,   VI.4
595–608.   VI.3

Studia indoeuropejskie

1974   *Studia indoeuropejskie/Études indo-européennes*
[Fs. J. Sarafewicz], J. Kuryłowicz *et al.*, eds.
(Wroclaw: Ossolineum).

Studia linguistica

1978   *Studia linguistica Alexandro Vasilii filio Issatschenko
        a collegis amicisque oblata*, H. Birnbaum *et al.*, eds.
        (Lisse: Peter de Ridder).

Studies for Stankiewicz

1982   *Slavic Linguistics and Poetics. Studies for Edward Stankiewicz
        on his 60th Birthday 17 November 1980*, K. E. Naylor *et al.*, eds.
        (= *IJSLP* 25/26, Columbus, OH: Slavica).

Symbolae in honorem Shevelov

1971   *Symbolae in honorem Georgii Y. Shevelov. Zbirnyk na
        pošanu prof. d-ra Jurija Ševel'ova*, W. E. Harkins, O.
        Horbatsch and J. P. Hursky, eds. (Munich: Ukrainische
        Freie Universität) (= *Naukovyj zbirnyk* 7).

Symonovič, Ė. A.

1978   ∗ "Kul'tura karpatskix kurganov i ee rol' v ėtnogeneze   VI.4
           slavjan," *Istorija, kul'tura …*, 197–209.   VI.3

Szymański, T.

1980   ∗ "Prasłowiańskie dial. wsch. *zolkъ*," *RS* 40,   V.3
           43–4.   VI.3

Šaumjan, S. (Shaumyan)

1977   ∗∗ "Roman Jakobson's Contribution to the Study of Slavic   II.1
           Historical Phonology and Phonetics," *Roman
           Jakobson: Echoes*, 421–33.

Šaur, V.

1975   ∗∗ *Etymologie slovanských příbuzenských termínů*   V.3
           (Prague: Academia).   V.2

1977a   ∗ "Kup(a)/kopa-kuč(k)a/kočka," *Slavia*   V.3
           46, 12–20.   V.2

1977b   ∗ Review of *Slawische Wortstudien. Sammelband des   V.1
           internationalen Symposiums zur etymologischen und
           historischen Erforschung des slawischen Wortschatzes* by H.
           Schuster-Šewc, ed., *Slavia* 46, 84–7.

1978   ∗∗ "Orzga, oržьnь, orditi, orbъ(?)" *Slavia*   V.3
           47, 30–8.   II.3
                                                                         II.2

1979   ∗ "Zametki po slavjanskoj ėtimologii," *ZfSl*   V.3
           24, 115–19.   V.2

1980a   ∗∗ "Ke genezi sloves typu 'baviti, slaviti',"   V.3
           Slavia 49, 19–25.   V.2

1980b   *   "Etymologie ruského *naróstit' sja* a výrazů   V.3
           příbuzných," *Slavia* 49, 208–14.   VI.3

1980c   *   Review of *Bălgarski etimologičen rečnik.* Tom 1, A-Z by   V.1
           V. Georgiev, *Slavia* 49, 415–17.

1981   **   "O deverbativním původu některých adjektiv   III.3
           (*gluchъ, slĕpъ, prostъ, pustъ* i jiných),"   V.3
           Slavia 50, 52–60.

Šrámek, R.

1979   *   Review of *Slawische Personennamen in*   VI.4
           mittelalterlichen Quellen zur deutschen Geschichte by
           G. Schlimpert, *Slavia* 48, 405–9.

Taszycki, W.

1972   *   "Kilka uwag o rzeczownikach na -*y* (*-ū-),"   III.3
           RS 33, 3–6.   III.4
                                                    VI.4

Timberlake, A.

1974   **   *The Nominative Object in Slavic, Baltic, and West*   IV
           Finnic (Munich: Sagner) (= *Slavistische Beiträge* 82).   VI.1

1981   **   "Dual Reflexes of *dj* in Slavic and a   VI.3
           Morphological Constraint on Sound Change," *IJSLP* 23,   II.4
           25–54.   II.6

Tolstoj, N. I.

1973   **   "K rekonstrukcii praslavjanskoj frazeologii,"   IV
           Slavjanskoe jazykoznanie VII, 272–93.   V.2

1978a   **   "O neposledovatel'nosti pervoj palatalizacii   II.4
           slavjanskix zadnenebnyx soglasnyx," *Linguistica* 17, 33–47.

1978b   **   "O slavjanskix nazvanijax derev'ev: V.3
           sosna-xvoja-bor," *Vostočnoslavjanskoe i obščee*
           jazykoznanie, 115–27.

Tolstoj, N. I. & S. M. Tolstaja

1978   **   "K rekonstrukcii drevneslavjanskoj duxovoj kul'tury   V.3
           (lingvo- i ètnografičeskij aspekt)," *Slavjanskoe*
           jazykoznanie VIII, 364–85.

Toporov, V. N.

1973   **   "O dvux praslavjanskix terminax iz oblasti drevnego   V.3
           prava v svjazi s indoevropejskimi sootvetstvijami,"   V.2
           Strukturno-tipologičeskie issledovanija, 119–39.

1975a   **   "Neskol'ko soobraženij o proisxoždenii fleksij   III.2
           slavjanskogo genitiva," *Bereiche der Slavistik*, 287–96.   III.4

1975b   ** "K ob″jasneniju nekorotyx slavjanskix slov   V.3
          mifologičeskogo xaraktera v svjazi s vozmožnymi   VI.1
          drevnimi bližnevostočnymi paralleljami," *Slavjanskoe
          i balkanskoe jazykoznanie*, 3–49.

1975c   * Review of *Indo-European and Indo-Europeans: Papers*   VI.1
          *Presented at the Third Indo-European Conference at the
          University of Pennsylvania*, by G. Cardona *et al.*, eds.
          (Philadelphia: University of Pennsylvania Press, 1970),
          IJSLP 21, 71–89.

1980   * "Baltijskij èlement k severu ot Karpat: VI.4
          Ètnonimičeskaja osnova *Galind-* kak znak baltijskoj   VI.1
          periferii," *SlOr* 29, 247–52.

Trost, K.

1978   * "Slav. *idetъ* : *šьdъ* : *choditi* und das   III.5
          Problem der Fortbewegungsverba," *WdSl* 23, N. F. 2.1,   III.3
          115–121.   II.3

Trubačev, O. N.

1973   * "Leksikografija i ètimologija," *Slavjanskoe   II.4
          jazykoznanie VII*, 294–313.

1974   ** "Rannie slavjanskie ètnonimy—svideteli migracii   V.3
          slavjan," *VJa* 1974.6, 48–67.   VI.3
                                                             VI.4

1974-   ** *Ètimologičeskij slovar' slavjanskix jazykov.*   V.1
          Praslavjanskij leksičeskij fond. O. N. Trubačev, ed.,
          Vyp. 1-(8-) (Moscow: Nauka).

1977   ** "Lingvističeskaja periferija drevnejšego   VI.1
          slavjanstva. Indoarijcy v Severnom Pričernomore,"   VI.3
          VJa 1977.6, 13–29. Reprinted in *Slavjanskoe   VI.4
          jazykoznanie VIII*, 386–405.

1978   ** "Serebro," *Vostočnoslavjanskoe i obščee   V.3
          jazykoznanie*, 95–102.   V.2

1979a   ** "'Staraja Skifija' *Archaíē Skufíē* Gerodota   VI.4
          (IV, 99) i slavjane. Lingvističeskij aspekt," *VJa*
          1979.4, 29–45.

1979b   ** "Zur Vorbereitung des Etymologischen Wörterbuches   V.1
          der slawischen Sprachen," *ZfSl* 24, 143–9.

1980a   ** "Ob odnom slučae glagol'nogo suppletivizma: III.2
          praslav. *něti* 'nesti, prinosit'," *V čest*   III.5
          Georgiev, 273–4.

1980b   ** "Rekonstrukcija slov i ix značenij," *VJa* 1980.3,   V.3

3–14.

1981	* "Replika po balto-slavjanskomu voprosu,"	VI.1
	Balto-slavjanskie issledovanija 1980, 3–6.	
1982	** "Jazykoznanie i ètnogenez slavjan. Drevnie	VI.4
	slavjane po dannym ètimologii i onomastiki,"	V.2
	VJa 1982.4, 10–26; 1982.5, 3–17.	V.3
		V.4

Trummer, M.

1978	** "Zu den slavischen Nasalvokalen und den Partners	II.3
	-y (-a): -ę (-ē)- in der Flexion," *WSlJb* 24, 254–6.	II.5
		III.2
		III.4

Tschiżewskij, D.

1977	** "Remnants of a Common Slavic Declension Group,"	V.3
	Papers in Slavic Philology, 302–3.	III.3
		III.4

Udolph, J.

1979a	** *Studien zu den slavischen Gewässernamen und*	VI.4
	Gewässerbezeichnungen. Ein Beitrag zur Frage nach der	
	Urheimat der Slaven (Heidelberg: Winter).	
1979b	** "Zum Stand der Diskussion um die Urheimat der	VI.4
	Slaven," *Beiträge zur Namenforschung*, N. F. 14.1, 1–25.	
1980	** "Slavische Etymologien und ihre Überprüfung an	VI.4
	Hand von Gewässer-, Orts- und Flurnamen,"	V.1
	Lautgeschichte und Etymologie, M. Mayrhofer, M. Peters	
	O. E. Pfeiffer, eds. (Wiesbaden: Reichert) (= *Akten der*	
	VI. Fachtagung der Indogermanischen Gesellschaft,. Wien,	
	24.–29. September 1978), 523–41.	
1981a	** "Zur Toponymie Pomesaniens," *Beiträge zur*	VI.4
	Namenforschung 16, 422–43.	
1981b	** "Die Landnahme der Ostslaven im Lichte der	VI.4
	Namenforschung," *Jahrbücher für Geschichte*	VI.3
	Osteuropas 29, 321–36.	
1981c	** "Südslavische Appellative in nordslavischen Namen	VI.4
	und ihre Bedeutung für die Urheimat der Slaven,"	V.2
	Proceedings of the Thirteenth International Congress of	
	Onomastic Sciences, Cracow 1978, *K. Rymut, ed.*	
	(Wrocław: Ossolineum), 565–74.	
1982	** "Zum slavischen Namen des Lachses," *WdSl*	V.2
	27, 269–300.	VI.4

VI.2

Ureland, P. S.

1979   ** "Prehistoric Bilingualism and Pidginization as   VI.3
        Forces of Linguistic Change," *JIES* 7, 77–104.   V.4
                                                                     IV

V čest Georgiev

1980   *V čest na akademik Vladimir Georgiev. Ezikovedski
        proučvanija po slučaj sedemdeset godini ot roždenieto
        mu*, K. Čolakova *et al.*, eds. (Sofia: BAN).

Vaillant, A.

1971   ** "Slave *užina* 'déjeuner'," *Symbolae in*   V.3
        honorem Shevelov, 448–9.   III.3
                                                                     III.4

1974   ** *Grammaire comparée des langues slaves*. Tome   I.2
        IV: *La formation des noms* (Paris: Klincksieck).   III.3
                                                                     III.4

1975   * "Vieux-slave *sŭvrapěti sę* 'se contracter',"   V.3
        ZbFL 18.1, 223.   V.2
                                                                     III.3
                                                                     III.5

1977   ** *Grammaire comparée des langues slaves*. Tome V: I.2
        La syntaxe (Paris: Klincksieck).   IV

Vanagas, A. P.

1981   * "Litovskie gidronimy slavjanskogo proisxoždenija,"   VI.1
        Balto-slavjanskie issledovanija 1980, 151–7.   VI.4

Varbot, Ž. Ž.

1974   * "Ètimologičeskie zametki," *Balto-slavjanskie*   V.3
        issledovanija, 34–48.   V.2

1978   ** "K sootnošeniju slavjanskoj ètimologii i   II.6
        praslavjanskoj morfologii (v istolkovanii složnyx   III.3
        imen)," *Slavjanskoe jazykoznanie VIII*, 105–19.   III.4
                                                                     V.1

1981   * "Ešče odin tip vtoričnogo ablauta v slavjanskix   II.3
        jazykax," *Slavjanskoe i balkanskoe jazykoznanie.*
        Problemy morfonologii, 52–60.

Vasilev, C.

1973   ** "Ist die Konstruktion 'u meja est'' russisch oder   IV
        urslavisch?" *WdSl* 18, 361–7.

1975   * "Möglichkeiten und Grenzen in der Erforschung der   VI.3

urslavischen Wortgeographie am Beispiel lexikalischer   V.3
Übereinstimmungen zwischen Serbokroatisch und   V.4
Westslavisch," *WSlJb* 21, 280–9.

Vavrus, A. R.

1977   * Review of *A Historical Phonology of the Slovak*   II.1
Language by R. Krajčovič, *SEEJ* 21, 286–7.

Velčeva, B.

1978   * "Rannata diferenciacija *ǫ*/*u* v slavjanskite   II.3
ezici, *Slavjanska filologija VIII*, 279–85.

1980   ** "Otnovo za praslavjanskija izglas," *V čest*   II.5
Georgiev, 323–8.

Vincenz, A. de

1975   ** "Zur semantischen Rekonstruktion des Urslavischen,"   V.3
Bereiche der Slavistik, 307–19.

Vostočnoslavjanskoe i obščee jazykoznanie

1978   *Vostočnoslavjanskoe i obščee jazykoznanie*,
O. N. Trubačev, B. I. Belozercev and V. V. Ivanov, eds.
(Moscow: Nauka).

Vuković, J.

1975   ** "Praslovensko *ě* i *y* u sistemu fonoloških opozicija,"   II.3
Xenia Slavica, 235–7.   II.6

Wallfield, J.

1971   * "Viex-slavon *rana* 'plaie' et latin *rāna*   V.3
'grenouille'," *Symbolae in honorem Shevelov*, 459–62.   V.2

Watkins, C.

1978   * "On confession in Slavic and Indo-European,"   V.3
FS 2, 340–59.   V.2

Wenzel, W.

1979   * Review of *Slawische Personennamen in*   VI.4
mittelalterlichen Quellen zur deutschen Geschichte
by G. Schlimpert, *ZfSl* 24, 919–22.

Werner, J.

1981   * "Bemerkungen zum nordwestlichen Siedlungsgebiet der   VI.4
Slawen im 4.–6. Jahrhundert," *Archäologische Funde und*
Denkmäler, Berlin. Beiheft 16, *Beiträge zur Ur- und*
Frühgeschichte I, 695–701.

Wexler, P.

1977   ∗∗ *A Historical Phonology of the Belorussian*   II.1
           Language (Heidelberg: Winter).   I.4

Windekens, A. J. van

1971   ∗∗ "Une correspondance lexicale entre le tocharien et   V.2
           le balto-slave," *IF* 76, 54–8.   VI.1

Winter, W.

1978   ∗∗ "The distribution of short and long vowels in stems   II.3
           of the type Lith. *ě̃sti* : *vèsti* : *mèsti* and   II.2
           OCS *jasti* : *vesti* : *mesti* in Baltic and Slavic   VI.1
           languages," *Recent Developments in Historical Phonology*,
           J. Fisiak, ed. (The Hague: Mouton), 431–46.

Witkowski, T.

1977   ∗ "Urslaw. *∗tep-* 'warm, wärmen o.ä.'," *ZfSl*   V.3
           22, 56–9.

Wojtyła-Świerzowska, M.

1974a   ∗∗ *Prasłowiańskie nomen agentis* (Wrocław: III.3
            Ossolineum) (= *Monografie slawistyczne* 30).   III.4
                                                 V.3

1974b   ∗ "Słowiańskie nomen agentis na *-ь* < *∗-i-s*,"   III.3
            Studia indoeuropejskie, 279–83.   III.4
                                                 V.3

Worth, D. S. (Vort)

1978   ∗∗ "Div = Sīmurg," *Vostočnoslavjanskoe i obščee*   V.3
           jazykoznanie, 127–32.   V.4

Wójcikowska, E.

1978   ∗∗ "Wykładniki funkcji włączania do zbioru i   V.3
           wyłączania ze zbioru w językach słowiańskich,"   VI.3
           Z polskich studiów slawistycznych, Seria 5:
           Językoznawsto (Warsaw: PWN), 217–20.

Wukasch, C. M.

1974   ∗∗ *Two Topics in Late Proto-Slavic Velar*   II.4
           Palatalization [unpubl. Univ. of Texas diss.].   II.3
                                                 VI.2

1976a   ∗ "A Rule Reordering in Late Proto-Slavic,"   II.4
            IRSL 1, 119–27.   II.3
                                                 VI.2

1976b   ∗∗ "A Rule-Collapsing Problem in Late Proto-Slavic   II.4
           and OCS," *Papers in Linguistics* 9, 161–71.   II.3

			VI.2
1977	*	Review of *Old Church Slavonic Grammar* (sixth ed.) by H. G. Lunt, *Language* 53, 700–2.	I.4

Xaburgaev, G. A.

1980	*	"Nekotorye voprosy istorii praslavjanskogo jazyka,"	VI.2
		Problemy teorii i istorii russkogo jazyka, K. V.	VI.1
		Gorškova, ed. (Moscow: Izd-vo Moskovskogo	VI.3
		Universiteta), 183–213 (= *Voprosy russkogo jazykoznanija*, vyp. 3).	

Xazagerov, T. G.

1973	**	*Razvitie tipov udarenija v sisteme russkogo*	II.2
		imennogo sklonenija (Moscow: Izd-vo Moskovskogo	III.4
		Universiteta).	III.2
			VI.3

Xenia Slavica

1975   *Xenia Slavica. Papers Presented to Gojko Ružičić
on the Occasion of His Seventy-fifth Birthday*, R. L. Lencek
and B. O. Unbegaun, eds. (The Hague and Paris: Mouton).

Z polskich studiów slawistycznych

1972   *Z polskich studiów slawistycznych. Seria 4:
Językoznawstwo. Prace na VII Międzynarodowy
Kongres Slawistów w Warszawie 1973*, W. Doroszewski
et al., eds. (Warsaw: PWN).

Zaimov, J.

1976a	*	"Die bulgarische Onomastik als Spiegel des	VI.4
		altbulgarischen und urslawischen Wortschatzes,"	V.1
		ZfSl 21, 806–13.	VI.3
1976b	*	"Slavjanskie ėtimologii," *IJSLP* 22, 7–17.	V.1

Zakonomernosti

1977   *Zakonomernosti na razvitieto na slavjanskite ezici*,
I. Lekov, ed. (Sofia: BAN).

Zaliznjak, A. A.

1977	**	"Akcentologičeskaja interpretacija dannyx	II.2
		drevnerusskogo 'Merila Pravednogo' XIV veka,"	VI.3
		Konferencija …, 18–20.	
1982	**	"K istoričeskoj fonetike drevnenovgorodskogo	II.4
		dialekta," *Balto-slavjanskie issledovanija 1981*,	II.5
		61–80.	VI.3

Zaręba, A.

1973   ** "Ze słowiańskich zagadnień semantycznych   V.3
       'czuć', 'słyszeć', 'pachnieć'," *JF* 30, 117–24.

1976   ** "Zur Geschichte und Geographie der slavischen   III.3
       Wörter: ursl. *velijь, velikъjь* 'gross'," *WdSl*   V.3
       21, 180–5.   III.4

1978   ** "Cerkiewne *drugъda, drugъde* i formacje   III.3
       pokrewne," *ZbFL* 21.2, 19–24.   VI.3

Zástěrová, B.

1975   * "Otázky etnogeneze z prvotní jednoty Slovanů,"   VI.4
       Slavia 44, 69–72.

Žuravlev, V. K.

1974   ** "Genezis akan'ja s točki zrenija teorii   II.3
       nejtralizacii," *VJa* 1974.4, 37–47.   VI.2

1976   ** "Vvedenie v diaxroničeskuju morfologiju,"   III.1
       Linguistique Balkanique/Balkansko ezikoznanie 19.2,
       49–71; 19.3, 23–47.

1977   ** "Pravilo Gavlika i mexanizm padenija slavjanskix   II.3
       reducirovannyx," *VJa* 1977.6, 30–43.

1977/78 ** "Die Dynamik baltoslavischer morphologischer   III.2
       Oppositionen," *IF* 82, 191–225.   VI.1

1978   ** "K tipologii refleksov reducirovannyx v   II.3
       slavjanskix jazykax," *Studia linguistica*, 509–17.

1980   * "Praslavjanskoe smjagčenie soglasnyx glasnymi   II.4
       perednego rjada (K probleme rekonstrukcii)," *V čest*
       Georgiev, 335–40.

Žuravlev, V. K. & V. P. Mažiulis

1978   ** "Iz diaxroničekoj morfologii slavjanskix i baltijskix   III.1
       jazykov" (Vilnius: Preprint, VIII Meždunarodnyj s″ezd   VI.1
       slavistov).

Žuravlev, V. K. & V. P. Neroznak

1981   ** "Problemy rekonstrukcii prajazykovogo sostojanija,"   VI.2
       Slavica 18, 5–20.

Other Books From
Slavica Publishers, Inc.

Ruth L. Pearce: ***Russian For Expository Prose***, Vol. 1 Introductory Course, Vol. 2 Advanced Course

Robert A. Rothstein and Halina Rothstein: ***Polish Scholarly Prose*** A Humanities and Social Sciences Reader

Oscar E. Swan: ***First Year Polish***

Charles E. Townsend: ***Continuing With Russian***

Charles E. Townsend: ***Czech Through Russian***

Charles E. Townsend: ***Russian Word Formation***

Susan Wobst: ***Russian Readings and Grammatical Terminology***

Catherine V. Chvany and Richard D. Brecht (eds.): ***Morphosyntax in Slavic***

Frederick Columbus: ***Introductory Workbook in Historical Phonology***

R. G. A. de Bray: ***Guide to the South Slavonic Languages***

R. G. A. de Bray: ***Guide to the West Slavonic Languages***

R. G. A. de Bray: ***Guide to the East Slavonic Languages***

Bruce L. Derwing and Tom M. S. Priestly: ***Reading Rules for Russian*** A Systematic Approach to Russian Spelling and Pronunciation, with Notes on Dialectal and Stylistic Variation

Dorothy Disterheft: ***The Syntactic Development of the Infinitive in Indo-European***

Charles E. Gribble (ed.): ***Medieval Slavic Texts, Vol. 1, Old and Middle Russian Texts***

William S. Hamilton: ***Introduction to Russian Phonology and Word Structure***

Roman Jakobson, with the assistance of Kathy Satnilli: ***Brain and Language Cerebral Hemispheres and Linguistic Structure in Mutual Light***

Emily R. Klenin: ***Animacy in Russian   A New Interpretation***

Demetrius J. Koubourlis (ed.): ***Topics in Slavic Phonology***

Rado L. Lencek: ***The Structure and History of the Slovene Language***

Maurice I. Levin: ***Russian Declension and Conjugation*** A Structural Description with Exercises

Thomas F. Magner (ed.): ***Slavic Linguistics and Language Teaching***

***The Comprehensive Russian Grammar of A. A. Barsov*/Обстоятельная грамматика А. А. Барсова**, Critical Edition by Lawrence W. Newman

Lester A. Rice: ***Hungarian Morphological Irregularities***

David F. Robinson: ***Lithuanian Reverse Dictionary***

Ernest A. Scatton: ***Bulgarian Phonology***

Other Books From
Slavica Publishers, Inc.

John M. Foley (ed.): *Oral Traditional Literature*

Raina Katzarova–Kukudova and Kiril Djenev: *Bulgarian Folk Dances*

Yvonne R. Lockwood: *Text and Context   Folksong in a Bosnian Muslim Village*

Felix J. Oinas (ed.): *Folklore, Nationalism, and Politics*

Henrik Birnbaum: *Lord Novgorod the Great   Essays in the History and Culture of a Medieval City-State. Part One: The Historical Background*

Charles E. Townsend: *The Memoirs of Princess Natal'ja Borisovna Dolgorukaja*

Daniel C. Waugh: *The Great Turkes Defiance   On the History of the Apocryphal Correspondence of the Ottoman Sultan in its Muscovite and Russian Variants*

American Contributions to the Ninth International Congress of Slavists (Kiev 1983), *Vol. 1: Linguistics,* ed. by Michael S. Flier; *Vol. 2: Literature, Poetics, History,* ed. by Paul Debreczeny

American Contributions to the Eighth International Congress of Slavists (Zagreb and Ljubljana, Sept. 3-9, 1978), *Vol. 1: Linguistics and Poetics,* ed. by Henrik Birnbaum; *Vol. 2: Literature,* ed. by Victor Terras

Henrik Birnbaum and Thomas Eekman (eds.): *Fiction and Drama in Eastern and Southeastern Europe: Evolution and Experiment in the Postwar Period*

Karen L. Black (ed.): *A Biobibliographical Handbook of Bulgarian Authors*

Thomas Eekman and Dean S. Worth (eds.): *Russian Poetics   Proceedings* of the International Colloquium at UCLA September 22-26, 1975

Richard Freeborn, R. R. Milner–Gulland, and Charles A. Ward (eds.): *Russian and Slavic Literature*

George J. Gutsche and Lauren G. Leighton (eds.): *New Perspectives on Nineteenth-Century Russian Prose*

Pierre R. Hart: *G. R. Derzhavin: A Poet's Progress*

Andrej Kodjak, Krystyna Pomorska, and Kiril Taranovsky (eds.): *Alexander Puškin Symposium II*

Andrej Kodjak: *Pushkin's I. P. Belkin*

Andrej Kodjak, Michael J. Connolly, Krystyna Pomorska (eds.): *Structural Analysis of Narrative Texts (Conference Papers)*

Other Books From
SLAVICA PUBLISHERS, INC.
P.O. Box 14388
Columbus, Ohio 43214
(614) 268-4002

John D. Basil: *The Mensheviks in the Revolution of 1917*

Gary Cox: *Tyrant and Victim in Dostoevsky*

Vasa D. Mihailovich and Mateja Matejic: *A Comprehensive Bibliography of Yugoslav Literature in English, 1593-1980*

Edward Możejko: *Yordan Yovkov*

Walter N. Vickery (ed.): *Aleksandr Blok Centennial Conference*

Sophia Lubensky & Donald K. Jarvis (eds.): *Teaching, Learning, Acquiring Russian*

Martin E. Huld: *Basic Albanian Etymologies*

Gilbert C. Rappaport: *Grammatical Function and Syntactic Structure: The Adverbial Participle of Russian*

Ernest A. Scatton: *A Reference Grammar of Modern Bulgarian*

R. D. Schupbach: *Lexical Specialization in Russian*

D. Rowney & G. E. Orchard (eds).: *Russian and Slavic History*

Papers for the V. Congress of Southeast European Studies (Belgrade, September 1984), Kot K. Shangriladze (ed.)

William R. Schmalstieg: *Introduction to Old Church Slavic*

Michael Shapiro: *Aspects of Russian Morphology*   A Semiotic Investigation

Dean S. Worth: *Origins of Russian Grammar*